BIG YEARS, BIGGEST STATES

NUMBER SIXTY-TWO
W. L. Moody Jr. Natural History Series

BIG YEARS,

Lynn E. Barber

BIGGEST STATES

Birding in Texas and Alaska

TEXAS A&M UNIVERSITY PRESS
College Station

Copyright © 2020
by Lynn E. Barber
All rights reserved
First edition

All paintings are by Lynn E. Barber.

This paper meets the requirements of
ANSI/NISO Z39.48–1992 (Permanence of Paper).
Binding materials have been chosen for durability.
Manufactured in China through Four Colour Imports.

Library of Congress Cataloging-in-Publication Data

Names: Barber, Lynn E., author.
Title: Big years, biggest states : birding in Texas and Alaska / Lynn E.
   Barber.
Other titles: W.L. Moody Jr. natural history series ; no. 62.
Description: First edition. | College Station : Texas A&M University Press,
   [2020] | Series: W.L. Moody Jr. natural history series ; no. 62 |
   Includes bibliographical references and index.
Identifiers: LCCN 2019035581 | ISBN 9781623498573 | ISBN 9781623498580
   (ebook)
Subjects: LCSH: Bird watching—Texas. | Bird watching—Alaska. |
   Birds—Counting—Texas. | Birds—Counting—Alaska.
Classification: LCC QL677.5 .B328 2020 | DDC 598.072/34764—dc23
LC record available at https://lccn.loc.gov/2019035581

CONTENTS

List of Paintings by Lynn Barber vi
Preface ix
Acknowledgments xi

1. A Big Year: What, Why, and When   1
2. Help for Big Year Birders   16
3. Two States   21
4. Two Big Years   36
5. Favorite Birding Places in Texas and Alaska   65
6. Spotting Birds in Texas and Alaska   79
   RARE BIRDS   80
      Rare in Both States   80
         Seen in Both States   80
         Seen Only in Texas   82
         Seen Only in Alaska   103
      Rare in Alaska   109
         Seen in Both States   109
      Rare in Texas   128
         Seen in Both States   128
   OTHER BIRDS   142
         Seen in Both States   142
         Seen Only in Texas   171
         Seen Only in Alaska   242
7. An Outrageous Idea   273

Appendix 1. Birds Seen in Texas and Alaska   275
Appendix 2. Big Year Comparison   294
Appendix 3. Month by Month   295
Appendix 4. Useful References in Planning Big Years   297
Index   299

PAINTINGS BY LYNN BARBER

Bald Eagle   vii
Northern Pygmy-Owl   xiv
Bald Eagles   34
Snowy Owl   73
Bald Eagle   74
Northern Pygmy-Owl   106
Wood Duck   109
Western Meadowlark   125
Trumpeter Swan   128
Rufous Hummingbird   147
Sanderling   151
Great Horned Owl   157
Short-eared Owl   158
Northern Flicker   159
Steller's Jay eating dried mealworms   162
Cedar Waxwing   164
American Tree Sparrow   169
Scaled Quail   173
Whooping Crane   183
Least Bittern   191
Snowy Egret   192
Black-crowned Night-Heron   193
Ferruginous Hawk   199
Barn Owl   200
Ferruginous Pygmy-Owl   201
Burrowing Owl   202
Vermilion Flycatcher   207
Scissor-tailed Flycatcher   209
Hooded Warbler   223
Black-throated Sparrow   233
Harris's Sparrow   234
Emperor Goose   242

Horned Puffin 256
Boreal Owl 262
Northern Saw-whet Owl 263
Bohemian Waxwing 269
McKay's Bunting 272

PREFACE

Anyone who reads my biography can easily see that I love doing big years. That love began in Texas in 2003 and continues to the present. When I did the second Texas big year in 2005, I delivered a talk about it to birding and general interest groups. Many people told me they would love to see a book about my adventures, especially from the point of view of a woman birder. So I wrote it up but was unable to find a publisher despite much effort, and I set it aside to get on with my life, including more birding and more big years.

When I learned that Texas A&M University Press might be willing to publish an account of my ABA (American Birding Association) big year (at that time, an ABA big year was defined as a big year done in the continental United States and Canada), I took careful notes during that year (2008), wrote it up, and got it published as *Extreme Birder: One Woman's Big Year*.

Time and another big year in South Dakota (2012) passed. I considered self-publishing my Texas account, and possibly including South Dakota information, but did nothing. When my husband and I moved to Alaska in August 2014, I vowed not to do another big year, knowing the effort, and particularly the expense, would be tremendous. However, I could not resist revisiting some of the island sites I had birded in 2008 during my ABA big year, so in August and September 2015 I traveled to Gambell on St. Lawrence Island, and to St. Paul Island. As I was bouncing along a road on St. Paul Island, I suddenly realized that without much effort I had already seen 227 species for the year. Hesitantly at first and then with great excitement, I revised my plans and decided to try an Alaska big year in 2016. I figured I could just do what I had done in 2015, plus some, and I already had experience doing statewide big years.

It turned out, unsurprisingly, that doing a big year in Alaska was remarkably different from doing one in Texas. As with my first effort in Texas in 2003, I gained much of my knowledge about Alaska's birding while I did my big year, and not before. I learned on the job, so to speak. Starting out, I assumed there would be some similarities between the states. Instead, I was often amazed by the differences—when was the best time to bird and what it was like to plan and travel to bird. Although many avid birders have birded in Texas and Alaska or have high-priority plans to do so, I am not aware of anyone who has done or even thought about doing a big year in both states or written about the differences between birding in Alaska and Texas.

Doing a big year requires more extreme planning than what is needed to bird in a less intense year. In a big year a birder is repeatedly, day after day, trying to see new birds for the year. It occurred to me that a book comparing my big year experiences in the two states and the birds found there would help others who wish to bird in Texas and Alaska, two of the largest and most ornithologically rich states in the country.

ACKNOWLEDGMENTS

What this book covers has been an ongoing joy—from the delicious anticipation of doing each of my big years, to the delightful requirement to bird as much as possible during them, to the final reliving of the wonders of the years through reviewing my notes and photographs and writing about my adventures.

These two years would not have been possible without the help and encouragement of many people. First and foremost, I give my heartfelt thanks to my husband, David Barber (who should really be called "Saint David").

Thanks also to Shannon Davies, Patricia Clabaugh, Stacy Eisenstark, and others at Texas A&M University Press, without whom this book would not have happened.

Special thanks to all the people at First Congregational Church and Fort Worth Audubon in Fort Worth, and those at First Congregational Church in Anchorage, who didn't complain too much about my frequent absences in 2005 and 2016, respectively.

Thanks also to those who gave me moral support, birding companionship, expert advice, information about sightings and birding locations, and identification assistance; to Texas and Alaska birders generally; and to all those who helped me before my big years, including all who helped in my preliminary effort in Texas in 2003.

Specifically, I give thanks for help in 2005 to Mark Adams, Pam and Reid Allen, Charley Amos, John Arvin, Shawn Ashbaugh, Mike Austin, Ron Baltzegar, Rob Bates, Susan Beree, Brandon Best, Colin Bludau, Jim Booker, Sarah Bourbon, Monica Bradford, Ron and Marcia Braun, Sally Breed, Lucie Bruce, Tim Brush, Eric Carpenter, Larry and Carol Carpenter, Sheridan Coffey, Scarlet and George Colley, Greg Cook, Mel Cooksey, Nick Cooney, Joe Cox, Mike Creese, D. D. Currie, Pat DeWenter, the Dewinds, Steve Dillinger, Bob Doe, Lawrence Duhon, Charles Easley, Marianne and Mark Eastman, Carol Edwards, George Eggenberger, David Elkowitz, Dodge and Lorna Engleman, Ted Eubanks, Jesse Fagan, Frank Favre, Tim Fennell, Jean Ferguson, Mark Flippo, Brush Freeman, Bert Frenz, Terry Fuller, Lena Gallitano, John Gee, Brian Gibbons, Ken Griffin, Halff Brothers Ranch, Juliet Hanson, Shelia Hargis, John Haynes, Tim Hicks, Jim Hinson, Petra Hockey,

Gary Hodne, John Hoogerheide, Ann Hoover, Pierre Howard, Marshall Iliff, Newton and Ginger Jackson, Simone and Bill Jenion, Dan Jones, John Karges, Jerri Kerr, Jim Kessler, Selena King, Keith Kingdon, Richard Kinney, Mollie Kloepper, Mark Klym, Howard Laidlaw, Cin-Ty Lee, Lee Lemmons, Dell Little, Mark Lockwood, Stefan Lorenz, Charlie Lyon, Steve Mayes, Jon McIntyre, Brad McKinney, Gail Morris, Bob Norris, John Odgers, Carolyn Ohl, Brent Ortego, Mike Overton, Jimmy Paz, Dwight Peake, Glenn Perrigo, Barrett Pierce, David Powell, Gary Powell, Sumita Prasad, Bob Rasa, Martin Reid, Helen Rejzek, Thomas Riecke, Joel Ruiz, David Sarkozi, Susan Schaezler, Willie Sekula, Andy Shetley, Tom SoRelle, Tom Stehn, Jim Stevenson, Paul Sunby, Sandra Tholen, Rob Tizard, Jack and Dee Turner, Richard and Sonya Turner, Darrell Vollert, Cara Wade, Pat Wade, Rick Waldrup, Jerry Walls, Chris Watenpool, Ro Wauer, Jim and Lynne Weber, Ron Weeks, Ken and Ann West, Matt White, John Whittle, Allen Williams, Jan Wobbenhorst, Mimi Wolfe, and Sue Yost.

I give thanks for help in 2016 to Bev Agler, Cindi Avery, Gwen Baluss, Brad Benter, Bob Bird, Aaron Bowman, Norm Budnitz, Toby and Laura Burke, Barbara Carlson, Claudia Cavazos, Dale Chorman, Ed Clark, Amy Courtney, Michael and Peggy Craig, Dan Crowson, Caitlin Davis, Luke DeCicco, Bob Dittrick, Nat Drumheller, Ava Eads, Louann Feldmann, Enriq Fernandez, Cathy Foerster, Lena Gallitano, Connor Goff, Matt Goff, Suzi Golodoff, Carol Griswold, Scott Hauser, Steve Heinl, Mike Herndon, Joanna Hubbard, Brad Hunter, James Huntington, Donna Hurley, Clarence Irrigoo Jr., Laura Keene, White Keys, Bev and George Kirsch, Rich Kleinleder, Jerry Koerner, Laurie Lamm, Aaron Lang, Paul Lehman, James Levison, Jim Lewis, Ben Lizdas, Stephan Lorenz, Rich MacIntosh, Jeff Mason, Jimmer McDonald, Misty Patison, Andy Piston, Dave Porter, John Puschock, Martin Renner, Sunny Rice, Patty Rose, Rya Rubenthaler, Justin and Travis Saunders, Scott Schuette, Ellen Schwenne, Peter Scully, David Sonneborn, Tim Stevenson, Ken and Connie Tarbox, Thede Tobish, Kenna Sue Trickey, Gus Van Vliet, John Weigel, Sue Westervelt, and Eric Youngblood.

And for all those other birders I met, or who posted a good bird sighting, whose names just got lost in my obsessive birding frenzy:

I've studied a list of all my birds, trying to remember who, by their words, helped me to put these birds on my list. Yet I'm quite sure I may have missed some of you. So please forgive. My bird-brain's small and like a sieve.

BIG YEARS, BIGGEST STATES

1

A BIG YEAR

What, Why, and When

Although there are many types of birding big years and many ways to do them, they have commonalities. During one full year, generally begun on January 1, the birder tries to find as many species of birds as possible in a selected geographic area. The birder can choose how big the geographic area is, whether it be the whole world (others have done it but I am *not* doing that), the ABA area (defined by the American Birding Association as the continental United States and Canada, which I did in 2008, or recently redefined to include Hawaii), a single state (I have done Texas, South Dakota, and Alaska), a single county (I have done three overlapping big years in Pennington County, South Dakota), or a single yard (some South Dakota friends do those in their very bird-friendly yard). Of course, a birder can also choose the year itself and in fact can choose to start it at a nontraditional time, as Ted Floyd, ABA editor of *Birding* magazine, proposed in 2011.

The big year birder may be quite casual about it, taking day trips or weekend trips to different parts of the chosen geographic area and seeing what can be found. At the other extreme, some birders do extensive, detailed, long-range planning to maximize the birds observed and then spend nearly every waking hour during the year looking for birds and chasing the rare ones reported by others.

The "rules" used by big year birders vary considerably, with some birders making their own rules as to what will count for their year and others using general birding rules, such as those set forth by the ABA. Some birders do not allow themselves to count any bird species unless they see it well, while other birders also count birds that are only heard (as is allowed by the ABA rules). The choice is up to the birder.

Tallying of species is generally done on the honor system, since it is often very difficult for birders to "prove" that they have seen or heard a particular species. For me, taking photographs of birds allows a visual record of birds I have seen and, when appropriate, provides documentation to submit to a bird record committee that makes official decisions on the accuracy of rare bird reports and whether the birds are officially countable. Of course, nothing requires birders to submit bird reports to the relevant bird record committee, and birders can ignore an official decision and count anything they wish for their own list.

REASONS TO DO A BIG YEAR

Although I have systematically tried to cover my many reasons for loving to bird and especially for doing year-long birding quests, it is especially important that birding allows me to live stories—stories of adventure, stories of persistence, stories of despair, stories of successful plans made and other plans gone astray, stories of wonderful vistas explored—and then to relive them for days and years to come. When I think back on my early birding life, I remember finding my first bird nest (Brown Thrasher) at about age seven; spotting an out-of-range Scissor-tailed Flycatcher in central Wisconsin while I was in high school; being awakened from days of nonbirding by a scolding Ruby-crowned Kinglet in a sapling next to me in North Carolina in the 1970s; and many more beautiful moments.

During my intensive big years, the stories sometimes piled up so rapidly that it was sometimes difficult to grasp what was happening. Keeping detailed records and taking photographs of birds and people and scenery allowed me to later extract and then treasure my stories—hurtling down gravel roads in Arizona during my ABA big year trying to finally see a Spotted Owl that had reappeared at Miller Canyon; locking my keys in the car in my mad haste to be somewhere to find an owl before daylight in Texas; queasily locating a seabird as a boat rocked back and forth in the Gulfs of Mexico or Alaska; picking out the glowing reddish head of a Eurasian Wigeon in the midst of a flock of American Wigeons; marveling at swarms of Texan blackbirds or Alaskan shearwaters; being surrounded by tweets and whirring wings of hummingbirds in West Texas; tracking an American Dipper in Anchorage as it dove into water beneath an ice shelf and popped back up elsewhere on the ice; seeing a Mountain Bluebird pop her head out of a gold dredge pipe in Chicken, Alaska; locating a vocalizing warbler high in the trees in April at Sabine Woods in Texas; and so much more!

Just as there are many reasons to get out and watch birds, there are many reasons a birder might decide to undertake a year-long birding endeavor. It is often very difficult to pinpoint what these reasons are. A nonbirder friend asked me years ago, "Why do you like to bird?" I was not able (then or now) to give a single, accurate, succinct answer, although I have been continually trying to figure it out since. Similarly, it is difficult to say why I like doing big years and why I have done so many of them. While I have tried to provide some answers here, I believe they can also be summarized by "I love birds"—I love their beauty, their liveliness, their songs, their variety, their unpredictability, and the fact that these feathered wonders can be found almost everywhere.

Most people who watch birds have favorites, birds that they wish to see more than other birds, birds that to them are especially "good" birds. Often for beginners, birds they can identify become their favorites. For many people, birds that are very colorful (such as Northern Cardinals, Painted Buntings, and orioles), spectacular (such as Scissor-tailed Flycatchers), or charismatic (such as owls and hummingbirds) are often more appreciated than dull-colored ones such as sparrows. For a big year birder, while it is still exciting to see colorful, spectacular, and charismatic species, it is rarities that are most sought to add to the year list. Of course, the identity of such "good" birds changes with the locale, the year, the time of year, and the birder's knowledge and experience. The challenge of finding each rarity and the excitement that attends each finding are part of what attracts me to birding and to doing big years.

I think one reason I became such an avid birder is my love of keeping lists. Before I listed avian creatures, as a child I kept lists of many things, such as movies seen and books read. Although I no longer keep so many lists of nonbird things, for some reason my bird lists have become increasingly important. I have lists not only of all the birds I've observed, but also for each country, state, and year. Many birders routinely keep year lists of the birds they see each calendar year. Each January, they can have the pleasure of seeing their new year list grow right away and can compare the current year with past years. Having a new year list gives them the challenge of leaping into the unknown of a new year to discover how many birds they can see. Thus, in high school, even before I knew what a big year was or tried one, I started doing annual lists. This made each January in the middle of a Wisconsin winter seem less cold and more fun, as each bird was new for the year and helped the year list grow.

Not only is a year list a way to compare the number of avian creatures seen each year, but it also gives the birder a way to watch a year unfold in day-by-day detail. Unlike sporadic visits to favorite locations to look for birds, birding intensely throughout a year allows the birder to see patterns of bird distribution as the numbers of different species of birds change throughout the year, such as when they arrive and leave on migration in spring and fall. Thus, being part of spring migration as new species of warblers and tanagers and orioles flit through the trees every day is often exciting and unpredictable and is always interesting.

In addition to making lists of things seen and done, I have also always loved to make planning lists, even to-do lists. To me it is fun to sit down with a calendar, Post-it notes, and bird books and plan where I might go in an upcoming year and then revise and augment the plans during the year.

I think another reason I do intense birding all year long is it gives me (at least in my mind) a valid excuse to just go out and look for birds, and not do whatever else I or someone else had in mind I should be doing. If I am doing a big year, the clock is ticking and if I don't go out and bird today, today is gone and I have lost the opportunity to find new birds today. Today will never happen again. During such a year, I regularly find myself uttering some variation of "I am doing a big year so I can't do (fill in the blank)—I just must go birding." If I handle it right, this might allow me to get out of daily chores or meetings or doctor appointments or other less fun things.

Because serious big year birding requires looking for birds as much as possible during the year, it gets me outside, which I love, often to places I have never been. There is very little that is as wonderful as being outside all the time, or at least most of the time. In Texas, doing big years gave me more time to be at High Island and Sabine Woods during migration, which I always enjoyed even on rainy days and days when biting insects abounded; to climb mountain trails at Big Bend National Park or in the Guadalupe Mountains; and to explore the many hotspots in the Rio Grande Valley (known simply as the Valley). In Alaska, my big year took me to areas I had never expected to visit—in January to Hoonah for a Brewer's Blackbird and to Gustavus to try to find a Barred Owl, in November to Petersburg for Lewis's Woodpecker, and multiple trips to Sitka for Wood Duck, Cape May Warbler, and Tropical Kingbird. I once met someone who had never seen a sunrise—as a big year birder, I regularly see sunrises and sunsets and rainstorms and rainbows . . . and of course, many birds.

Nonstop birding also provides more opportunities to hear avian sounds—the varied and borrowed melodies of a Northern Mockingbird, the gurgles and squawks of a Black-billed Magpie, the liquid music of a Wood Thrush, the nearly inaudible songs of kinglets and Blackpoll Warblers, the low nighttime hoots of a Great Horned Owl, and the hollow drumming of distant woodpeckers.

Big year birding gives the birder the fun of trying to second-guess the birds. I do try to plan my big years in advance, but I continually modify my plans based on which birds I have not yet found and which ones others are reporting, trying to figure out when and where each species is possible in the chosen geographic area and where it will appear. When do I need to fly to Juneau, to Utqiagvik (Barrow), to St. Lawrence Island, and all the Alaska locations that might have birds?

For many people, a big year is primarily a competition. Although I have many, varied reasons for doing big years, I must admit to being competitive as well. I did my second Texas big year in 2005 primarily to beat my own previous number (485 in 2003), to see whether I could do better than I had already done. In 2005 I was also very aware of the previous big year records for other Texas birders (505 for Eric Carpenter in 2003, and 511 for Howard Laidlaw in 2004). That awareness kept me going to reach and then pass their totals, ending at 522 species for 2005. As far as I know, as of mid-2019, that record still stands.

In Alaska, I had seen 227 species by the end of 2015, which I had done without trying. In 2016, I initially just hoped to exceed that number. I was also aware of earlier Alaska records. I was originally told that the previous Alaska record was 275, but as I approached that number in late June, I learned of an earlier, now deceased birder who was believed to have reached 287 species in one year. So, I worked for that higher number and then passed it in mid-July, finally finding 307 species by the end of the year. Yes, competitive.

A big year allows birders to obtain many types of advanced education. It enables them to learn what birds are in an area and about the area itself by doing rather than just by reading. It allows them to have a much better idea of how bird distribution and numbers change as the year progresses and to realize how amazing the differences are from year to year and from area to area. The more you watch birds, the more you can learn about them—their identification, habits, songs, ranges. This is just magnified if you do a big year and bird nonstop. It may be somewhat analogous to cramming for exams—the older I get the more I realize that doing a big year, especially in an area new to me, is an intense way to cram in learning about birds, their habits, and their habitats so that I become better informed. It takes too much time to learn by doing if I go out only every now and then.

Much is known about bird habits and distribution, and in its magnitude this information is almost impossible to comprehend completely. Often I am unwilling to sit down and just read about birds. I don't even know where to start. The more I bird, however, the more I can gain firsthand knowledge of birds, and then reading about them becomes more interesting. No longer is the known information just a collection of abstract facts compiled by others. Even better, every time I go out in the field, I may learn something new, maybe even something new to science.

In many ways, doing a big year "takes a village," especially if the big year is done in a large area or includes many birding locations that are distant from where the birder lives or are unfamiliar to the birder. In the best of big years, the birder will meet other birders along the way, both to share the birding and to learn from those more experienced or knowledgeable about the area and its birds.

While I like to bird with others, I also like exploring and bird-watching on my own. By necessity doing a big year gives a birder time, generally much time, to bird alone. Very rarely can birders find someone else who is both willing and able to always accompany them in nonstop bird-watching.

I love to write and talk about birding. Doing a big year gives me unique and interesting (at least to me) material to talk and write about. I could never have produced a daily blog about bird things, or about anything, if I had not been birding every day in my 2016 big year. Before my Alaska big year ended, I was working to line up talks about it and looking forward to putting together presentations.

I enjoy taking pictures of birds to remind me of the wonderful things I have seen—multicolored Painted Buntings and Wood Ducks, soaring Bald Eagles, friendly chickadees and Red-breasted Nuthatches, comical American Dippers, and huge flocks of Purple Martins and Sandhill Cranes. The more I am out birding, the more opportunity I have to take bird photographs. Also, because I like to illustrate my talks with photos, doing a big year gives me not only something to talk about, but also the opportunity to obtain other illustrations for my talks, including habitats, scenery, and other bird-watchers.

One reason I enjoy doing a big year is I do not like to be bored. Even when I am not doing a big year I fill my time with many activities. When I am

Red-breasted Nuthatch

doing a big year, it is very difficult to be bored for long. Even if I do not have any rarities to look for, I am planning where I might go next, and best of all, I can be watching birds. Even if I am not seeing any exciting birds, one might appear any second. There is almost always a sense of anticipation of what might be just around the corner.

As with many other undertakings, there is a wonderful feeling of accomplishment from completing a big year, despite the cost, effort, failures, and so on, whether or not any records have been set. It is a huge endeavor to keep on keeping on for a whole year, when there is no pay but much expense and effort involved. It is a commitment of great magnitude and a labor of love. During every big year, I have seriously contemplated giving up before the year was done, but the thought of "wasting" so much effort by not completing the journey kept me going, as did the encouragement of my friends and fellow birders.

The older I get, the less I worry or care about being so odd, one of the nuttiest of nutty birders, and in fact, it is sort of fun to be noteworthy for being odd and different from "normal" people. At least for now, being a serial big year woman birder gives me an identity, a uniqueness.

WOMEN AND BIG YEARS

I believe that more people, including more women, are doing big years than when I first did one. It may be, however, that because I am such an enthusiastic big year birder, I am more aware of others undertaking such an effort. Even so, I must admit that because I would rather go looking for birds than keep track of others' birding adventures, I am undoubtedly unaware of what many other birders are doing, especially birders in other states.

When I first attempted a big year in Texas in 2003, I was unaware of anyone else doing a big year, and at first I told no one about it. Early in the year, I met Eric Carpenter, who was then doing a serious, record-breaking big year and told me that he found it was important to tell others that you were doing a big year. In addition to encouraging other birders to let you know about their bird sightings, telling others about your big year allows them to do a vicarious big year by closely following your adventures as the year progresses. In my experience, this is especially true of many women birders.

When I give a talk about one of my big years, it is usually the women in the audience who come up to tell me they cannot believe that I do so much birding, and that I do most of it alone. Women often approach me with a look of both amazement that I would do and have done such a thing, and concern for my sanity in making such an effort, and doing it mostly alone.

Most of my life I have birded alone, however, unlike many other women. I think that in addition to time and money constraints, a big reason that women are less likely to do a big year is that it is often a solo endeavor. It seems to me that needing to bird with others limits many women's flexibility as to when and where to bird and keeps them from birding except when their friends are available. I am not sure whether they are just more sociable than I am, or whether they are afraid to go birding alone.

Because solo birding has always been my norm, I usually do not spend the time and effort to try to find people to accompany me. In my ABA big year, I took fewer than 10 percent of my extended birding trips with others (all women). I was lucky that during the first portion of my Texas big year, Simone Jenion was often able to accompany me. In Alaska, I usually traveled to my various destinations alone but was often able to bird with others for a portion of my stay there.

When I go birding in places, especially unfamiliar places, where there is absolutely no one else around or in places where people for some reason appear threatening, I am of course concerned about my safety or about losing my expensive optics. Rarely, however, does that keep me from birding there. At least stereotypically, many women are more timid than men in unfamiliar or potentially scary situations, or are more willing to admit to such timidity. While I am often timid and an admitted worrywart about what might happen in an unknown place or possibly scary situation, I tend to try to ignore the possibility that something bad might actually occur. This brings to mind an experience in North Carolina (long before I did big years). I went birding on a trail to a lake to look for eagles. After nearly a mile of walking through the woods, seeing no one along the trail, I came to a small clearing where I saw about eight big tattooed bikers sitting around on logs and talking, their bikes parked nearby. They seemed to ignore me and I pretended they did not exist as I walked the trail through their gathering. I got to the shore just past them, pretended to bird a bit, and casually strolled back through them, my tripod and scope over my shoulder and my big telephoto lens hanging down by my side, my heart in my throat. Nothing happened, which reinforced my feeling that solo birding is mostly okay to do.

I have been lucky, of course. I know that many would consider such behavior foolhardy, but my drive to go birding, especially during a big year, usually overrides my fears, and perhaps my common sense. I often rationalize it by thinking that even if there were two (or three) of us, we would probably be unable to prevent something bad from happening. For me, my motivation to do the best I can during a big year, and the rewards and pleasure I find in exploring new areas, seeing and hearing new birds, and experiencing each new day's adventures make doing big years a highlight of my life.

In spite of these concerns, I hope that more women will learn what a joy it can be to do a big year. As I was writing this, Laura Keene was nearing the completion of her ABA big year, the second woman (as far as I know) to make such a huge effort. I was the first. Laura was one of four birders to make this effort in 2016, all of whom broke all previous big year records. A third woman, Yve Nagy Morrell, was doing an ABA big year in 2017 as I continued work on this book.

Although doing a state big year does not require as many miles of travel as an ABA big year, it is still an intense effort that few birders are willing and able to make. Many women have done state big years, but more men have done them. I understand the many other reasons fewer women do big years. Those who want to do a big year must of course be interested in and willing to devote themselves to this effort. Stereotypically, men are more interested in watching and participating in competitive sports and more interested in breaking records than are women. Although most women have not traditionally thought of themselves as competitive, as more women have found careers outside the home in fields where goal setting and striving are important, more women have also become involved in competitive sports, among which I include big years.

In addition to a willingness to undertake one, doing a big year requires both time and money. Women are more likely than men to have long-term responsibilities for caring for children and making a home for their families, leaving little opportunity for "taking off" a year to go birding, at least until after their children are grown. Women who work outside the home may also not be able to take the time necessary to do a serious big year, unless they are self-employed or otherwise have control over their work schedule. Unless they have found the time to go birding and nourish their love of avian creatures for many years, women may not feel the drive to go all out to do a big year when they finally have a chance. Even if they eventually have the time, they may not have the financial resources to make such an effort. Very importantly, they also may not have a supportive spouse who is willing to let them use the family's funds and to be left home alone.

I was lucky—I had the drive to do my big years, I was self-employed and able to take the time, I was able to juggle career and credit cards to make them happen, and I have an extremely supportive spouse. For me, it is rewarding to do something very few women do, and to try to show the way so others can follow. I know there are many enthusiastic women birders. I hope more of them who want to do a big year will find a way to do so. In any case, I hope that women will increasingly experience the rewards of birding.

REASONS *NOT* TO DO A BIG YEAR

Unless your big year is a very low-effort year, a local green year, or a year in a very small area, a big year costs money, often a lot of money.

Setting out on my Alaska big year, December 31, 2015

Anytime you leave home, you must pay travel expenses, including gas, airfare, and rental car costs. If you stay overnight somewhere, you pay for a motel or campsite unless you are lucky enough to find someplace free to stay. The cost of food on the road is generally higher than if you stayed home. If you hire a guide or go with a group, there are additional costs. If you are employed, your hours and income may be reduced. It all adds up, and particularly if you are doing an ABA area (or world) big year, the cost may be prohibitive.

Doing a big year by definition takes time, a lot of time. Unless you are doing a big year with your significant other and have no other close friends, it takes you away from family and friends. It also takes you away from other nonbirding activities you enjoy.

While I like to plan, the birds aren't on the same page. It is very difficult to second-guess them because their habits change all the time. No matter how much you know about them, it is impossible to know everything. This leads to disappointments, wasted trips, and bad days when you may not find your target birds, or any birds at all. Thus, after careful study of prior records, I determined that my best chance for Mountain Bluebirds in Alaska was to go to Juneau in late April, and I scheduled my Juneau flight for then. I was busy birding elsewhere in mid-April and did not realize until I arrived in Juneau that the bluebirds had migrated through earlier and I was too late.

Not only do birds not always follow a birder's plans, but it is very difficult to make plans, particularly far in advance when tickets are likely to be less expensive and more available. Do you make all those plane and motel and car reservations far in advance to lock them in and possibly reduce cost, or do you stay flexible to allow for last-minute chases? Whatever you do, it will never completely fit what the birds do. They will go where you have not planned to go, will arrive earlier or later than you have planned to see them, or will not come at all. It's all part of the challenge, of course, but it can also be a big headache.

A big year can be and often is a source of great physical and mental stress, particularly as one ages. The mountains seem higher, the terrain more difficult to traverse, the days shorter, and the body less willing and able to obey one's commands. No matter one's age, however, it takes stamina and endurance to keep on the move day after day after day, often at a forced-march pace or faster, on the run. I have alluded to causes of the mental stress—knowing you cannot be in more than one place at any one time and you will miss birds because you cannot get there in time or maybe at all. There is also mental stress when what you "need" for your big year list refuses to be found, which can be particularly stressful if you are doing a big year at the same time as someone else and that birder sees your needed bird. No matter how good your plans are and how cooperative the birds are, there will always be many, many days, especially as the year draws to a close, when no new birds are possible.

Although doing a big year is often a cure for boredom, there is some boredom involved. Maybe there are no feathered creatures present, or worse, maybe the weather or a cancelled plane flight causes an enforced break in the searching. If you cannot bird during a big year and cannot do the other things you normally choose to occupy your time, boredom can be problematic.

For me, a major problem is the fuel required to get from place to place in a big year, increasing my carbon footprint. Maybe it is better to take a flight that is already scheduled to go to my destination whether I go on it or not, rather than hop in my car and drive for many miles. I tell myself that many people travel many places, many birders who are *not* doing big years travel many places, and big year birding is a drop in the bucket compared to all the other travel that goes on. This is not negligible, however, and I feel guilty about it. I try to support environmental causes in other ways, but the guilt remains, just not enough to keep me from doing another big year. In between big years, I try not to do bird chases and to reduce my travel.

It is a difficult issue, unresolvable in a satisfactory way for me. In an attempt to do something for the birds and their environment, and to understand why some birds are threatened or endangered, a few years ago I did substantial research and then wrote *Birds in Trouble*. It is my hope that this book will also help others understand what we can do to conserve and improve the environment and to help the most endangered bird species in the continental United States. These actions will of course also be valuable to other bird species, to other animals, to plants, and to human beings.

WHEN TO DO A BIG YEAR

Although Neil Hayward did an "accidental big year" in the ABA area, not starting in earnest on January 1, most birders make conscious decisions about this sometime before the calendar year begins. Sometimes, such years are years in the planning. In any case, because big year planning usually and most preferably involves at least some advance plans, including reservations of rooms, flights, and rental cars, as the year before the possible big year nears its end, it becomes easier to see whether rare birds will be around the next year. Of course, it also becomes less and less easy to back out and decide the next year may not be the best year to do a big year.

How can a birder know when to engage in such an undertaking? There are a couple of things to consider. Ideally, it would be best if we could know whether the upcoming year will bring rarities to where we hope to do a big year. Unfortunately—it is possibly too obvious to say it, but I will—every year is different, in the birding world as elsewhere. We know each new year will be different from the past, but none of us can predict how it will be different and what will happen in the future.

It is tempting to think knowledge of future weather would be helpful in deciding whether to do a big year. We know weather patterns affect bird movement, but while it is possible to make some weather predictions a few weeks out, we cannot with any accuracy make predictions for a whole year. Even if we could, how particular weather patterns will affect the number of rare bird species that may appear in the geographic area we plan to visit is almost completely unknown. If we are trying to decide whether to do a big year next year or wait until the year after that, our weather forecasting ability is of no help in comparing bird likelihood in the two years. We can look at global weather patterns such as the timing of El Niño, but we still cannot know how a particular El Niño will affect birds' wandering, particularly into a remote state. We cannot know which rarities will arrive in a particular geographic area in a particular year or whether the next year will be spectacularly empty of rare birds.

The best we can do, if anything, is to become familiar with what is happening at the end of the current year in our particular chosen area. It can help to know whether rarities are there now that might remain until the new year. In late 2004, there were reports of multiple Crimson-collared Grosbeaks in the Lower Rio Grande Valley (LRGV) of Texas, and other rarities were also reported in the state. It looked like 2005 would be a good year, and it was a wonderful year for rarities in Texas.

That is the only time this type of prediction has worked for me. My ABA big year in 2008 was not very good for rarities in the United States. In 2016, while many Alaskan springtime rarities were present, in the last half of the year rarities from Asia on the western islands were considerably less frequent than in previous years. In both cases, I was ready to do a big year and did not try to figure out whether it was a good idea to choose those years for my next adventure. I just did it.

In my opinion, picking a "good" year is less about trying to figure out whether rarities will appear, and more about being ready to do a big year that year. Although ideally, you are ready to do it because you are knowledgeable about and experienced in the geographic area of the big year and where the birds are likely to be found in that area, I admit this factor has been less important to me than it probably should have been. My impatient nature, and the fact that I am never sure how long we will live in a particular area, has led me to do big years when I felt like doing them and as soon as I thought I could manage it. With the help of other birders and much cramming of information, I managed to do big years without being a longtime birder in an area, but more experience is undoubtedly preferable.

I think it mainly comes down to a question of whether you are psychologically prepared to leave family, friends, other hobbies, sleep, and a comfortable life behind for a year. Have you been able to figure out how to spend the needed time and money that year to chase birds? Because doing a big year is not something most people can do repeatedly in a particular area, when you finally choose to do a big year somewhere, you need to be ready to jump into it completely. Once the journey has begun, there is absolutely no going back, no way to ask the birds to wait around until you get plans in order. If you do not put full effort into it, beginning immediately on January 1 if possible, you will still spend much time and money. When you finally begin the year in earnest, you will have missed birds, and birds and time will have passed that you can never regain. Many times during my various big years, I have thought about quitting but realized that I would forever regret it. Why pour your heart into something only to make a half-hearted effort or quit when the going gets tough or boring or chaotic?

The bottom line for me is, if you are going to do a big year, choose where and when to do it to best fit your life. Whether it turns out to be a really good year for rarities is not nearly as important as being ready and motivated to find as many birds as possible, rare or not.

2
HELP FOR BIG YEAR BIRDERS

In my Texas big year in 2005 and especially in my Alaska big year in 2016, I was a relative novice to birding in those states, and I needed all the help I could get to figure out when and where to go. I found that other birders were often the best way to get help before and during a big year. My friends in each state were sometimes able to leave their normal lives and travel with me on a portion of my adventures. Also, in both states by the time I did my big year I had met other birders who often gave me information about where and when to look for birds, and when they found rarities, they let me know. Before both years started, I enhanced the usefulness of this natural tendency of most birders to share what they find by emailing those I knew personally as well as many of those I knew about but had not yet met, telling them about my upcoming year and asking them to let me know of rarity sightings. In addition, in Alaska where it was difficult to just go explore in my spare time (as I had done in Texas), and where I had to fly to many areas I had never been, birders I had contacted in advance and those I learned of during my big year were extraordinarily helpful in giving their knowledge, their time, and often their company when I arrived.

In both states, before and during my big years, I talked to others who had done big years or were longtime birders in the state. In Texas I talked to Eric Carpenter, who broke the record in 2003, and during 2005 I talked to many birders I met as I wandered about the state, always adding tidbits of bird lore and wisdom to what I already knew. During my Texas big year I did the Yellow Rail walk at Anahuac National Wildlife Refuge (NWR), enlisting the help and eyes of the other participants and the leader, David Sarkozi, so I could add that species to my year list.

In Alaska, I met with a few birders before my adventure, including Ed Clark, who was in Anchorage from Fairbanks over Thanksgiving weekend in 2015; Aaron Bowman, who then lived in Anchorage and regularly broke his own Anchorage big year record; and other Anchorage birders including David Sonneborn, Luke DeCicco, and Louann Feldmann. To help with logistics and to provide myself with companions and leaders in 2016, I signed up for Wilderness Birding Adventures trips to Adak and Gambell in May, Nome in June, Juneau and the Gulf of Alaska in August, and Gambell in September, and in November I participated in a trip to Utqiagvik with Zugunruhe Birding Tours.

EMAIL, LISTSERVS, AND eBIRD

As far as I recall, in 2005, electronic state bird listservs were just replacing the older state-by-state system where you could call a state hotline to listen to rare bird reports. Before the advent of listservs, people who did big years had to call (and before cell phones, find a pay phone) to find out about rare bird reports; call their friends to find out what was being seen; or just go looking to see what they could see. In 2005, while I had a cell phone and I could find a computer with internet access to determine what had been reported to Texbirds, I did not have access to email or the internet on my cell phone.

In 2016, when I did my Alaska big year, not only did I have cell phone access to my email and the internet (where there was Wi-Fi), but I also signed up with eBird (which started in 2002, but which I had not subscribed to by my Texas big year in 2005), so that I received targeted tailored emails telling me which birds had been seen in Alaska, with separate emails on sightings of species that I had not yet reported for the year. Not only did I use eBird daily to learn about sightings by other birders, but it was an invaluable tool that allowed me to post my sightings and review what I had and had not seen so far. I was also signed up with a number of Alaska listservs and periodically received emails reporting sightings in the areas they covered: AKBirding, Boreal Birders (Interior), Eagle chat (Southeastern Alaska), Kodiak Birding, Sitka Birds, and kpbirding (Kenai Peninsula).

eBird was also extremely helpful in allowing me to review historical sightings of birds to find out where and when various species had been reported in Alaska in previous years, and to see how regularly a bird species was found in the state. I could thus determine the rarity of a species by looking at actual observation reports, which helped me determine which birds were important to chase if someone else saw them, and where I should look for birds that no one had yet reported.

BOOKS, TAPES, CDS, APPS, AND MAPS

Texas, being a more populated and long-settled state than Alaska in many areas, has many more books to use in planning and carrying out a big year.

Many of these books, which are listed in appendix 4, cover places to bird in different sections of the state, such as the Texas Hill Country, the Rio Grande Valley, the Trans-Pecos, and the Panhandle. I used these to determine where to go in a certain part of the state to maximize the number of birds I could find and to increase my chances of finding rarities. My favorite statewide books during my Texas big year were *The Texas Ornithological Society Handbook of Texas Birds*, second edition, by Mark Lockwood and Brush Freeman (TOS Handbook) and *Birding Texas* by Roland Wauer and Mark Elwonger (Wauer guide). Although I am sure there have been many changes in local information about some of the sites and their access, as well as many new sites that have come into being since its publication, the Wauer guide is invaluable in providing historical information about what rarities have been seen and about the usual birds that might be found at each site. I also used the TOS Handbook often, particularly when planning where and when to go to find birds I had not yet seen, as well as to figure out whether a bird I had found but was unsure of was likely to be what I thought it was.

In Alaska, I used only one Alaska birding guide during my big year, *A Birder's Guide to Alaska* by George West. Although I bought the first edition (2002) long before I moved to the state in 2014, just before my big year started I purchased the second edition (2008), so the information was as current as possible. This book covers locations across the state that birders have found to be good places to bird, from Utqiagvik to Southeastern (Juneau, Ketchikan, Sitka, Petersburg, Haines), Western (Gambell, St. Paul, Attu, Adak), and South-Central (Anchorage, Kenai, Homer, Seward) Alaska. Each chapter, written by one or more people most familiar with birding at the covered location, includes maps, site descriptions, directions, and logistics (accommodations, campgrounds, contacts).

During both big years, I often referred to birding field guides that covered the whole country. While my favorite for both Texas and Alaska was National Geographic's *Field Guide to the Birds of North America*, I used others such as *The Sibley Guide to Birds* to flesh out details about species of interest, such as the different plumages of many species as they mature and as they molt into breeding plumage.

In Texas, I carried a tape player or a CD player to allow me to hear what a bird sounded like. So many times I would hear a bird I could not see, such as a warbler, and need to know what it was so I would know whether I had already observed it during the year, and if not, I could add it to my year list.

By 2016, my bird book and tape/CD usage was often replaced by iPhone apps. Access to a single handheld source of multiple apps, each with pictures, descriptions, and range maps, together with multiple taped songs for most species, is extremely valuable in birding. My favorite bird apps are iBird Pro, Sibley Birds, Bird Tunes, Audubon Birds, and National Geographic Birds.

During my Texas big year, in addition to maps of birding sites in the Wauer guide, I always had a Texas road atlas in my car and regularly pulled over to consult it. In 2016, I rarely carried a paper map. Instead, I used apps on my cell phone to figure out where I was or where I was going. My favorite, primarily because it was one of my first map apps, is Where Am I At? However, I also used Google Maps.

FACEBOOK

Although Facebook was in its initial stages at the time I did my Texas big year, I was unaware of it. By 2016, however, I used Facebook regularly and found that in Alaska, the public Facebook group Alaska Rare Bird Alert was a very useful source of information and usually contained pictures of rarities that had been found in the state. Also useful at times were other Facebook groups, including Kodiak Birding, Ketchikan Birders, Haines Birders, and Birds of Alaska.

PRIOR BIG YEAR RECORDS

In both big years, from the beginning I was comparing my results to other people's big year numbers and always working toward them. Until the year was well along I had no real expectation that I could actually reach the previous records.

Texas has a long history of birders doing big years. The book *Chasing Birds across Texas* tells Mark Adams's tale of finding 489 species in his Texas big year in 2000, which tied the previous record of Brush Freeman and Petra Hockey in 1995. He provides a table of the top ten Texas big years as of the year he wrote the book, beginning with Brush Freeman (453 in 1996), followed by the multiple big years of Red and Louise Gambill (458 species in 1991 and 1995), Petra Hockey (463 in 1999), Don Alexander (465 in 1986), Greg Lasley (468 in 1994), and Petra Hockey and Brush Freeman (variable numbers given by Adams as 485 and 489 in 1995). Eric Carpenter's 505 species in 2003 and Howard Laidlaw's 511 species in 2004 were the records most in my mind during my big year.

Five of us did a Texas big year in 2005—three men, Simone, and me. As I recall, two of the men did not keep up the effort all year, but those of us who finished the year all did very well. I reached 505 species on October 5, and 511 on November 11. My final total of 522 species remained the Texas record as I wrote this. Although at least two people did a serious Texas big year in 2017, they did not surpass my total.

In Alaska, I was initially told that a couple of birders had previously observed 274 or 275 species in a single year, but I was also told that these people (Scott Schuette, Brad Benter, and maybe more) had outdoor jobs that helped boost their numbers, and they had not set out to do a big year. As my big year progressed, I was also told of Pete Isleip, now deceased, who was believed to have seen 287 species in one year, but no one seemed quite sure. I decided that 287 was the number to reach, and maybe beat if all went well. Some of the expert birders I talked with during the year felt confident I could reach 300 species, but I was dubious. As it turned out, I reached 287 species by July 14 in Ketchikan with a Rose-breasted Grosbeak, and I finished the year with 307 species, which is currently the record.

TWO STATES

Before I discuss what it is like to plan and do a big year in two such varied states as Texas and Alaska, I need to talk in some detail about the differences between the states themselves. The size, climate, and geography of each state dramatically affect which birds can be found there and where, greatly influence how a big year is best done, and place specific limitations on what a birder can do in a big year.

SIZE

While both Texans and Alaskans take great pride in the size of their state, there is no question which state is the largest. Alaska has an area of 663,000 square miles, while the area of Texas is 267,000 square miles.

Texas extends more than 800 miles from east (Sabine River) to west (El Paso). In Alaska, the distance from Attu at the western end of the Aleutian Islands to Ketchikan in the southeast is over 2,350 miles, similar to the distance from California (across all of Texas) to Florida. The distance from Utqiagvik in the north to Amatignak Island in the southernmost area of the Aleutian chain is 1,390 miles (similar to the distance from Fargo, North Dakota, across all of Texas to Brownsville).

Not only does the size of a state affect what it is like to try to bird the entire state, but the amount of coastline and its accessibility also affect which shorebirds and ocean birds can be observed in the state. According to the National Oceanic and Atmospheric Administration's Office for Coastal Management, the mostly inaccessible coastline of Alaska is 33,904 miles (the longest of any state), and that of Texas is 3,359 miles (seventh longest of any state).

CLIMATE

Utqiagvik in northernmost Alaska is over 3,400 miles (straight-line air distance) from Fort Worth in the Northern Plains of Texas, and nearly 3,900 air miles from Brownsville in southernmost Texas (no road goes from Utqiagvik to the rest of Alaska, so you cannot drive from Utqiagvik to Texas unless the northern portion of the driving is over frozen tundra). From Hyder in southern Alaska, it is 2,778 driving miles to Fort Worth and 3,218 miles to Brownsville. As expected with two states so far apart from each other, there is basically no overlap between their climates.

Another way to see the difference in their location on the globe is to note that Utqiagvik, at a latitude of about 71 degrees, is about 67 percent of the way from the equator to the north pole, while Brownsville, at a latitude of about 26 degrees, is about 30 percent of the way from the equator to the north pole. Clearly Alaska has a more Arctic climate and Texas a more arid/temperate/subtropical climate, which affects the vegetation and, very importantly, the birds that can survive and thrive there.

The climate of Texas is quite diverse, ranging from tropical and subtropical to very arid. The Northern Plains region is semiarid and drought prone, with 16–32 inches of annual rainfall and 15–30 inches of snow. Temperatures can go below freezing in winter and above 100 degrees Fahrenheit in summer. The Trans-Pecos region is much drier, with rainfall of 16 inches or less and snow rare except at high elevations. The Hill Country is semiarid, with cool winters and hot summers. Most of the up to 48 inches of rain falls in spring. The Pineywoods has a humid subtropical climate, with more than 60 inches of annual rainfall and a lot of severe weather. Winters are fairly cool because of Gulf of Mexico waters. The South Texas climate ranges from arid away from the Rio Grande Valley to wet and tropical in the Valley. While winter can be cold and there can be some snow, most of the year is hot and humid, especially in April and May. If you are birding across Texas, you must be prepared for anything from humid 100-degree heat in southern and south-eastern Texas in spring through fall, to below freezing temperatures and blizzards in West Texas and the Panhandle in winter.

The temperatures during the summers in Alaska can reach 60–80 degrees, and 40–50 degrees at night. Birders are advised in George West's book to be prepared for cold, wet, and windy weather at any season. While the temperature of the Interior may reach 90 degrees in summer, it is generally much cooler, and it can drop to many degrees below zero in the winter. Along the coast, temperatures are in the low 20s in winter and rarely above 60 in summer. Rain gear, knee-high rubber boots, and gloves are almost always essential in many areas, particularly in Southeastern Alaska and along the Gulf of Alaska.

GEOGRAPHY AND HABITAT

It is well known that Texas and Alaska differ in their geography, which results in different habitats available for both flora and fauna. Texas is basically flat or rolling, with relatively few mountains, and is hot much of the year. It stretches from wet flatlands along the Gulf of Mexico in the east to low mountains in the dry west. None of the Texas mountains are snow covered all year, and most do not regularly receive snowfall or have anything like the tundra found in Alaskan mountains. The highest mountain in Texas is Guadalupe Peak, at 8,749 feet above sea level, while the highest Alaskan mountain is Denali (formerly Mt. McKinley), at 20,308 feet above sea level. There are nearly 70 named Alaskan mountains that are higher than Guadalupe Peak in Texas.

In contrast to Texas, most of Alaska is mountainous, stretching westward from the mountains of western Canada to cold northern waters and rocky islands, north to the Arctic. The different terrain and climate affect all the life that can flourish, or even survive, in these two states, controlling and limiting the plants and animals (mammals, birds, reptiles, insects, and everything else) found there.

Of course, these differences affect what it is like to do a big year and what you can see and experience in the two states. A major difference between the two is that you can drive across Texas, and with the exception of some mountain foot trails and areas out on and near the Gulf of Mexico, travel by car is doable. No flights are necessary. In Alaska, with the exception of the South-Central area and roads south and north of Anchorage (south to Homer, north to Fairbanks and Delta Junction), you must fly or take a boat to get to all the other areas, whether the very birdy Southeast region, islands in Western and Southwestern Alaska, or Utqiagvik in Northern Alaska.

While many bird species may be found in both Texas and Alaska, many are found in one state but not the other. In addition to the different habitats in Texas and Alaska, each state has regions that are distinctly different from those in the other state. The great differences between the two states in climate, geography, plant life, and habitat usable by birds result in bird populations in each state that are not found in the other.

TEXAS

Birding Texas by Roland Wauer and Mark Elwonger describes 10 biogeographic regions in Texas. Other sources, such as the TOS Handbook, set forth similar but somewhat differently defined "natural areas of Texas." Here I summarize Wauer and Elwonger's discussion of the biogeographic regions of Texas, which is helpful in describing the state, followed by notes about some of the Texas birds I found in each region during my big year. With rainfall, soil, and vegetation as criteria, these 10 regions, each with its characteristic bird populations, are as follows.

Trans-Pecos

The Trans-Pecos, all of Texas west of the Pecos River, includes arid lowlands and deserts as well as the highlands of the Guadalupe, Davis, and Chisos Mountains, which have areas of moist coniferous forest. On the southern edge of the region along the Rio Grande are canyons and floodplains of cottonwoods, willows, mesquite, and nonnative salt cedar. This area is the primary location for western specialty birds, both as nesting breeders and as vagrants from the west. Although Big Bend National Park (NP) and Fort Davis in the Trans-Pecos are more than 550 miles and 470 miles, respectively, from Fort Worth, I traveled to the Trans-Pecos 12 times during my Texas big year.

My favorite two places in the Trans-Pecos region are (1) Big Bend NP, where Cassin's Kingbirds are ubiquitous and Common Black-Hawks, Band-tailed Pigeons, Western Screech-Owls, Elf Owls, Lucy's and Colima Warblers,

Trans-Pecos scene

Montezuma Quail

and Painted Redstarts are regularly found, and (2) the Davis Mountains and Davis Mountains State Park, where Montezuma Quail and Buff-breasted Flycatchers are most likely to be found in Texas. Except for Band-tailed Pigeons in Ketchikan and Western Screech-Owls in Southeastern Alaska, none of these West Texas birds is found in Alaska. Ruddy Ground-Dove is difficult to find in the United States, and although I did not find it anywhere during my ABA big year, I did see it in Big Bend during my Texas big year.

Other sites I visited in the Trans-Pecos during my big year include Guadalupe Mountains NP and El Paso.

Panhandle and Western Plains

This region extends from New Mexico on the west and Oklahoma on the north and east to the Trans-Pecos and Edwards Plateau regions to the south. The elevation is 1,000–4,500 feet. Stream valleys, playa lakes, and vast former prairie areas with large amounts of mesquite and yucca cover much of the mostly unpopulated area. This area is particularly important in Texas for wintering waterfowl and land birds.

The Texas Panhandle for me was the main area to find wintering raptors, such as Rough-legged Hawks, some of which migrate to Alaska in April, and Ferruginous Hawks, which are not found in Alaska. The Panhandle also had reliable locations for wintering American Tree Sparrows, which breed in Alaska.

Sites I visited in the Panhandle and Western Plains include Rita Blanca National Grassland, Lake Meredith National Recreation Area, Lake Marvin, Gene Howe Wildlife Management Area (WMA), Muleshoe National Wildlife Refuge (NWR), Lubbock, Texline, and Monahans Sandhills State Park.

Edwards Plateau

The Edwards Plateau, often called the Hill Country, is in Central Texas. Vegetation includes grasses, live and shinnery oaks, junipers, and mesquite. This area is the breeding home of two particularly important Texas bird species, the Golden-cheeked Warbler (found only in Texas and Mexico) and the Black-capped Vireo (found only in Texas, Oklahoma, and Mexico), which I found there during my Texas big years. It is also a good area to search for migrating birds in the spring.

Sites that I visited in the Edwards Plateau include Balcones Canyonlands NWR and Lake Buchanan.

Northern Plains

This region covers north-central Texas from Oklahoma south to the Edwards Plateau and the Central Plains and east to the Pineywoods region. It includes cross timbers and prairies in the west, blackland prairies in the center, and post oak savannah in the east. The area has flatland, rolling hills, and stream valleys and includes the Dallas–Fort Worth Metroplex, where I lived for 10 years. It is an area of major overlap between closely related western and eastern bird species. Thus, I found Tufted and Black-crested Titmice, Eastern and Western Kingbirds, Eastern and Western Meadowlarks, and Ruby-throated and Black-chinned Hummingbirds in the Northern Plains region during my big year. I saw only two of these species during my Alaska big year—one Eastern Kingbird and one Western Meadowlark, both rare in Alaska.

Sites I visited in the Northern Plains include the Metroplex (including many areas in Fort Worth), Hagerman NWR, Arlington's River Legacy Park, and Lake Tawakoni.

Bluebonnets on the Northern Plains

Pineywoods
This region is adjacent to Arkansas and Louisiana and extends down to the Upper Coast region. It includes much forested land with lowland hardwoods and upper hilly areas of conifers, primarily pines. Many of the species are the same as in pine woods of the eastern United States, such as the at-risk Red-cockaded Woodpecker and other woodpeckers including Pileated, Downy, and Hairy, Brown-headed Nuthatches, Fish Crows, eastern warblers, and Henslow's and Bachman's Sparrows. Except for Downy and Hairy Woodpeckers and a few of the warblers, none of these species is found in Alaska.

Sites I visited in the Pineywoods include Nacogdoches and surrounding pine forests.

Central Plains
This region extends between the Northern Plains in the north, the Pineywoods and Upper Coast in the east and south, and the Brush Country and Edwards Plateau in the south and west. East Austin is near the western edge and Houston toward the eastern edge of this region. It includes savannahs and prairies as well as bottomlands and floodplains. Although many of the

birds in the Central Plains are found elsewhere in Texas, it was a particularly good area for wintering ducks, such as scoters, and shorebirds, including Mountain Plovers.

Sites I visited in the Central Plains include Austin, especially Hornsby Bend, Williamson County, Attwater Prairie Chicken NWR, and west Houston.

Upper Coast

This region extends from the Louisiana border south to the San Antonio River and includes flat lowland coastal plains and barrier islands. The Upper Coast is one of the main migration hotspots in Texas for flycatchers, vireos, thrushes, warblers, grosbeaks, tanagers, and buntings, especially well-birded areas such as Sabine Woods, High Island, and Anahuac NWR. Birders from around the world can also be found there, especially from mid-April to early May, and to a lesser extent during fall migration.

Sites I visited on the Upper Coast include Sabine Woods, Sea Rim State Park, McFaddin NWR, Anahuac NWR, High Island (Boy Scout Woods, Smith Oaks), Bolivar Flats Shorebird Sanctuary, Galveston Island, Houston (Jesse H. Jones Park), Brazos Bend State Park, Brazoria NWR, Port O'Connor, and Matagorda County.

Coastal Bend

This area lies below the San Antonio River south to the eastern portion of the Rio Grande Valley. On the east is a chain of barrier islands. There are many water areas, from streams to estuaries and saltwater wetlands. Similar to the Upper Coast, the Coastal Bend is on the Central Flyway, and both areas are therefore very important during migration, particularly for eastern warblers, tanagers, grosbeaks, and buntings. These migrants generally do not go as far north as Alaska, except for a few that make it to Southeastern Alaska, particularly the most southern area around Hyder.

Sites I visited in the Coastal Bend area include Aransas NWR, Goose Island State Park, Rockport-Fulton, Port Aransas, Packery Channel County Park, Padre Island National Seashore, Corpus Christi, and Hazel Bazemore County Park.

Brush Country

This is the South Texas plains region and extends from the Edwards Plateau south of San Antonio, south to the Rio Grande Valley along the southwestern edge of Texas (e.g., Laredo). The original grassland and savannah have been changed, primarily by grazing, to dense Tamaulipan scrub, mesquite, live oaks, acacias, and cacti. Important birds in this area include Harris's Hawk, Crested Caracara, Greater Roadrunner, Ringed and Green Kingfishers along the river and other waterways, Golden-fronted Woodpecker, and Long-billed and Curve-billed Thrashers, none of which is found in Alaska, which does not have a similar habitat. Rufous-capped Warbler was a particularly rare bird for Texas (not found in Alaska) that I was able to see in the Brush Country in 2005.

Sites I visited in the Brush Country include San Antonio South (Mitchell Lake) and other areas south and southwest of San Antonio.

Rio Grande Valley

The Rio Grande Valley on the South Texas border stretches from the Gulf of Mexico for about 165 miles upriver to the northwest, and it includes the land about 20–30 miles north of the river. As I learned within a month of moving to Texas, for Texan birders there is only one Valley, the elongated megahotspot more fully known as the Lower Rio Grande Valley (LRGV). Because of its wet habitat in a generally very dry area and its proximity to Mexico for wandering Mexican vagrant birds, this area is the main region in the state for visiting birds and birders all year long. To the casual observer the Valley is merely a ragtag assemblage of gas stations and stores strung out along US 83 parallel to the Mexican border and catering to winter Texans. But tucked between and in the towns are numerous tree and water oases that attract Mexican birds, which in turn attract birders from around the world. Although Brownsville is over 530 miles from Fort Worth, I visited the region over 12 times during my big year, at times for fairly extended stays. Other than Texas specialties regularly found in the Rio Grande region (such as Plain Chachalaca, Long-billed Thrasher, White-tipped Dove, Great Kiskadee, Clay-colored Thrush, Buff-bellied Hummingbird, Couch's Kingbird, Olive Sparrow, Green Jay, Groove-billed Ani, and Muscovy Duck), rare birds I found in the Rio Grande Valley during my big year (in the order found) include Crimson-collared Grosbeak, Green-breasted Mango, Black-legged Kittiwake (added to the Texas Review List midway through 2005), White-throated Thrush, Social Flycatcher, Elegant Trogon, Blue Mockingbird, and Golden-crowned Warbler.

Sites I visited in the Rio Grande Valley include Laguna Atascosa NWR, Boca Chica, Brownsville, Santa Ana NWR, Bentsen–Rio Grande Valley State Park, Salineño, and San Ygnacio.

Upon Being Asked:
"How do you like Texas birding?"

Do you fancy a mountain with junipers, pines?
Or maybe a forest with thick, hanging vines.
Perhaps you like yucca stretching for miles,
Or is it the beach that brings on your smiles?
You might like the plains that stretch to the sky,
Or the canyons with beauty no one can deny,
Or maybe you really like rivers that flow,
Or deserts, or big lakes, or marshes, or snow.
All of these places are in Texas somewhere,
And in each of these places are birds that are there.
The diversity—astounding; the landscape—so vast,
The birding—stupendous! I'm glad that you asked.

Although I have enjoyed birding in both states, I wrote a poem only about the vast diversity found in Texas.

ALASKA

A Birder's Guide to Alaska describes the six major biogeographic regions of Alaska first characterized by Brina Kessel and Daniel Gibson in 1978, which I have summarized below with a brief listing of some of the birds I found in each region during my Alaska big year.

Northern Alaska

Northern Alaska includes the North Slope and extends from the Brooks Range north to the Beaufort Sea and west to Point Hope. Between the mountains and the coast the land is very flat and has water-filled lowlands in the summer, a perfect area for breeding waterfowl and shorebirds. Although in 2008 I birded the North Slope to find the Gray-headed Chickadee, I decided in my Alaska big year that the time and expense of a week-long river float trip were prohibitive because the birding season is so short in Alaska. I did go to Utqiagvik, however, on four different brief trips. Ross's Gulls are the main expected goal there (October), as are Snowy Owls (also seen elsewhere in Western Alaska). In 2016, another major goal, Ivory Gull, usually seen in Alaska associated with floating ice off the coast, did not appear in Utqiagvik on any of my three winter trips, presumably because no sea ice was visible from the shore in the fall before the darkness of winter, when I could no longer bird there.

Sites I visited in Northern Alaska in my big year include locations in Utqiagvik.

Western Alaska

Western Alaska extends along the Chukchi and Bering Seas south to the mouth of the Kuskokwim River. It includes the Seward Peninsula and islands in the Bering Sea. St. Paul and St. Lawrence are the main islands that are birded, where in addition to nesting seabirds, Asian migrants and strays are regularly found.

Sites I visited in Western Alaska include St. Paul Island, St. Lawrence Island (Gambell), and Nome.

Highlights on St. Paul in spring were shorebirds not usually found in other parts of the United States and certainly not in Texas (Wood Sandpiper, Common and Curlew Sandpipers, Long-toed Stint, Common Greenshank, Lesser Sand-Plover), nesting alcids not ever found in Texas (Parakeet, Crested and Least Auklets, Horned and Tufted Puffins), and Siberian Rubythroat (rarely found in the United States except in Western Alaska). Late summer on St. Paul Island was less noteworthy in 2016 than in many other years, but I was able to add Jack Snipe, Eurasian Skylark, and Red-flanked Bluetail to my year list.

Spring highlights at Gambell on St. Lawrence Island were White Wagtail and Common Ringed Plover (regular breeders there), Terek Sandpiper, Red-necked Stint, Dovekie, and Eyebrowed Thrush (only one of each viewed), and White-tailed Eagle (very rare anywhere in the United States). In late summer, it was relatively slow for the season, but new for the year were Sharp-tailed Sandpiper (regular fall migrant in Western Alaska), Siberian Accentor (the second year I saw one there), and Gray-tailed Tattler (regular but not common migrant). Although I had not planned it, I took an unexpected trip to Gambell in late November because a Pine Bunting was reported and was easily watched as it hopped on the snow eating weed seeds.

My spring trip to Nome, part of another Wilderness Birding Adventures trip in early June, was very productive of new birds for the year. Birds I saw in Nome that are uncommon or difficult to find in most other places in Alaska were Arctic Warbler, Bluethroat, Bristle-thighed Curlew, Eastern Yellow Wagtail, Spectacled Eider, Sabine's Gull, Say's Phoebe, and Red Knot. I saw two of these in my Texas big year, Sabine's Gull and Red Knot. Astoundingly, a pair of Eastern Phoebes, an extremely rare bird in Alaska, nested just outside Nome. I went back to Nome in late November to see McKay's Buntings, which winter there and are difficult to find in Alaska the rest of the year (never reported in Texas).

Southwestern Alaska

Southwestern Alaska includes the Alaskan Peninsula and the Aleutian Islands. The westernmost islands, such as Attu (essentially no longer accessible to birders by air) and Adak, have a long history of observations of Asian migrants and rarities.

During my Alaska big year, I went to Adak with Wilderness Birding Adventures in mid-May, where we saw Gyrfalcons, Tufted Ducks, Bar-tailed Godwits, Kittlitz's Murrelets, Common Snipe, and Ruffs, none of which are normally found in Texas, nor did I see them during my Texas big year. In late June with members of the Anchorage Audubon Society, I took the state ferry from Homer to Kodiak and out the Alaskan Peninsula to Dutch Harbor, followed by a charter boat trip from Dutch Harbor, and was rewarded by seeing thousands of Whiskered Auklets, plus wonderful views of Short-tailed, Black-footed, and Laysan Albatrosses just behind the charter boat.

Interior

The Interior of Alaska extends south from the Brooks Range to the Alaska Range and east to the Yukon border. Much of the area is boreal forest, bogs in permafrost, and glacial rivers that empty into the Bering Sea. There is alpine tundra at the higher elevations. The area is excellent for nesting waterfowl and shorebirds.

My main birding in this region during my big year was near Delta Junction. Target birds I found there in late April included displaying Sharp-tailed and Ruffed Grouse, the first of only a few American Kestrels seen during the year, and many singing Hammond's Flycatchers. I returned to the Delta Junction area later in the summer and added Upland Sandpiper and Yellow-breasted Sapsucker. I went once to the Yukon border and once in June to Chicken, Alaska, which was hosting a pair of nesting Mountain Bluebirds, birds with a very limited summer range in Alaska. I had missed Mountain Bluebirds when they migrated into the state in spring (they winter in West Texas). I made a special trip to Kenny Lake, which is along the Edgerton Highway between Glennallen and Valdez, where Ruddy Ducks nest (not expected to be found elsewhere in Alaska, but commonly found in many areas of Texas).

South-Central (South Coastal) Alaska

South-Central Alaska extends south from the Alaska Range to the Gulf of Alaska. It includes boreal forest, farming country, and extensive mudflats that are critical for migrating shorebirds. Because Anchorage is in this area, as are areas to the south that can be reached by car (Seward, Kenai, Soldotna, and Homer), I found many birds of my Alaska big year in this area. Most were the regular residents and migrants there, such as Steller's Jay, Black-capped, Boreal, and Chestnut-backed Chickadees, Bohemian Waxwing, Arctic Tern,

Sandhill Crane, and Osprey. Alaskan rarities and uncommon birds I first saw for the year in this region were Brambling, White-throated Sparrow, Yellow-billed Loon, Eurasian Wigeon, Townsend's Solitaire, Franklin's Gull, and Blue-winged Teal.

On the way from Anchorage to Kenai is Summit Lake, which until August 2016 I had not particularly noticed. It, however, was the starting place for a great hike in late August, where I was finally able to see a few White-tailed Ptarmigan.

Mountains south of Anchorage

Turnagain Arm south of Anchorage

Although my original big year plans did not include it, Kodiak Island was where I began my Alaskan journey on a quest for a Common Pochard reported there, a bird I had never seen. The pochard was the second bird for the year (after Bald Eagle). Because every bird there was new for the year, I saw more new birds on Kodiak Island than I did anywhere else in Alaska that year.

Southeastern Alaska

Southeastern Alaska has large areas of Pacific coastal rain forest with large spruce, hemlock, and cedar trees that are attractive to the lumber industry. For birders trying to obtain large Alaska life or year lists, the proximity to western and southern Canada and a warmer climate than in the rest of the state make this region the best and usually only place to add birds more typically found outside Alaska. I made numerous flights to this area during my Alaska big year, primarily to Juneau and Ketchikan. I also made a special trip early in the year to Hoonah, where a Brewer's Blackbird (rare in Alaska) had wintered, and another to Sitka for a Wood Duck (which surprisingly remained throughout the year).

Bald Eagles

At first most of my flights to Southeastern Alaska were aimed mainly at finding the regular Southeastern Alaska birds that are difficult to find or rare in the rest of Alaska, such as Anna's Hummingbird, Western Grebe, Brandt's Cormorant, Hooded Merganser, Red-breasted Sapsucker, Vaux's Swift, Sooty Grouse, Band-tailed Pigeon, and Caspian Tern (early May, Ketchikan), as well as the state rarities that had wintered there (Spotted Towhee, Pied-billed Grebe, Western Meadowlark, American Coot). I also went to see other rarities that came in later (Cinnamon Teal in late April and Palm Warbler in October in Juneau; Brown-headed Cowbird in June, Rose-breasted Grosbeak in July, and House Finch in October in Ketchikan; Tropical Kingbird in October and Cape May Warbler in November in Sitka; and Lewis's Woodpecker in November in Petersburg).

The most amazing outing in this area was a four-day trip to Hyder, the southernmost mainland Alaskan birding site adjacent to British Columbia, where under the leadership of Steve Heinl, three of us were able to see 20 birds new for my year. Some of these are regular (at least not rare) in the area, while others are quite rare for the state. New birds for my year in Hyder were American Crow, Chipping Sparrow, MacGillivray's, Magnolia, and Black-throated Gray Warblers (first state record), American Redstart, Western Wood-Pewee, Black Swift, Yellow-bellied, Least, Willow, and Alder Flycatchers, Western Tanager, Eastern Kingbird, Veery, Bullock's Oriole, Black-headed Grosbeak, Northern Rough-winged Swallow, Cassin's Vireo, and Swainson's Hawk. Other than the Black Swift, these are found in Texas much more regularly than in Alaska.

4
TWO BIG YEARS

By the time I started my 2005 Texas big year, I had lived in Texas for five years and had explored the state quite extensively. That exploration was aimed not at preparing for this endeavor but rather at adding birds to my Texas county lists. Texas has 254 counties and I was trying to see at least one bird in each county and then repeatedly visit the counties to increase each county list as much as I could. It helped me learn much about the state and its birds.

I had also done what turned out to be a Texas big year in 2003. My arbitrary goal that year had been to see 400 species in the state. As a relatively inexperienced Texas birder, I was trying to maintain a low profile, hoping to avoid other birders' comments on my efforts and results. Early in that year while chasing some bird rarity, I met Eric Carpenter, who was doing a serious Texas big year. I had never met anyone like him before. Hearing about him and his plans caused me to change my goal of 400 species to "as many as possible." I wasn't calling it a big year because I had done no preliminary planning to speak of and at that point did not fully understand the whole concept. I just kept birding as much as possible, paying close attention to what Eric was doing and following the rare bird reports. To my amazement I did very well, ending the year at 485 species, not far from previous records. Eric, however, saw 505 species for that year, breaking the previous record.

After 2003, I was ready to do it again:

PLANNING THE BIG YEARS

Late in 2003, in the midst of racing around Texas, I casually broached the idea of doing a serious Texas big year to my husband. His response was not overenthusiastic, just silence and a

On Big Year 2003
(written January 11, 2004)

It got me to camp; it got me to climb;
It got me to bird, most all of the time.
It got me to hear; it got me to see;
It made my life buoyant, exciting and free.
It drove me to drive every road of this state.
It got me up early and kept me up late.
You ask if I'd do it all over again—
Don't ask me "if," just ask me "when."

look that needed no words. So, perhaps I wouldn't do one in 2004. Howard Laidlaw did a Texas big year that year, setting a new record of 511 species. Midway through 2004, I began to consider how I might plan a big year, a serious Texas big year. Little did I know that when I decided to do this in 2005, with what my sister called "Lynnie's luck," I had picked an astounding year for birding in Texas.

Inspired by Eric's advice to let other birders know about my endeavors so they would let me know about the birds they were seeing, I decided to send emails to most of the Texas birders I knew as well as other active birders I did not know but whose posts on the Texbirds listserv indicated that they seemed familiar with their local birds and might have useful and current knowledge. Most states have listservs that electronically distribute messages about bird sightings to subscribers.

I studied bird books that described bird habitats and habits, and books about places to bird in Texas. Toward the end of 2004, I had collected a bulging notebook of rare bird reports in Texas in the hope that at least some would remain into 2005. It was a great winter season in late 2004, with many wanderers from Mexico and some from the far northern United States. I traveled to see some of them in 2004, even though I knew I would have to return to see them in order to count them for my 2005 big year.

I readied my website by adding new pages where I planned to list the birds I observed in 2005 by date seen and by taxonomic order. Experts classify bird species and arrange them in taxonomic order, based on how the species are believed to be naturally related. My planned lists were designed not only to help me keep track of things but to allow other birders to easily know whether I had already seen a particular species during the year.

My main preparation was trying to figure out when to go where to maximize the number of bird species. To help in this attempt, I used sticky notes on a dedicated planning calendar, with notes such as "need to go to Big Bend now" or "Golden-cheeked Warblers arriving now in Austin." This allowed me to begin scheduling trips. I could move the notes around to juggle the timing when they overlapped or other scheduling problems arose.

In the excitement of what I was about to undertake, I babbled continually to everyone I met about my plans, which included an initial 10-day marathon drive around Texas starting January 1. Simone Jenion, a Fort Worth birder I did not know very well, was also excited about the project and became part of the plan for the 10-day marathon. Little did either of us know that the momentum of those 10 days would propel her into doing her own big year, so our big year travels were often together, particularly during the first half of 2005.

I knew that no matter how much I planned, I would never be ready, really ready for another big year, but I was surely more ready than in 2003. I knew that the relentless march of time was the enemy. Once spring migration is over, the birds depart and you can't go back to get those you missed. Many of these migrants travel different routes in fall and might miss Texas entirely. The bottom line was becoming clear—you have to plan to go everywhere a species might be when it is likely to be there. This required more knowledge and less spontaneity than I liked. What I really wanted was just to bird all the time and see as many birds as possible. I was also worried that in my attempts to add rarities to my list I would be racing blindly back and forth, forgetting to see and count the nonrarities, the usual birds.

In contrast to my planning for my Texas big year, by the time I planned my Alaska big year in late 2015, I felt like an old pro at planning and doing big years. After all, I had done not only my two Texas big years but also an ABA big year (2008) and a South Dakota big year (2011), as well as a few county big years in South Dakota. I updated my website and started a blog so I could tell the story of my Alaska big year day by day.

A main problem with planning an Alaska big year was that although I had been to Alaska multiple times during my ABA big year, I was unfamiliar with much of what I needed to know about Alaskan birds and where and when to find them, especially those more common outside Alaska than in Alaska. I did study books and internet reports. Another big problem was my lack of knowledge on just how to get to some of the Alaska bird sites and the logistics of being there, including places to stay, availability of rental cars, road conditions, weather/snow/ice problems, remoteness, difficulty of getting around, the need to be prepared for bears, and on and on.

As part of my planning, similar to what I had done in Texas, I made a list of Alaska birders I gleaned from talking to Anchorage birders I had met and from looking at reports on the AKBirding listserv. In addition to emailing them an announcement of my upcoming big year, I contacted some to ask whether they might be willing to help me with bird locations in their part of the state. Also, as I had done with my ABA big year, I told some women birders, primarily in the Anchorage area, about my planned big year in the hope they might be able to join me for a major trip or two to split expenses as well as be companions on my journey.

Unlike in Texas, in order to bird in Alaska it is necessary to fly to most destinations. I realized it would make sense to make advance plane, motel, and car reservations for as many places as possible, particularly during tourist season, which is the time of year to see birds in Alaska. In Texas I did not need to rent a car or get airline tickets—I just got in the car with my map and gear (and Simone, if she was going) and headed out. In Alaska I either made long-range plane reservations or paid a lot more for spur-of-the-moment reservations, or risked not being able to go where I wanted. That clearly reduced spontaneity, which was very different from my Texas big year. I knew that the more I fixed my future travel plans, the more likely I was to run into the problem of wanting or needing to be in one place when an unexpected rarity showed up somewhere else and being unable to get there.

DOING THE BIG YEARS

Unlike in Alaska, where most birds leave the state as it gets colder in the fall and winter, many birds go to Texas in the winter. Also, more birds pass through Texas during spring migration and stay a while, and many others come back through the state in the fall, providing a second chance to see them before they leave for Central and South America.

In contrast to Alaska, because there are so many wintering species and such diversity in the different areas of Texas, starting a big year in Texas is best done by covering the entire state and its vast and varied wintering bird population in January and February. To that end, my Texas big year began with a 10-day drive around the state. Simone Jenion joined me on that drive, from Fort Worth southeast to the Upper Coast and Coastal Bend to the Lower Rio Grande Valley, then through the Brush Country to the Trans-Pecos, up to the Panhandle, and back to Fort Worth. After that, much of my birding for the rest of the year was not planned but occurred in response to reports of rarities around the state, and during that time I tried to see the nonrare birds wherever I went. I also took targeted trips, particularly as migrants started arriving, for birds likely to be found in different areas of the state. All these trips were by car (adding 90,000 miles to my odometer that year, over 10,000 of which were driven in January), and the only planning usually required was to put gas in the car and call Simone to see whether she wanted to come. There was no need for advance reservations, nor were they usually possible because of the last-minute nature of many trips. Most often I had no definite plan as to where I would be come nightfall, so I often did not make motel reservations at all, and of course I didn't require a rental car (except for the period when one of our cars broke down and we had not yet bought another one).

Later in my Texas year when birders and birds were everywhere, occasionally no motels were available so I had to sleep in my car, but usually being last-minute worked out fine. On March 14 I was in Big Bend NP, which for some reason (perhaps it was spring break) was packed with people. This trip was unplanned, and I found out there was no room at the inn, or in the motel, or in the campgrounds, or anywhere. I wasn't quite sure whether it was against the rules to sleep in your car in the park, but that seemed to be my only option, other than going home (at least nine hours away) and trying again another day. The hour was late, I was tired, and I wanted to bird in Big Bend the next day. I knew that camping was allowed only in marked sites, and all sites were full, so I couldn't just put up my tent in some vacant corner.

I birded until after dark, until after the closing of the Chisos Basin store and restaurant, and then parked relatively near the restrooms by the store and crawled into the back of my car behind the front seats. Thank goodness the back seats of a RAV4 are removable and we had removed them to make room for all my travel gear. As the sky darkened, the car lights of a few departing employees and late guests washed over my vehicle. I was a bit worried that what I was doing was against some rule, so I huddled beneath a blanket in the back of my car every time I saw approaching lights or heard footsteps, flattening out to look like a piece of luggage and not a human body. Eventually I dropped off to sleep without being ejected from the park, and I awoke a bit stiff, but eager to bird.

By midyear, a big year can seem very long, especially when the easy-to-find birds have been found. This was particularly true during my Texas big year when even I, a lover of driving, became very weary of the whole thing. Although I am aware that others, even enthusiastic birders, find the big-year concept insane at best, generally the excitement of the endeavor keeps this information repressed. As the excitement fades, worry about what will come in the remaining months begins to surface.

During my Texas big year, I found that venting my frustrations by writing them down in doggerel helped me deal with my anxiety—about spending so much money, about deciding where to go and when, about whether I would see a hard-to-get rarity, about how things were going, about being anxious, and so on. It also helped to take breaks periodically, birding only "for fun" for a change, or doing something completely different.

In Alaska, most birds endeavor to leave the state as it gets colder in the fall and winter. Starting an Alaska big year in January involves spending time trying to see those that winter there, primarily in the generally warmer Southeastern and South-Central areas, so that when the very brief weeks of migration and summer arrive, bird-seeking time can be devoted to the arriving breeding birds.

Although I did not plan to begin my Alaska big year in Kodiak (it was due to a rarity, Common Pochard, present there at the end of 2015), the result was that I saw many more species (52) on January 1 and 2 than I would have if I had started in Anchorage as planned. The Kodiak birds reduced the number of trips I would have had to take elsewhere to see those species during the winter. After the first two days, I followed my initial plans, with trips to Southeastern Alaska (Juneau, Ketchikan, and Hoonah).

In Alaska the arrival of spring and migrants mostly does not occur until late April at the earliest, and many of these depart by the end of June and July. For this reason, it is wise to bird nonstop during these two or three warmer months. Because so many bird species breed in Alaska, it was tempting to cease my chase and revel in the feverish nesting activity as I did in June in Utqiagvik, where there were fluffy shorebird and waterfowl babies galore. While fall migration in late August through early October consists mainly of birds leaving the state, arriving rare-to-the-United-States Asian migrants are regular in Western Alaska, requiring another stint of nonstop birding. Slow times in Alaska are mostly February to late April, July to early August, and mid-October to December.

Five Months into the Big Year

The problem with driving across this broad state
Is that it gives me time to contemplate
The idiocy of the five months past,
And seven more—I hope I last!
With each bird reported not yet on my list,
I must hop in my car—it cannot be missed.
The miles fly by, as do the birds,
It really is too nuts for words.
Yet there's an odd pleasure as the total rises,
Filled with wondrous, bizarre surprises
With "easy" birds that can't be found,
But rarities that much abound.
No one could've predicted what's happened to date
Nor what will be my Big Year's fate.
Let's hope it's not what happened to my car,
Which died from being driven too far.
Let's hope that birds keep being spotted,
That t's are crossed and i's are dotted,
That migrants are manifest and days are long,
That snows are early and fronts are strong,
That I hold out and my new car does too,
That finds are many and misses are few,
As I roam the state both far and near,
And that there's time to sleep in the coming year.

HOW AND WITH WHOM I BIRDED

My Texas big year was mostly either a solo endeavor or trips with Simone Jenion, who decided to try a big year after the first 10 days of January. It was rare for me to bird with anyone else except for spontaneous group gatherings at hotspots or where rarities had recently been reported. My typical birding trip during my Texas big year was to hop into my car (a Toyota RAV4) and head either to an area where I thought there might be some birds I had not yet seen in my big year or to a spot where something rare had been reported. These trips lasted anywhere from 1 to 10 days and were often at least 3 to 4 days, as I headed south from Fort Worth to the Lower Rio Grande Valley (over 500 miles), to the coastal area (300 miles or so), or to West Texas (over 500 miles). The average miles I drove per day each month was nearly 250, and I drove a total of about 90,000 miles. I never got on a plane, and only a couple of times did I reserve a motel room at my destination before arrival.

In major contrast to my Texas experience, most of my Alaskan travels were by plane to a chosen destination, where I reserved a room and a rental car in advance. It is impossible to drive to most Alaskan destinations from Anchorage, and many of these destinations have no road access from anywhere else. Southeastern Alaskan birding destinations are isolated, with the exception of Hyder and Haines, which are 756 and 1,354 miles, respectively, by road from Anchorage (much of the route is through Canada and therefore time spent in these areas cannot contribute to an Alaska big year), and are therefore much easier to get to by plane. I birded the southern and western islands (Kodiak, Amaknak, where Dutch Harbor is located, Adak, St. Paul, and St. Lawrence, where Gambell is located) as well and of course had to fly there. Only in South-Central Alaska (Kenai and Homer, south of Anchorage), north of Anchorage (Palmer, Wasilla), and in the Interior (Glennallen, Delta Junction) did I drive my car. For some of my Alaska travel, to help with logistics (room and board, transportation, leadership) I also signed up with bird tour companies—Wilderness Birding Adventures (Adak, Juneau, Gulf of Alaska, Gambell) and Zugunruhe Birding Tours (one of my Utqiagvik trips).

Because I was relatively new to Alaska, I did not know my way around many of my destinations and could not just inexpensively drive around to explore. Therefore I found it particularly useful and critical to get to know local birders who could help me figure out where to bird, and they were invaluable in helping with my bird searches. I owe them a great debt of thanks, especially Steve Heinl (Ketchikan), Gus Van Vliet, Bev Agler, and Patty Rose (Juneau), Aaron Lang (Homer), Rich MacIntosh (Kodiak), Matt Goff (Sitka), Jeff Mason (Delta Junction), Amy Courtney (Hoonah), Brad Hunter (Petersburg), Nat Drumheller (Gustavus), Bob Bird (Summit Lake area), and Ken Tarbox and Toby and Laura Burke (Kenai area). Clarence Irrigoo Jr. kept birders informed of birds at Gambell, and Jerry Koerner regularly welcomed me to his astoundingly bird-friendly yard in Ketchikan. I also thank all those who helped but whose names I did not know or have forgotten.

SIMILARITIES AND DIFFERENCES

There were both similarities and very large differences between how my big years progressed in the two states. In both cases, migrants arrived in spring. In Texas, spring migration is exciting and dramatic, especially in hotspots along the coast. The trees and fields and woods in these hotspots can be filled with warblers, buntings, grosbeaks, orioles, thrushes, and hummingbirds. Most birds arriving in Texas have just made a long trip either across the Gulf of Mexico or over vast dry lands in Mexico. They are tired and hungry and tend to stay put for a while, resting and eating. This allows a birder to concentrate efforts at the hotspots and have a good chance of seeing most of the possible species relatively easily. In Alaska, however, once the birds arrive, they are almost at their Alaskan destinations. They do not stop to rest but quickly move through and spread out over areas mostly inaccessible to birders.

Once birds migrating through Texas leave the state in spring, of course, they are gone for a few months or more. The big year birder that misses them must try to catch them as they come back through in the fall, usually without staying very long. In Alaska, the migrants that arrive in spring can in theory be found during the summer if you miss them during migration, but you must be lucky or must spend a great deal of time and effort trying to find the birds at their widespread breeding locations.

In both states I saw the greatest number of new species, as expected, in January. In Texas, the numbers per month were similar from February through May, but after that I noted very few new species each month. In Alaska, after January there was a two-month lull, after which I saw the majority of species from April to June with a peak in May, as shown in appendix 3.

In both states the cumulative number of species I found during the big years rose gradually until May, after which it began to level off.

FEAST OR FAMINE

Big year birding is not evenly paced throughout the year. At times the schedule is frenetic because the expected migrants *must* be found before they are gone, mainly during spring migration. Before spring migration, birding is rewarding because the resident birds are all new to the year list as you wander about the state. In both Texas and Alaska (and I assume in other states as well), after spring migration there are times when there are absolutely no new birds. Usually this is most evident in mid to late summer before fall migration, and late in the year when, with any luck, all the possible usual birds have been seen and last-minute rarities begin to show up.

During my Texas big year, after I found 294 species in January and 40 to 50 new species each month from February through May, in June the number of new birds dropped to 14. It was difficult to find new birds. In July, land birds were all ones I had seen, and I saw only one new species (Parasitic Jaeger), which I saw only because I went on a pelagic trip (a boat trip on the open sea). In August I added six more species by traveling to West Texas, climbing mountains, and literally beating the bushes. September's four new species were either hard to find (Cassin's Vireo, Sabine's Gull, and Ferruginous Pygmy-Owl) or rare (Fork-tailed Flycatcher), as were the five new species in October. In November I was finally able to add all three fall-migrating scoters I had missed earlier in the year plus the rare American Flamingo, Lewis's Woodpecker, Eurasian Wigeon, and, difficult for me, the Juniper Titmouse. December's four new species were Texas rarities: Trumpeter Swan, Mew Gull, Red Crossbill, and Snow Bunting.

In Alaska, the feast was in January (105 species), especially January 1 and 2 on Kodiak Island (52 species). The next two months kept me going as I searched Southeastern and central Alaska for resident species as well as overwintering rarities, but the new monthly species numbers were only 13 and 6, respectively. By April new birds increased to 25 species, including hawks, some shorebirds and warblers, and east-central Alaskan birds (Delta Junction area). May and June, with 76 and 56 new species, respectively, were the high points following my initial January feast. These high numbers were due to migrants arriving and my intense schedule, including, in the west, Nome (16 species), Adak (16), Gambell (11), and St. Paul (17), and in the east, Hyder (20), plus a few species each in Anchorage, Gustavus, Homer, Anchor Point, Ketchikan, and Juneau. After June, the number of new species each month was 1 to 7, very slow going. Most of those species were rarities at least in Alaska, including Short-tailed Albatross (Dutch Harbor), Eastern Phoebe (Nome), Rose-breasted Grosbeak and House Finch (Ketchikan), Siberian Accentor and Pine Bunting (Gambell), Red-flanked Bluetail (St. Paul), Palm Warbler and Tropical Kingbird (Sitka), and Lewis's Woodpecker (Petersburg). Others were more usual fall migrants (Gray-tailed Tattler, Sharp-tailed Sandpiper) and early winter migrants (Ross's Gull in Utqiagvik), or species I had missed earlier (White-tailed Ptarmigan, Great Gray Owl).

WHAT A DIFFERENCE A YEAR MAKES

One of the amazing things you learn with startling clarity if you keep a bird list during more than one year is that there can be huge differences. In Texas, where I finished my first big year in 2003, I thought I had a good idea of which birds would be difficult and which would be easy to find. Wrong. Here are some examples: in 2003, I found some birds relatively easily that were very difficult to find or not found in 2005, including Williamson's Sapsucker (found in March 2003), Juniper Titmouse (April 2003), Lazuli Bunting (May 2003 in Fort Worth), Yellow-nosed Albatross (September 2003; never seen again anywhere else), and Thick-billed Kingbird (never found in 2005, despite much looking). Unlike in 2005, in 2003 I did not see Rose-throated Becard even though I traveled to the Lower Rio Grande Valley just to try to find it after others posted sightings, nor could I find a Red-faced Warbler in Big Bend NP, where it is usually present in August. In 2003 I saw 46 species of warblers and in 2005 I saw 50 species. Throughout the two years I found many birds at different locales, with more or less difficulty, and at different seasons in the two years. In April 2006 after my 2005 Texas big year was over, I went to Beaumont to give a talk about it. The day before my talk I easily saw two species at Sabine Woods that I had not found in my big year—Hermit Warbler and Sulphur-bellied Flycatcher.

Although I have done only one Alaska big year, I kept good records in 2015 and went to many of the remote areas that I also visited during my big year in 2016, keeping close track of birds. In 2015 I saw 227 species. Of course that list obviously lacks birds that are found only where I did not go in 2015, such as those found only in Southeastern Alaska. An important consideration is the differences year to year in Alaska as to what Asian or other rarities will be found. In 2016 I did not see Tundra Bean Goose (seen on Adak in 2015) or Black-headed Gull (seen in 2015 on St. Paul). I also did not see Pink-footed Shearwater (observed on a Gulf of Alaska trip in 2015), Ivory Gull, or Great

Black-backed Gull (seen in October in Utqiagvik in 2015), Stilt Sandpiper (found in Juneau in 2015), Costa's Hummingbird (viewed in Anchorage in 2015), or Brown Shrike (seen in Gambell in 2015). Of course after my big year in Alaska, as in Texas, rarities showed up that no longer counted for my big year, such as the Hawfinch that came to Anchorage in early March 2017 and the Pied Wheatear in Nome in July 2017.

ISLAND BIRDING

Island birding is not a big feature of Texas, except for Matagorda Island, which I visited a few times over the years I was in Texas, and South Padre Island. The latter location was important, especially early in the year for shorebirds. The large number of first-of-the-year sightings in Cameron County (66), the great majority of which were on South Padre Island, makes its importance clear (appendix 1).

In contrast, unless a birder in Alaska spends considerable time on the Alaskan islands, the number of species seen in the year will be low. The importance of islands is apparent from the number of times I flew to islands in 2016. I took 2 flights to Kodiak, 11 to Ketchikan, 3 to Sitka, 3 to Gambell, 2 to St. Paul, and 1 each to Hoonah, Gustavus, Adak, and Petersburg, a total of 25 flights. The other flights during the year were, with the exception of flights to Homer, flights to mainland sites not reachable by road (Juneau, Nome, and Utqiagvik), and areas reachable by road from Anchorage but requiring more than a few days' drive (Hyder and Haines).

Sitka forest

Birding in the rain in Gustavus

WEATHER—TEMPERATURE, SNOW, AND HEAT

Weather of course plays a role anywhere. Winter in Alaska can be a very difficult time to bird, and Alaskan winters seem to last forever. The extreme cold in many areas is an obvious limitation to how long you can stay outside and to where you can bird in winter. Roads and trails may be impassable, dangerous, or possibly closed because of heavy snow or ice. As spring approaches, ice-covered or mud-covered roads can still be problematic. Some years at higher elevations and in the north, snow and road problems return in late summer only a couple of months after the roads have finally cleared. Storms or lack of visibility due to clouds and fog often means flights are delayed or cancelled, particularly in winter (e.g., Juneau being fogged in during early January) and on flights to and from the western islands (particularly flights to St. Paul, in my experience).

In addition, because the days are so short in an Alaskan winter the farther north you go, the time you can bird each winter day is very short. In contrast, in the summer, days are long and roads are usually passable, but unfortunately the birds are spread out over a vast area.

In Texas, while winter weather can be unseasonably cold and rainy in some areas, it is usually possible to bird wherever desired. Exceptions are mountainous areas and the Panhandle in harsh winter weather. In early February in Texas I went west looking for more wintering birds. On February 7, I drove for over an hour to the Guadalupe Mountains to continue my search. While in the Davis Mountains, I had noticed a light trace of snow on the distant peaks but hadn't thought much about it. In the half light when I arrived at Guadalupe Mountains NP, I could see some whiteness on the far-off mountains, which I first thought was sunlight touching the mountaintops. I began to realize that my intended goal, the "Bowl," a wide forested valley near the top of the mountain, might be up in that area, and that the whiteness was snow, a rare concern in my previous Texas experience. It looked as if it was going to be such a nice day that I didn't give it much thought as I gathered my hiking gear from the car (walking stick, water, snacks, extra clothing, camera, lenses, and binoculars) and headed up the Tejas Trail just before 8:00 a.m.

There were quite a few birds along the lower parts of the trail, including Dark-eyed Juncos, Ladder-backed Woodpeckers, Bewick's and Rock Wrens, a Townsend's Solitaire, Chipping, Rufous-crowned, and Lincoln's Sparrows, and Canyon Towhees. I saw no other hikers on this quiet, eerily beautiful sunny day. In about an hour and a half at my usually slow pace, I reached the lower edge of the snow. As I continued upward the snow got deeper and deeper, and prettier and prettier. The temperature was crispy; the snow wasn't melting or getting my nonwaterproof boots wet—and after all, I grew up in snowy Wisconsin, so not a problem.

Dark-eyed Junco

When I reached the Bowl, tired and disgruntled by the lack of birds, the snow was nearly a foot deep in places and a bit slippery, but I was determined to see new birds. So I started walking one of the snow-covered Bowl trails. Imagine my surprise when I realized that under the lovely white snow, icy puddles had formed as the day turned warmer. Ooh, that was cold as the icy water filled my boots. Oh well, I couldn't get wetter, could I? So I kept going. But I could get colder, and I could definitely get more miserable.

After seeing just a single Steller's Jay and a single Mountain Chickadee and not another bird in the Bowl, I turned around in disappointed disgust to head back. Sprinting up the last part of the trail toward me were two energetic hikers who cheerily hailed me. I muttered an icily sodden hello and headed down the now slippery, icy, slushy trail. The hiking kept my feet from freezing and I gradually cheered up as I hiked down. In a little while, I heard voices behind me and the two bouncy hikers caught up to me. I decided that it wouldn't hurt me to be civil for a change, so we had a little polite conversation. When I inanely asked whether they were birders (no binoculars were visible), they replied that they were not but their son was. When I asked who he was, on the off-chance I might have heard of him, they told me he was Mark Lockwood, whom I had met a couple of times and knew to be secretary of the Texas Bird Records Committee, the committee that decides which sightings of rarities to officially accept. I didn't beg them to put in a good word for me, but I did ask them to tell their son when next they talked that they had met a goofy lady who was doing a big year.

It is usually not winter but summer that presents problems in Texas. Texas is hot. Not only do people slow down in midday and have difficulty zipping around to find new birds, but the birds often disappear to wait out the heat. Therefore, to see birds in summer it is usually best to get up very early to avoid the heat and then bird again in the late afternoon and early evening. Siestas or midday travel can be part of the routine, especially in summer.

In both states, bad weather makes it more difficult to bird, but bad weather can produce "good" (rare) birds. Storms in Texas, especially during migration, can bring rarities in from the Gulf of Mexico and can also bring western or northern birds to the state. In Alaska, nasty western storms are the preferred weather during migration, especially on the western islands. Many birders analyze weather maps for fronts and other weather patterns to determine the chances of rarities arriving.

WEATHER—RAIN

Although rain and flooding can occur almost anywhere in Texas, it can be a big problem in the western mountains of Texas, as I experienced when I went to a hummingbird festival in the Davis Mountains. On August 20, I was booked to go on an all-day field trip up to Mount Livermore. On the drive from Fort Davis to the Davis Mountains Preserve, I noticed a very dark sky with some distant lightning and rain, but it wasn't raining right around me so I pushed it to the back of my mind.

I was thankful our leader, John Karges, paused periodically to, in his words, "stop and look at the oxygen." We were high enough that I definitely needed to find a little more oxygen after clambering up some inclines. There were House, Rock, and Canyon Wrens along the climb, which he termed a "high wren district." Humor is always a good thing, especially when you are feeling a bit light-headed. Also along the trail were Zone-tailed Hawks, White-throated Swifts, and Townsend's Warblers, in addition to the birds observed the previous day.

As we climbed I became more and more aware of the looming thunderclouds. No one else seemed particularly perturbed as we continued hiking. When we got to the top of the dirt road, a narrow trail led upward, which some of the group explored. We had lunch and then went back down the mountain as a few raindrops began to fall. Soon it was raining steadily, with a bit of thunder now and then. We were a long way from our cars, high up on a mountain, with nothing to do but keep going. We got out our rain gear and continued plodding downward. After a heavy rain, it gradually let up and then stopped. We all hastened to remove our rain gear, which was now helping hold our perspiration inside our clothing. Eventually we reached our cars, stowed our rain gear, climbed aboard, and started down the hill.

One thing I think most of us had forgotten (or repressed) was that all that water falling on the top and sides of the mountain had to go somewhere. Where that somewhere was became obvious as we rounded a bend in the road and heard the rush of water. There we beheld a very high river of water crossing the road ahead of us where it had previously been dry. The roiling water carried branches and clumps of debris churning their way down the mountain. All three cars managed to cross that portion of the river. We were aware that all the rivers were winding their way down faster than we were, and as we got farther down the mountain the rivers were going to be more full of water than they had been higher up. It was only going to get worse.

The driver leading the parade knew the various possible roads down the mountain and suddenly cut off on a side road, which apparently allowed us to reduce the number of streams we'd have to cross (or maybe got us to the streams more quickly). In any case, while we were able to cross a couple of times, we ultimately came to a complete stop.

Ahead of us was a roaring river that appeared to be at least as deep as halfway up a car, or more. Huge branches and tree trunks were being carried across the road ahead of us, and there was absolutely no chance we were going to get across it anytime soon. By now it was about 4:00 p.m. We all glanced at each other, wondering about our food supplies (probably close to none, since we'd just eaten the lunches we'd brought), about where we were going to sleep that night, and about other questions too worrisome to contemplate.

The leaders all convened near the edge of the torrent in the now-pouring rain, pacing about or standing miserably and watching the mayhem ahead. We waited in the cars, peering out through the bucketing rain and worriedly conversing. The rain up the mountain seemed to have stopped, and the rain around us, while steady, wasn't too heavy, and very gradually the level of the gushing water started to go down. One of the leaders found a pole and waded partway into the water to take periodic depth measurements. The flow was too deep and rapid for anyone to venture farther out for about two hours, but by then, the leaders decided to make a run for it. Our car went first, as fast as the driver dared, across the rocky river crossing, with perhaps nearly two feet of very rapid water pushing at us from the left. We made it, but we had the highest clearance. The other two drivers sat awhile on the opposite bank (probably praying) as we waited for them on the other side, and then they too made a successful run for it. We had a few more rivers to cross after that, but they weren't as difficult.

Rain in Alaska in my experience was mainly an uncomfortable ever-present reality, even in winter sometimes. Everywhere I went I took rain gear, either lightweight (rare) or heavyweight so it could fit over my parka and I could stay both warm and relatively dry. Much of the rain in Alaska occurs in the southeast, and it was a particularly rainy winter there at the beginning of my big year. Rather than snowing a lot, it rained and froze on the roads and trails and trees. The people I often got together with in Juneau (Bev Agler, Patty Rose) birded every Saturday no matter what the weather. On many days when I was in Juneau I would wake up in my motel, see that it was pouring outside, and know that we were going birding anyway. Anything for a big year, I would think. We would slog across the Mendenhall Wetlands, barely able to see through the downpour, and eventually we would find birds, sometimes new ones, in the now-soaked wetlands.

BIRDING BY BOAT

Early in my Texas big year, the five of us who were doing a big year noticed that the World Birding Center (WBC) had not included pelagic trips in its schedule. For the past couple of years it had organized and run the only pelagic trips off the Texas Gulf Coast. I was worried that perhaps these trips might not happen in 2005, which would have been a catastrophe for me. I posted a survey on Texbirds asking people to indicate their interest in doing one or more pelagic trips. I planned to give this information to the WBC as proof that pelagic trips were important events for the birding community, and if it was not interested in organizing them, I might try some other way.

The results of my survey were clear—there was a lot of interest in Texas pelagics. The WBC quickly informed birders that it was indeed going to run pelagic trips in 2005. As soon as the announcement came out, I signed up for all the trips. I usually do not love pelagic trips. In fact, until I moved to Texas I almost always got sick on them. It had been a while since I had been seasick, but whether I felt like it or not, I had to go on every pelagic trip I could during my big year. It was very unlikely that most of the real oceanic birds of the Gulf would be visible from land, and I couldn't write off a whole group of species just because getting to see them might make me ill.

The first pelagic trip was scheduled for Friday, June 17, leaving the dock at South Padre Island at 6:00 a.m. About an hour and a half after departure, two Masked Boobies were flying around the boat. Masked Boobies are not a real rarity on these trips, but they were a very welcome sight. Much more rare and exciting was the adult Red-billed Tropicbird that flew right over our boat about 15 minutes later. We got spectacular views, and it was a lifer for many aboard. I settled down to rack up the more usual pelagic birds for the year, Cory's and Audubon's Shearwaters, Bridled and Sooty Terns, and Band-rumped Storm-Petrels along with the much rarer (in Texas) Leach's Storm-Petrels. As I had hoped, the first pelagic trip was productive, and I was at 490 species for the year when my day ended in Brownsville.

On the second pelagic trip at the very end of July, we had a Parasitic Jaeger, my one and only new bird for July. It was not around for long. I believe I was the first one on the boat to see it as it attacked a group of gulls, but it hightailed it out of there right after that. The real highlight of that trip, however, was seeing sperm whales—sometimes breaching nearby and causing excited shouts of "there's another one" all around the boat. Even monomaniacal birders can be enthusiastic about whales too (especially when they're the only game in town).

The pelagic trip out of South Padre Island on September 17 produced a Barn Swallow, two Magnificent Frigatebirds, a Red-billed Tropicbird, Bridled, Black, and Sandwich Terns, Cory's Shearwater, and a Red-necked Phalarope, but no new birds for the year.

The last pelagic trip for the year was on Saturday, November 5. As I drove to the boat dock that morning, I had a very mixed mind about going out. The weather forecast was for high waves and I was concerned that the boat might not go out; it was my last chance for a couple of regular pelagic species, Long-tailed and Pomarine Jaegers. Of course, I was also afraid that the boat might go out and that it might capsize, or maybe worse, I'd be seasick. I'd been fortunate that the previous trips had actually been pleasant and I had not gotten sick. As it turned out, on this November trip, which did go out, I was ghastly sick almost the entire time. I even felt sick a couple of days after the trip, every time I thought about the waves. I did see both a Long-tailed and a Pomarine Jaeger, as well as Bridled Terns and Cory's Shearwater. So, I guess the trip was a success.

The Last Pelagic Trip

The waves were as forecast—six feet, maybe more.
We kept keeping on—distinctly hard-core.
At the back of the boat, I provided the chum
Though wobbly my knees and the rest of me numb.
Two more jaegers we saw, completing the set,
But my fear of the waves was not over yet.
If the truth could be known, I wanted to die
But I wouldn't have seen the jaegers fly by.
No gain without pain—'tis trite but 'tis true.
I rejoice in the gain; as for pain—I came through.
It's a story to tell when I'm older and grayer,
Not now on the sidelines, now I'm actually a player!

Although Alaska has much more coastline than Texas, much of it is rocky and inaccessible, and very few pelagic trips are offered. Exceptions were John Puschock's trips in Western Alaska, including a spring trip to Attu, but because of schedule and cost concerns I did not go on one during my big year. I did go on two organized birding trips on Alaska state ferries.

The first Alaska ferry trip was organized by the Anchorage Audubon Society, a project I took on and made happen so I could get to Dutch Harbor to see Whiskered Auklets. We left Homer at around dawn (4:45 a.m.) on June 29. Almost all day during the long days of the entire trip the birders and our leader Aaron Bowman stared out across the waters, looking for, and often seeing, pelagic birds. The morning of the first day was a bit rough and rainy and I was concerned that while this might increase the number of bird species, we might all be too sick to see them. The remaining days were wonderful and not rainy, but we did have periodic high winds. Early on the trip we started seeing many, many Sooty Shearwaters. Soon, there were Tufted and Horned Puffins, at least one Rhinoceros Auklet, Red-necked Phalaropes, Common and Thick-billed Murres, light and dark Northern Fulmars, a few Fork-tailed Storm-Petrels, and a few Black-footed Albatrosses.

We stopped for a few hours at Kodiak and then we were off for Chignik, which we reached about noon on June 30. We saw the same species along the way as before plus a Parakeet Auklet, Pomarine and Parasitic Jaegers, at least three Cassin's Auklets, and three Black Oystercatchers. Late on the thirtieth we reached Sand Point and saw a few Arctic Terns and Bald Eagles. At numerous places along the route we saw Pigeon Guillemots, particularly near the harbors.

Early on the morning of July 1 we reached King Cove on a beautiful clear day. When we reached Cold Bay, some of us took a bus to Izembek NWR. Highlights there were a fox, a couple of Northern Wheatears, Lapland Longspurs, a Semipalmated Plover parent and chicks along the road, and Bank Swallows. In the early evening we reached False Pass, where there were

Whiskered Auklets at Dutch Harbor

Harlequin Ducks, Wilson's and Yellow Warblers, and Savannah, Fox, and Golden-crowned Sparrows, plus fields full of purple lupines. Before it got dark (midnight or so) we saw Ancient Murrelets and more Northern Fulmars.

On Saturday, July 2, we stopped briefly in Akutan before reaching our Dutch Harbor destination about 10:00 a.m. On the way we saw large numbers of puffins, Northern Fulmars, three Kittlitz's Murrelets, and our first Whiskered Auklets. After the ferry arrived in Dutch Harbor, six of us took a taxi to the very new harbor for our boat trip on the *Miss Alyssa*, a 43-foot charter vessel captained by Jimmer McDonald, who fed and guided us very well.

Our charter boat trip lasted from about noon until 9:00 p.m. Because of the timing of tides, the normal route was changed and we headed first to a deep-water bank (Chelan Bank). For what seemed like hours we were in heavy fog with no visibility, but gradually we emerged and could see a few birds, including Pigeon Guillemots, Kittlitz's Murrelets, and both puffins. The captain made a chum line with lumps of meat, which gradually and then dramatically attracted thousands of birds, primarily Northern Fulmars. There were also thousands of Short-tailed Shearwaters, mostly resting on the water.

The excitement began when instead of a few distant albatrosses, we had one and then two Laysan Albatrosses on the water close to the boat. Then a very rare, immature, pink-beaked **Short-tailed Albatross** appeared and landed behind the boat, followed immediately by a black-beaked Black-footed Albatross. We could see all three albatross species together.

Eventually we were able to pull ourselves away from the feeding frenzy and amazing albatross spectacle and motor on to the Baby Island area for the main bird goal of the whole Dutch Harbor trip, Whiskered Auklets (seen only in the far distance from the ferry earlier). Here there was a great multitude of these auklets, usually in tight-knit rafts on the water that exploded in flight as we approached. Often they were too distant for photos, but not always. There were also many Ancient Murrelets on the water, as well as

Three Albatross species seen from charter boat off Dutch Harbor

Cassin's and Crested Auklets and other usual seabirds. With great satisfaction we returned to Dutch Harbor and crawled into real beds for the first time in nearly a week.

The next day (July 3), we explored Dutch Harbor and Unalaska with our guide, Suzi Golodoff. It was also an enjoyable day, with beautiful scenery and wildflowers.

The second ferry trip, organized by Wilderness Birding Adventures, was the same one-and-a-half-day trip that I had gone on the year before from Juneau to Whittier. Unfortunately, this trip, beginning on August 23, was not nearly as productive as it had been the year before. We observed very few birds on the foggy, rainy ferry trip and there were *no* new birds for my list. Every now and then the rain would seem to cease, but it wasn't long until fog on the water or serious rain cut visibility. Nevertheless we hardy birders persevered and kept watch during almost all daylight hours, although a few times the scopes kept watch alone. On the ferry we saw Sooty and Short-tailed Shearwaters (we usually just grouped these two similar species together when we saw the distant fog-shrouded birds), as well as ducks (Harlequin Ducks and Surf and Black Scoters), Pomarine and Parasitic Jaegers, Common Murres, Marbled Murrelets, and Black-legged Kittiwakes.

We docked in the early morning of August 24 at Yakutat and did a bit of land birding before setting out on the ferry again. Land birds included Eurasian Collared-Dove, Fox Sparrow, Bald Eagle, Northwestern Crow, Hooded Merganser (probably young of the year), Common Yellowthroat, and Barn Swallow.

On the second ferry day we saw quite a few Black-footed Albatrosses and Northern Fulmars as well as Cassin's Auklets, Ancient Murrelets, and Tufted Puffins. The ferry portion of our trip ended about 6:00 a.m. on August 25 in Whittier, where we boarded a van and were driven back to Anchorage. It rained most of the way, but when we arrived in midmorning at Potter Marsh just south of Anchorage, the rain stopped and we were able to bird some more before arriving back in Anchorage.

BIRD SPECTACLES

Both Texas and Alaska have many spectacular landscape views as well as spectacular birds. Both states also have bird spectacles, special bird happenings that to me seem impossibly wonderful. In many years, possibly most years in Texas, spring migration along the coast is such a spectacle. For at least a few days each spring, especially in late April, you can go to any of the many hotspots and see colorful birds everywhere—Rose-breasted and Blue Grosbeaks, Baltimore and Orchard Orioles, Ruby-throated Hummingbirds, up to 25 species of warblers, Summer and Scarlet Tanagers, and Indigo and Painted Buntings—to name just a few. It is never the same and you never know exactly what to expect or whether you will arrive in the midst of a fallout or between the waves of birds. Anytime you go to Sabine Woods, High Island, or numerous other, less well-known coastal sites, the trees and bushes could be full of these birds, plus flycatchers flitting about, slower-moving vireos, and cuckoos and thrushes in the undergrowth.

For me, Alaska's biggest spectacle is the cliff-nesting birds on St. Paul Island. Beginning in late May when most of the snow on the cliffs is gone, the area fills up with mostly black-and-white birds punctuated by splashes of red and orange—Common and Thick-billed Murres, Parakeet, Least and Crested Auklets, Horned and Tufted Puffins, Red-legged and Black-legged Kittiwakes, Red-faced Cormorants, and Northern Fulmars. Unlike the Texas spectacle, where one must peer upward to see many of the birds, the Alaska spectacle is viewed by looking down or across to the cliffs, and the Alaskan birds are not moving through but are there for the breeding season.

UNUSUAL OR RARE BIRDS

In Texas, rarities from other places in the United States are usually birds that wander too far south in the fall or winter and get all the way to North Texas, such as Northern Shrikes (found in the Panhandle in winter), or along the coast, such as Long-tailed Ducks. Less common is a rarity from the north that makes it all the way down to South Texas, such as the Snow Bunting on Christmas Day on South Padre Island. Other US species that are rare in Texas have wandered east across the southern United States far from their usual haunts, such as the Red-breasted Sapsucker and Olive Warbler in the Davis Mountains and the Lewis's Woodpecker

Christmas Snow

Little Snow Bunting, got sick of the cold,
So she headed south, out of the fold.
She kept on going; the world was all changed.
She was beginning to feel a bit deranged.
And then she finally found a shore,
She really couldn't fly anymore.
She fluttered down, sore to the bone,
And by George,* it looked just like a home.
The birders came from far away,
To see this bird on Christmas Day.
Around her little anchor bed,
They scattered seeds, and she was fed.
*and Scarlet Colley; thanks to all who cared for her!

Brown-headed Cowbird in Ketchikan

near Guadalupe Mountain that arrived in West Texas from farther west. In my experience most Texas rarities were found in the colder months.

In Alaska, rarities coming from elsewhere in the United States are generally found in Southeastern Alaska—for example, the first-for-the-state Black-throated Gray Warbler found in Hyder. This species is usually found in the western part of the Lower 48 and just into southwestern British Columbia. Other species unusual or rare for Alaska that came to Southeastern Alaska during my big year include many warblers: Tennessee (Juneau), Palm (Juneau and Sitka), Cape May (Sitka), and Magnolia (Hyder) Warblers and American Redstart (Hyder), as well as several Veeries (Hyder), Cinnamon Teal and Spotted Towhee (Juneau), Swamp Sparrow and Brown-headed Cowbird (Ketchikan), Brewer's Blackbird (Hoonah), and Tropical Kingbird (Sitka). Much less common is the sighting in Western Alaska of a rarity that comes from the east, not the west, such as the pair of Eastern Phoebes that made it not only to Alaska, but all the way west to Nome, and then nested there during my big year.

For border states like Alaska and Texas, birds that are rare not only for the state but for all of the United States cross the state's border at the edge of the country. For Texas, these rarities are typically from Central or South America and are often found near the border along the LRGV. In my Texas big year, such rarities included Crimson-collared Grosbeaks, an Elegant Trogon, and a White-throated Thrush, all observed at Frontera Audubon in Weslaco; a Social Flycatcher at Bentsen–Rio Grande Valley State Park in Mission; a Gray-crowned Yellowthroat at Sabal Palm Audubon Sanctuary; a Rufous-capped Warbler south of San Antonio; and a Golden-crowned Warbler at Los Ebanos Preserve north of Brownsville.

Rarities from outside the United States that come to Alaska are found most often on the western islands (Adak, St. Paul, and St. Lawrence

[Gambell]). These are normally Asian or Eurasian birds, which generally appear during migration in spring or fall. Many of these are shorebirds. Examples of rare shorebirds from west of the United States that I found during my Alaska big year include Lesser Sand-Plover, Curlew Sandpiper, and Long-toed Stint (St. Paul), and Terek Sandpiper (Gambell). Other foreign rarities I found in Western Alaska include the White-tailed Eagle, Eyebrowed Thrush, Siberian Accentor, and Pine Bunting at Gambell, and Siberian Rubythroat and Red-flanked Bluetail on St. Paul.

NONBIRD CRITTERS

As a birder, I am usually glad to see nonbird critters, at least ones without bared teeth or stingers. In both states I have seen many other animals while out looking for birds, usually a pleasant experience. In Texas, there have been bobcats, armadillos, antelope, porcupines, and deer (sometimes way too many in the Hill Country); and in Alaska, moose (backyard regulars), porcupines, deer, mountain sheep and goats, and caribou. I have been very lucky during my big years and have not had any dangerous encounters with bigger critters, but in many places I have birded, there have been moments when it seemed that something bad was going to happen.

I have been told that in West Texas you are always within the range of one or more mountain lions, but only rarely have I encountered one. Before dawn on May 11, I drove to the upper parking lot at Chisos Basin at Big Bend NP to cut my walking distance for the day, strapped on a very heavy pack with camping equipment and tons of water, a camera and telephoto lens, a bird book, food, and so on, and began my ordeal of climbing the Pinnacles Trail. I slowly walked the 4.5 miles and on the way saw the typical low- to midelevation birds—a perched Rufous-crowned Sparrow, noisy Mexican Jays and Black-crested Titmice, a Summer Tanager, a Spotted Towhee, singing Blue Grosbeaks and Hutton's Vireos, soaring Zone-tailed Hawks, chattering White-throated Swifts, and Canyon and Bewick's Wrens. Finally, I began to hear the main target species of the walk, Colima Warbler, and I saw it at somewhat higher elevations and at Boot Springs.

At Boot Springs, as I was birding contentedly, a passing hiker appeared, the first person I'd seen that day, who told me a mountain lion had been sighted just beyond the springs. I was undecided on whether to stay at the springs or go back to my tent away from the area where the lion was, but in the end I did neither. Slowly and very carefully, I walked in the direction where the mountain lion was supposed to be. Every little sound made me jump, and I was sure that on the overhanging rocks above my head the lion was watching me, waiting. I never did see it, and eventually I went back to my tent to recuperate a bit from all the walking I'd done that day. I have never been sure whether I was relieved or disappointed not to see the lion.

The only mountain lion I saw in Texas was at Big Bend, but I was safely in my car, and it was running across the road.

In Alaska it is bears, both black and brown (grizzly), that are a concern when you wander out in the woods. Even in Anchorage (which covers a huge area) there are hundreds of each of these species. The only time bears were noticeable during my big year was in Hyder, which is famous for its bear sightings. During the four days we were there, we were mostly on foot, wandering the streets and paths, including the brushy area around the dump, and we regularly saw black bears, sometimes more than one. We always carried our bear spray (an essential precaution in much of Alaska) but did not have to use it as we carefully backed away when we saw bears, and they mostly ignored us. There are also polar bears in Northern Alaska, but I have not had any close encounters with them either, and I always welcome seeing them at a distance from my car.

BIRD FAMILIES

In comparing the results of these two state big years, I found it interesting to look at the various species groups (families) found in the mainland ABA area. Some families have large numbers of species in the United States; some include species found in only one of these two states; and others include species found in both states. For example, the family that includes ducks, geese, and swans has 65 species in the United States, of which I saw 38 in Texas and 41 in Alaska, and 32 of which I found in both states in my big years. The shorebird family has a similar number of possible species (66), but I found many more in Alaska (41) than in Texas (29), and I noted only 23 species in both states. The warbler family (see below for a more detailed discussion) includes 57 species in the United States, 48 of which I noted in Texas. I found fifteen warbler species in Alaska, all of which I also saw in Texas. In contrast, of the 23 possible species in the family that includes auks, murres, and puffins, I found 15 in Alaska and none in Texas.

What follows is a more detailed discussion of a few bird families of particular interest to me.

Hawks

Hawk watches, where birders gather to count migrating hawks, are a part of birding in both Texas and Alaska (as well as in other states). In Texas, the most well-attended hawk watches are those along the coast in the fall. The spring migrations when hawks fly north, primarily from south of the Mexican border, seem to be more diffuse and unchanneled, presumably because the whole of the United States and Canada is open to them as they travel north to their breeding grounds. In fall, however, their southern movement is funneled to a narrower area by the Gulf of Mexico. Thus, during my Texas big year I included the Hazel Bazemore hawk watch in Corpus Christi in late September, where I hoped to see (but did not) the Short-tailed Hawk previously reported. I did see Broad-winged Hawks and Mississippi Kites, neither of which were new for the year.

In Alaska, the northward spring migration path of some hawks is affected by the mountainous terrain. Many years ago, Alaskan birders located

Hawk watch site north of Anchorage

mountain passes where more hawks could be seen during spring migration than at any other time or place in the state. For many years the Anchorage Audubon Society and the Mat-Su Birders have jointly done a weekend hawk watch in the middle of April about 119 miles northeast of Anchorage. Hawks and eagles coming from Canada are channeled past the hawk watch site, where birders have a view up and down and across a valley. For a couple of years, including my big year, HawkWatch International expanded the previous weekend hawk watch to last from early March to early May. As part of my big year, this hawk watch was important in allowing me to get my first Red-tailed (usually the darker Harlan's race) and Rough-legged Hawks, as well as my first Golden Eagles. Other, rarer raptors have been observed there, but those are the only three new raptors I saw at the hawk watch in 2016.

Owls

While the number of owl species I saw in my two big years was similar (11 in Texas and 10 in Alaska), I found only 4 owl species in both states (Western Screech-Owl, Great Horned Owl, Barred Owl [rare in Alaska], and Short-eared Owl). The owls I noted only in Texas were Mexican species (Ferruginous Pygmy-Owl, Spotted, and Elf), western mountain and plains species (Flammulated, Burrowing), eastern US species (Eastern Screech-Owl), or widespread Lower 48 species (Long-eared, sometimes found in Alaska but not by me).

The Alaska-only owls I saw during my big year are rarely seen south of Canada and the northern Lower 48 states: Snowy, Northern Hawk, Northern Pygmy-, Great Gray, Boreal, and Northern Saw-whet Owls. Most of these owls were difficult to see, usually requiring many more hours of searching than other types of birds and involving mostly hearing rather than seeing. I was fortunate during 2016 to see many of these owls in Anchorage (not found in Anchorage were Snowy, Great Gray, Northern Pygmy-, and Barred Owls).

Woodpeckers

I saw nearly twice as many woodpecker species during my Texas big year (15) as I did in my Alaska big year (8). I found 6 of these species in both states: Lewis's Woodpecker (rare in both states), Yellow-bellied and Red-breasted Sapsuckers (the latter rare in Texas), Downy and Hairy Woodpeckers, and Northern Flicker. Woodpeckers I observed only in Texas were typical eastern North American woodpeckers that are usually but not always seen in East Texas (Red-headed, Red-bellied, Red-cockaded, Pileated), typical western

North American woodpeckers seen in West Texas (Acorn Woodpecker, Red-naped and Williamson's Sapsuckers), and Mexican/Texas species (Golden-fronted, Ladder-backed Woodpeckers). The location of Texas makes it an ideal place to see both eastern and western species, and this is especially well illustrated by the woodpecker family.

I observed only two woodpecker species in Alaska only: American Three-toed and Black-backed, both of which are generally not found south of Canada, except in the northern midwestern Lower 48 and the western US mountains. Although I saw the American Three-toed Woodpecker in a park in Anchorage, the usual places to find both of these species are forested areas where trees have been killed by fire. In recent years, the Sockeye Burn north of Anchorage is where most birders travel to see them, and this is where I first saw the Black-backed Woodpecker during my big year. Later in the year I saw both of them there.

Warblers

During my Texas big year, I saw nearly all the warblers that are possible in Texas, a total of 50 species. In Alaska, while I saw only 15 warbler species, this too was almost all of the regularly occurring Alaskan species, plus a few rarities. Appendix 1 lists all the birds I found in my Texas and Alaska big years, including the warblers.

Although some of the Texas warblers remain there to breed, more of them are migrants only, flying through Texas to the northern Lower 48 states or to southern and central Canada, and most are not ever found in Alaska. Some, however, make the long trip to Alaska. Regular Alaskans that I saw during my big year are Northern Waterthrush (which I found in Anchorage and Kenai), Orange-crowned Warbler (common breeder in Anchorage and elsewhere), Yellow Warbler (common breeder in central Alaska), Blackpoll Warbler (migrant and breeder in large areas of the state), Yellow-rumped Warbler (common in summer in the Interior), Townsend's Warbler (breeder in South-Central Alaska) and Wilson's Warbler (common in summer in much of the state).

Less common in Alaska but found during my big year are Tennessee Warbler (one bird only, in Juneau), MacGillivray's Warbler (only in Hyder during my big year; they also come to other parts of Southeastern Alaska), Common Yellowthroat (in Ketchikan in my big year; one seen the previous year in Anchorage), American Redstart (only in Hyder during my big year),

Cape May Warbler (one only, seen only in Sitka), Magnolia Warbler (one only, in Hyder), Palm Warbler (seen in Juneau and Sitka), and Black-throated Gray Warbler (only in Hyder—a first state record).

BIG YEARS DO END, AND LIFE GOES ON

I wrote the poem below at the end of my 2005 Texas big year, but it applies equally well to my Alaska big year (except most of the miles were flown, not driven). The message I hope others garner from reading about my journeys and listening to me talk is that birding can be wonderful. For me it is especially wonderful the more I take the time to do it. Doing a big year gives me the best excuse to go birding: in a big year I *must* go birding as much as possible. Time is a-fleeting; gotta bird.

End of My Big Year

It's over. It's finished. It's done. I'm through
Though I'm glad it's over—am I sad? That too.
In fact, right now, I'm mostly sad.
Just think of all the fun I've had!
You might be thinking—what happens after?
Well, for starters, lots of laughter.
Celebration of what occurred.
A great rejoicing in each new bird.
Then, lots of thanks to one and all,
Who helped, encouraged, gave me a call.
The miles were driven, the birds appeared.
An incredible, astounding Great Big, Big Year!
Now, it's your turn. Get out there! Look!
But as for me—I'm writing a book.

5

FAVORITE BIRDING PLACES IN TEXAS AND ALASKA

Just like the song "My Favorite Things," the following are just a few of my favorite places in each state that were also important in my big years. In both states, the places I love to bird are too numerous to begin to describe. A short description of why I love these not quite arbitrarily chosen places gives someone not familiar with them an idea of what it is like to bird at a few of them. There are many other places in Texas and Alaska where birding is often phenomenal, whether or not you are doing a big year.

TEXAS
Big Bend National Park

Big Bend is almost as far away from Fort Worth as it is possible to go in Texas. Although the drive is over 10 hours (if done nonstop), and although some of the hikes are long and steep, I went there often during my big year (as well as in other years while I lived in Texas). The Pinnacles Trail is a 4.5-mile always-upward hike you can take to see the Colima Warbler after it arrives in spring. Although most of the park is hot except in the few cooler winter months, the air at the top of the Pinnacles Trail is almost always cool, and it can get down into the fifties at night in August. Many other rarities for the United States can also be found there, including Lucifer and Blue-throated Hummingbirds, Red-faced Warbler, and Black-capped Vireo, and there are numerous records for even rarer species from Mexico and farther south. The park has many miles of roads along which you can stop at various hotspots, usually containing a source of water to attract birds, before a quick retreat to the air-conditioned car. Some of my favorite hotspots, in addition to Boot Springs at the top of the Pinnacles Trail, are the Sam Nail Ranch (not much of the ranch is noticeable except a bird-attracting wet area at the base of a windmill), Cottonwood Campground (with large cottonwoods that can be filled with woodpeckers, warblers, and other migrants in spring; also a great place for Lucy's Warbler), and the Rio Grande Village campground at the eastern end of the park, a reliable place for Elf Owls.

In my big year I first went to Big Bend on January 6 and added Horned Lark, Roadrunner, Mountain Bluebird, Phainopepla, and a lovely Golden Eagle soaring over the nearby hills. At Cottonwood Campground we saw a Gray Hawk perched on a post, Common Ravens, and a mixed sparrow flock that included Clay-colored Sparrows. Black-tailed Gnatcatchers hopped about in the brush, and in the campground I saw my first Black-throated Gray Warbler of the year, foraging high. At Sam Nail Ranch, we got brief but fairly good views of a Green-tailed Towhee and a Spotted Towhee.

On May 10, I found Lucy's Warbler, Scott's Oriole, and Elf Owls at Big Bend. On August 9 I climbed the Pinnacles Trail to see a Red-faced Warbler for the year. A few days later I went on a festival field trip there and saw the usual Rufous, Black-chinned, and Broad-tailed Hummingbirds, White-throated Swifts, Band-tailed Pigeons, Hutton's Vireos, and Western Tanagers. Once I got to Boot Springs, Blue-throated Hummingbirds were their usual noisy but often invisible selves in the tall pine trees, Zone-tailed Hawks were calling in the distance, and Colima Warblers and Painted Redstarts were easily found. In early September while looking for (and not finding) a Hermit Warbler, I saw my only Cassin's Vireo for the year.

Sabine Woods

Sabine Woods is a sanctuary owned by the Texas Ornithological Society (TOS), located near the coast just south and east of Beaumont–Port Arthur. It comprises a main wooded area, wetlands, and openings containing smaller wooded areas. Beyond Sabine Woods the road traverses open brush along the Gulf of Mexico and passes a site traditionally known as "the Willows," where few willows currently exist because of hurricane damage, then passes a small area known as "the Mulberries," and ends at McFaddin NWR. While not as well known as the High Island area, Sabine Woods rivals High Island in the number and variety of migrants in spring and fall. In my opinion, the best plan in spring is to drive back and forth between Sabine Woods and High Island, leaving one of them when it is slow, because migration on the Texas coast is often uneven and constantly varies. It is not unheard of to find 25 or more warbler species there on a single day, many of them hopping on the ground or on lower branches, and others high and mostly obscured in upper branches. In spring the trees can also be dotted with Rose-breasted

Sabine Woods

Grosbeaks, Baltimore and Orchard Orioles, Ruby-throated Hummingbirds, and Scarlet and Summer Tanagers; the shady areas under the trees can have Ovenbirds and other warblers and a wide variety of thrushes; and the surrounding grassy areas can be filled with Painted and Indigo Buntings and Blue Grosbeaks. Summertime and fall migration are usually slower, but fall can produce Texas rarities such as Black-throated Blue Warbler.

    I first went to Sabine Woods in my big year on February 12, when I added Marsh Wren and also saw a Pine Warbler and Black-and-white Warbler as well as a Prairie Warbler I had heard was wintering over. While I was watching the Prairie Warbler, two Great Horned Owls were calling. Another trip to Sabine Woods on March 29 produced eight warbler species (Yellow-throated, Yellow-rumped, Hooded, Prairie, Black-and-White, and Black-throated Green Warblers, Common Yellowthroat, and Northern Parula), a young male Indigo Bunting, a Wood Thrush, a calling Fish Crow, and a perched, well-observed Whip-poor-will. On April 18 essentially all the spring migrants I had found elsewhere were also at Sabine Woods. Highlights were Blue Grosbeaks, a Veery, Chestnut-sided, Worm-eating, and Kentucky Warblers, Yellow-billed Cuckoo, and Baltimore Oriole. What a colorful array. I was there every few days for a couple of weeks, seeing my first Blackburnian, Bay-breasted, and Cerulean Warblers plus a Black-whiskered Vireo.

On May 26 I went back to Sabine Woods hoping for warblers I'd missed when the hordes had come through in April. I'd been worried about mosquitoes in the warmer weather, but it was the buzzing, clingy flies (I grew up calling them "deer flies") that nearly drove me nuts. After distracting me by smashing into my head, they'd sneak in, land on my arm, and raise a big itchy welt with a single bite. Insect spray seemed to attract them. On top of that, there were no new birds, or at least I couldn't find any through the flies. There were Blue Jays feeding young, Cedar Waxwings at mulberries, Ruby-throated Hummingbirds, Orchard Orioles, Magnolia Warblers, and American Redstarts as well as the more common birds.

On August 25 I added to my year list a bright Yellow-bellied Flycatcher and a Mourning Warbler that were frequenting the Sabine Woods birdbath and also saw Common Yellowthroats, Black-and-white, Yellow, Black-throated Green, Canada, and Blue-winged Warblers, and Yellow-breasted Chat.

On September 10 Sabine Woods produced Northern Waterthrush and Hooded, Black-and-white, Canada, Worm-eating, and Mourning Warblers, but no new birds for the year.

Frontera Audubon

Frontera Audubon is one of the many great hotspots in the Lower Rio Grande Valley. I like it primarily because I have noted many rarities there, often at close range. The site is almost completely wooded, with winding paths, feeder stations, seating areas, and water along its many paths. There is a very nice visitor center, an orchard, and nearby plantings for birds. In my big year, we went to Frontera Audubon on January 2, and in addition to a Crimson-collared Grosbeak, I saw all the expected Valley birds, such as Plain Chachalacas, Long-billed Thrashers, White-tipped Doves, Great Kiskadees, Black-crested Titmice, Buff-bellied Hummingbirds, Common Ground-Doves, and Couch's Kingbirds. I was back on January 14, when I saw a White-throated Thrush, and the next day an Elegant Trogon as well as the first Black-headed Grosbeak and Red-crowned Parrot of the year. The trogon and grosbeak were still there on February 18, when I returned and added the Tropical Parula to my year list.

Ode to Sabine Woods

Be there before dawn
With your bug-spray on,
Preferably buddied,
Bird-book well studied,
Your pants tucked in socks,
Your eyes seeking flocks.
Birds will be coming,
Hummingbirds humming.
No need to wait,
Whatever the date.
Though it seems absurd,
Get out there and bird.
So, it's off to Sabine,
The best place I've seen
For building the list
Or finding the missed
Birds from the spring,
Or some rarer thing.

Guadalupe Mountains National Park

Guadalupe Mountains NP is one of my favorite Texas sites even though it is so far from Fort Worth and usually requires lengthy hikes to see anything. On February 7, 2005, I did my first trip there, made the snowy climb to the Bowl discussed in chapter 4, and saw my first Steller's Jay and Mountain Chickadee for the year. On May 19 I saw my first Gray Vireo there, plus many Plumbeous Vireos and Olive-sided Flycatchers. On June 21 I went back and walked the Devil's Hall Trail and found a Spotted Owl for my year.

On the final day of August, I again made the long climb to the Bowl in strong winds. A couple of hours later as I paused to look around, I saw a slight movement on the rocks above my head. There, peering at me over the top was a brown head with two gently curved horns—what I found out later was a Barbary sheep (aoudad). I had heard they were introduced in the Guadalupes but had never encountered one before. As I watched, 14 more sheep pulled into view, all looking down at me. Some were half-grown, some even smaller. One giant had lots of "beard" hair and looked like a very old elder. They never bolted but just made their way across the nearby ridge and out of sight, my camera shutter snapping all the while. After I resumed my hike up the multiple switchbacks, I entered a very birdy area, with close-up Mountain Chickadees, Orange-crowned Warblers, White-throated Swifts, Hepatic and Western Tanagers, Black-chinned Sparrows, and Red-breasted Nuthatches. Finally arriving at the Bowl about 10:45, I was amazed at the large numbers of Townsend's Warblers. What I especially wanted was a Hermit Warbler, but I checked each new warbler and there were no Hermits. I did see Black-throated Gray, MacGillivray's, Wilson's, Yellow-rumped, and Grace's Warblers. Other species included Steller's Jays, a Rufous Hummingbird catching gnats, White-breasted and Red-breasted Nuthatches, a Brown Creeper, Dark-eyed Juncos, a Hermit Thrush, Plumbeous Vireos, Western Wood-Pewees, and an Olive-sided Flycatcher. Finally, there was a new bird. A Hammond's Flycatcher was working an area along one of the trails in the Bowl.

On October 19 Simone Jenion and I camped overnight at Pine Springs Campground in the Guadalupes and made an early start the next day up to the Bowl, Simone's first trip there. Along the trail were Lincoln's and Rufous-crowned Sparrows, Spotted and Canyon Towhees, Dark-eyed Juncos, Rock and Canyon Wrens, White-throated Swifts, and a soaring Golden Eagle. As we panted our way up the trail, we began to see Steller's Jays in the conifers ahead. In the Bowl were Pine Siskins, Mountain Chickadees, Red-breasted Nuthatches, Bushtits, a very high flock of overflying Sandhill Cranes,

Common Ravens, and a Red-naped Sapsucker. After wandering around for a bit, we sat down on a log, undecided as to whether we had the energy to explore more. It wasn't too long until we heard a mixed flock, which turned out to be more White-breasted Nuthatches and three Pygmy Nuthatches, new for the year. As with many birds that are initially hard to find, I saw them again later in the year.

Late on the afternoon of November 17, I arrived in New Mexico on my way to the Dog Canyon trailhead in the Guadalupes. The next morning I drove the required 65 miles through New Mexico to the northern park entry, arriving a bit before 8:00 a.m. It was 27 degrees and very crisp, but a brisk walk got my circulation moving enough that I could enjoy the walk. Along the hike were Mountain Chickadees, Dark-eyed Juncos, a Hermit Thrush, House Finches, Western Scrub-Jays (now Woodhouse's), Ladder-backed and Acorn Woodpeckers, White-breasted Nuthatches, Rock, Bewick's, and Canyon Wrens, and Pine Siskins. Just before noon I turned around to return to my car. Western Bluebirds were perching in some of the trees as I approached the corral, and I saw a single Red-naped Sapsucker. Then a little flock of chickadees materialized and amid the chattering, I heard the distinctive sound of a Juniper Titmouse, which to me sounds like a liquid "boink."

I was back on November 26 at Frijole Ranch in the Guadalupes, where I was delighted to see the only Lewis's Woodpecker I'd seen in my 10 years in Texas (see chapter 6).

On December 28 I made my last hike to the Bowl in the Guadalupes. I didn't add any new birds for the year, but I got a great look at another Pygmy Nuthatch, as well as Red-breasted and White-breasted Nuthatches, and even better, I heard the flight calls of a Red Crossbill.

Panhandle

I love the wide-open spaces of the Texas Panhandle, vast expanses of grass punctuated by small stands of trees and periodic water holes. We first visited the Panhandle on January 8, when we found our first American Tree-Sparrows, McCown's and Lapland Longspurs, Long-eared Owls, Prairie Falcon, and Yellow-headed Blackbirds. I was back on February 8 and saw wintering Loggerhead Shrikes, Ferruginous Hawks, Horned Larks, miscellaneous sparrows everywhere, Cooper's Hawk, Rough-legged Hawk, Great Horned Owl, Sage Thrashers, and Sandhill Cranes, as well as a new-for-the-year Cassin's Finch. On April 4 Simone and I returned to look again for

Lesser Prairie-Chickens, which we saw the next morning. We also saw our first Burrowing Owls of the year in Briscoe County. We then explored Gene Howe WMA and the Lake Marvin area near Canadian and were able to add a Franklin's Gull.

On November 22 I went to Muleshoe NWR on the far western side of the Panhandle and eventually located the previously reported Eurasian Wigeon at dusk at Upper White Lake.

On December 12 I went back to Texline, way up in the northwest corner of the Panhandle, which was full of even more Eurasian Collared-Doves than usual, including one being nailed by a Cooper's Hawk. Ferruginous and Rough-legged Hawks, a Prairie Falcon, and a Great Horned Owl kept distracting me from looking for rarities, but it was a great trip anyway.

ALASKA
St. Paul Island

While much of St. Paul Island is off-limits to those who do not live there, birders can go with a trained guide in one of the island's vehicles and see beautiful views, seals, and many birds up close.

My first trip to St. Paul during my big year was for a week at the end of May. As I usually do, I chose to go on my own rather than with a bird group because travel there typically includes airfare, lodging, food, and guides, and additional hired guides are not needed. I always recommend travel to St. Paul Island in late May and early June to birders and nonbirders alike for the spectacular views of cliff-nesting birds (such as puffins, murres, and auklets), as well as close-up viewing of seals and arctic foxes, and possible views of reindeer. Also there in the spring of 2016 were a Northern Wheatear, Siberian Rubythroat, Wood, Curlew, and Common Sandpipers, and Long-toed Stints.

My second (and last) trip for the year to St. Paul was for 11 days in September. New birds were difficult to come by, but I did add Jack Snipe, Eurasian Skylark, and Red-flanked Bluetail.

Utqiagvik (Barrow)

Utqiagvik is one of my favorite places because it is so Alaskan, so clearly "at the end of the world." In summer you can see nesting birds everywhere, never hidden by trees (there are no trees). My first trip there was in early July. While there were no state rarities, I did get to see my first Snowy Owl and many, many nesting shorebirds, primarily phalaropes and Pectoral

St. Paul Cliffs

Sandpipers. I went back in early October and saw my goal bird, migrating Ross's Gulls. Although I went back again twice in November to try to find Ivory Gulls, there were none to be found, presumably because the usual ice pack (where they are usually seen) was not even visible from shore.

Potter Marsh

Potter Marsh, on the south side of Anchorage, like much of Alaska, is mostly frozen over in winter. Even then Bald Eagles are usually present, and

Favorite Birding Places in Texas and Alaska | 73

Snowy Owl

Utqiagvik scene in July

sometimes rarer birds such as Northern Goshawks and Short-eared Owls. One of the attractions of Potter Marsh is the long boardwalk from which you can see the mountains and marsh. Beginning in spring you can easily see the returning gulls and Arctic Terns, shorebirds, warblers, and sparrows, often quite close to the boardwalk. During migration, there are often many Trumpeter Swans floating on the open water of the marsh, and whenever the water is not frozen there are usually Mallards, Green-winged Teal, Common Mergansers, and other ducks.

In March, when I had seen many of the regular wintering birds and was anxious for migrants to arrive, I went to Potter Marsh every two to three days all month long. Gulls arrived, as did Trumpeter Swans, and Black-billed Magpies were building nests. Migrating shorebirds arrived in April, as did Sandhill Cranes, and Mew Gulls seemed to be selecting nest sites. By the middle of June baby ducks and geese were increasingly common. In mid-July baby birds were still around and there were already gatherings of migrating shorebirds such as Greater Yellowlegs.

Bald Eagle

By late September Potter Marsh became very quiet, as most of the birds had departed for the south. Although Trumpeter Swans remained until early October, by the end of the month there was very little open water for waterfowl.

Ketchikan and Hyder

These two places are linked because the quickest way to get to Hyder is by flying from Ketchikan in a mail plane, and I birded both places with

Potter Marsh in April

Steve Heinl of Ketchikan. My first day in Ketchikan was January 6, when I found a previously reported Pied-billed Grebe, as well as Western Grebes, Red-breasted and Common Mergansers, Surf Scoters, Barrow's and Common Goldeneyes, Buffleheads, Mallards, and the omnipresent Bald Eagles. The next day Steve helped me find two Brandt's Cormorants and a couple of White-winged Scoters, plus at Jerry Koerner's house we saw a Yellow-rumped Warbler visiting a suet feeder, a White-crowned Sparrow, a few Varied

Potter Marsh in winter

Thrushes, a Northern Flicker, a Lincoln's Sparrow, Song Sparrows, Pine Siskins, Dark-eyed Juncos, Steller's Jays, European Starlings, Chestnut-backed Chickadees, and an Anna's Hummingbird. Later we found Fox Sparrows, Hooded Mergansers, an American Dipper, and a Thayer's Gull.

Toward the end of February I went back to Ketchikan and saw a wintering American Coot, plus Killdeer and California Gulls. In early May I was there again to see the first White-winged Crossbill of the year (it had been rare in previous months), my first Caspian Tern, and more new shorebirds for the year.

Common Goldeneye

Song Sparrow

June was the only time I went to Hyder. Just before Hyder, I birded in Ketchikan and added Brown-headed Cowbird, Pacific-slope Flycatcher, Common Yellowthroat, Warbling Vireo, Olive-sided Flycatcher, and Barred Owl to my year list. Hyder was amazing, with an additional 20 species in four days, most of which are rare or very uncommon in the rest of Alaska (in order observed: Chipping Sparrow, MacGillivray's Warbler, Western Tanager, Willow Flycatcher, American Redstart, Alder Flycatcher, Eastern Kingbird, Western Wood-Pewee, Veery, Least Flycatcher, American Crow, Bullock's Oriole, Black-headed Grosbeak, Northern Rough-winged Swallow, Black Swift, Yellow-bellied Flycatcher, Cassin's Vireo, Magnolia Warbler, Black-throated Gray Warbler, and Swainson's Hawk).

In the middle of July a Rose-breasted Grosbeak drew me back to Ketchikan (helping me tie the big year record for Alaska), and in late August I went back for young Ring-billed Gulls (found in both cases with the help of Steve Heinl). In mid-October, I was able to briefly see a House Finch that came to Ketchikan, and my last bird of the year was a very skulky Swamp Sparrow in Ketchikan in December.

Gambell and Nome

These two sites are grouped together here because to get to Gambell on St. Lawrence Island you must fly to Nome, and therefore both places are often birded on the same trip.

Birding in Gambell is unlike birding anywhere else I have been. Although portions of Gambell birding are similar to that elsewhere, such as doing sea watches and riding on ATVs around the lake to look for birds, the unique portion is "doing the boneyards." Gambell's boneyards are large areas where bones of killed sea animals, such as walruses, have accumulated over the years. Soil has filled in some areas around the bones, and plants have grown over them, year after year. Because the old bones and tusks can be used to create beautiful objects, native people, who may legally carve the bones and tusks, regularly dig in the boneyards to find useful pieces. Birds that arrive at Gambell find the maze of holes, bones, soil, and plants full of good hiding places, since there are no trees. Each day birders at Gambell line up at each of the three main boneyards and endeavor to walk across, with the goal of flushing any hiding birds that may be rarities from Asia.

My first (of three) trips to Gambell was from late May to early June, with Wilderness Birding Adventures, when I added 11 species to my list, highlights

Gambell scene

of which were Terek Sandpiper, Dovekie (small numbers nest there), White-tailed Eagle, Red-necked Stint, Eyebrowed Thrush, and Red-throated Pipit. After that I went to Nome with WBA and added another 16 species, highlights of which were Bluethroat, Bristle-thighed Curlew, Eastern Yellow Wagtail, Say's Phoebe, Sabine's Gull, and Red Knot.

In mid-July I took a day trip to Nome to see the nesting Eastern Phoebes there, a species I had not expected to see in the state.

At the very end of August I began my second trip to Gambell and saw three birds new for the year: Gray-tailed Tattler, Sharp-tailed Sandpiper (regular fall migrant), and Siberian Accentor.

My third trip to Gambell was in late November, a successful trip for the Pine Bunting first spotted by Clarence Irrigoo Jr. On the way there, and again on a quick trip in early December, I birded in Nome and was able to see McKay's Buntings, which winter there with Snow Buntings.

6

SPOTTING BIRDS IN TEXAS AND ALASKA

As expected, I saw most of the birds in my Texas big year in a different chronological order and often in different seasons than I saw the same birds in Alaska (if I did see them there), and of course I found many species in only one of these states.

Therefore, in the following comparison of my two big years, rather than list each big year chronologically, I have ordered each section taxonomically on a "bird-by-bird" basis, starting with ducks and ending with blackbirds. Each section covers species in a particular category related to rarity of the species and to the state(s) in which the species were sighted. The sections are briefly defined by their titles, such as "Rare in Both States" or "Seen Only in Alaska." Within each section, the relevant bird species I observed are listed in current taxonomic order as set forth in the ABA Checklist of July 12, 2016. For each species in each section, there is first a discussion of my first big year sighting of that species in Texas, if I found it in Texas during my big year there, followed by a discussion of where I saw it during my big year in Alaska, if I found it in Alaska that year. Appendix 1 lists all the species I saw in these two big years and provides the date and location of the first sighting of each species.

Because big year birding is often primarily about finding rarities, the following sections are organized by how rare the species are in Texas and Alaska. This classification is not necessarily related to how rare the species are in other states or in the United States as a whole.

In particular, there are separate sections according to whether the bird species are rare in Texas, rare in Alaska, rare in both states, or rare in neither state. I use the term "rare" somewhat loosely here, basically including species that are not common, or those listed by the relevant state authorities as "rare," "casual," or "accidental" in that state. Birds listed in the TOS Handbook as having some type of multiple status, such as "rare to locally uncommon" and other, similar overlapping classifications in Texas are not considered "rare" for the purposes of these accounts. In some cases, when the Texas status is difficult to determine or the bird is clearly variably rare, I have placed it in a section that reflects how difficult it was for me to locate the bird. Thus, placement in these sections is in some cases somewhat arbitrary. Also, species that have never been found in a state are placed in a section with birds considered to be "rare" in that state because they do not occur there at all.

In these accounts, the date of the first sighting of a species is given. For a big year birder, the goal is to see or hear as many bird species as possible during that year. Therefore, later sighting dates are generally not as important to the birder as the first sighting date. For many of the listed birds, dates in addition to the date first observed are given, but unless stated otherwise, these dates are just examples of when I found the species, and in many cases I saw the birds many more times during my big year than what is listed in these accounts. More information is given here for many of my Alaska sightings because that big year was much more recent than my Texas big year, and this information was posted to eBird and is more easily accessible than the data on my Texas sightings. Unless otherwise stated, the dates given for each sighting are dates during the respective big years—2005 for Texas sightings and 2016 for Alaska sightings. In the accounts for species observed in both states, to make things less confusing, at the beginning of each discussion, the state where I saw the bird is indicated by [TX] or [AK]; however, no such indication is used where the whole section relates to birds found in just one of the states.

RARE BIRDS
Rare in Both States
Seen in Both States
Lewis's Woodpecker

[TX] I was wandering around the northern Texas Panhandle in late November trying to find a new bird for my big year when a ranger at Guadalupe Mountains NP called me. Earlier in the year I had talked to her about my undertaking and had mentioned that although Lewis's Woodpeckers were quite rare in Texas, one of the most likely spots to find one historically was her park. On November 25, she called to tell me one had appeared at Frijole Ranch in the park. I left Dalhart in the Texas Panhandle at 2:00 a.m. the next morning and drove the approximately 400 miles to the ranch, arriving there just before 9:00. There was a very strong wind and the temperature hovered at freezing, with even stronger wind in the forecast, so I was worried the woodpecker would be holed up someplace to stay out of the elements. Although it was a Saturday and her day off, the ranger was there to meet me. Together we inspected the large trees around the buildings where the bird had been reported and where Lewis's Woodpeckers had been found in years past. After about an hour, a large black crow-like bird appeared out of nowhere, clearly just what we were looking for. As soon as it landed, we could see its red and black head, its gray collar, and its pink tummy—unmistakable.

AK On November 12, a Lewis's Woodpecker, extremely rare in Alaska, was reported in Petersburg. I waited a couple of days, figuring the bird would disappear, as do many wandering birds. When I realized it was apparently staying around, I immediately checked out where Petersburg was, contacted Brad Hunter, who had reported it, and scheduled an airline flight, motel, and rental car for November 17, the first chance I had to leave my scheduled tasks. I arrived there in midafternoon, met Brad, and together we walked a few blocks down the street from my motel to the crabapple tree where the bird had originally been found. Brad had skewered four large Red Delicious apples with a dowel and placed them in the tree to provide the woodpecker with a substantial food source. When we arrived, the woodpecker, which appeared to be a young bird of the year, was vigorously pecking on the frozen apples, as it was also doing the next morning when I returned. Every now and then it would leave the tree, sometimes seemingly without cause and other times when someone walked by on the sidewalk. A couple of times I was able to see where it went, which was a perch in a nearby spruce tree. I later learned it stayed around a week or so.

Lewis's Woodpecker in Petersburg

Cape May Warbler

^{TX} Cape May Warblers are rare spring migrants and very rare fall migrants in Texas, occurring primarily on the coastal prairies. On April 19 at the Willows near Sabine Woods, a single Cape May Warbler flew into a willow from across the road, even allowing a few pictures before vanishing.

^{AK} On November 7, I met Matt Goff at the Castle Hill area in downtown Sitka about 8:00 a.m. Within five minutes, we saw the Cape May Warbler he had found several days before in the same area. It constantly flitted about, peering under branches and leaves, busily feeding. There were also two Palm Warblers in the same wooded area.

Seen Only in Texas
Muscovy Duck

At Salineño in the LRGV on January 4, Simone spotted two black blobs perched in a grassy brushy area, way up the river but on the Texas side of the Rio Grande. Quickly training our telescopes on the blobs revealed big black ducks with white wing patches—Muscovy Ducks. They are often hard to find, usually moving fast along the river. We watched as they clambered around in the heavy vegetation until we lost sight of them.

Masked Duck

We learned as we were entering Corpus Christi on the evening of March 6 that a female Masked Duck had been found again at Padre Island National Seashore, having been seen there periodically for quite some time. At dawn the next morning Simone and I slowly drove up and down the road looking for the open water where the duck had been. Finally locating the area where it had been reported, a small lake surrounded by cattails, we began our vigil, but no Masked Duck appeared all morning. Before we departed from the seashore, however, we contacted George Eggenberger, who had originally found the Masked Duck some weeks earlier. About a month later he called saying he'd seen the Masked Duck again. After a quick call to Simone and rapid piling of our belongings into the car, we were on our way down to the seashore once again.

On the morning of April 11 at 7:25, we made our third attempt for this Masked Duck. After 15 minutes of searching, to our astonishment, she appeared. With a buffy trilined head and looking vaguely like a small dapper female Ruddy Duck, she emerged without fanfare from the reeds and grasses and meandered her way around the edge of the cattail-lined wetland. Every now and then she dove under the water, sometimes staying down for a while, and reemerged from the water or cattails somewhere else after we were sure she'd faded back into the vegetation for good.

American Flamingo

On October 14, a birder reported seeing a flamingo at Shoalwater Bay in Calhoun County. While American Flamingos have periodically appeared over the years in various beach areas in East Texas, their wild origins are usually in doubt, and they are dismissed as escapees from some zoo. When I heard that this bird was banded, I and every other Texas birder assumed that it was just another escaped flamingo. On October 19, a post on Texbirds (the Texas birders' listserv) discussed the leg bands worn by this flamingo, indicating that it was banded at a wild flamingo colony at the Rio Lagartos Biosphere Reserve in Mexico.

Masked Duck at Padre Island National Seashore

The chase was on, or at least I tried to begin the chase, but I couldn't figure out how to do it. The flamingo had been observed among the islands offshore from Port O'Connor, a place way off the beaten track. I finally found someone available in a couple of days to take Simone and me out to look for the bird. Unfortunately, the captain with whom I made the reservation cancelled our trip the night before we were due to go out, without any valid excuse. I finally found another captain, who took us out of Port O'Connor on October 23, a gorgeous crisp morning. The shallow water and islands were filled with egrets and herons and spoonbills. In spite of an excellent trip where we thoroughly explored every single inlet and waterway and scanned the tops of the treeless islands, there was no sign of a flamingo.

On November 8, a report on Texbirds stated that a federal agent had found a flamingo on St. Joseph Island ("St. Joe"), between Matagorda and North Padre Island. I found that Rockport was probably the best place to hire a boat to try to find the flamingo at its new location. The plan was to try to reach this new location with an airboat because the water was very shallow and not just any boat could navigate it. Also, the island where the flamingo had last been seen was private property, so we could not go ashore and explore away from the water. Even though grasses might block me from seeing the flamingo when I was in a boat, especially if the flamingo had its head down, it seemed that my only choice was to try to find a boat.

I finally located an airboat captain who not only would take me out to look for the flamingo but had extensive experience as a hunting guide for this very island and was quite familiar with the area. He was booked for the morning of November 11 but would take me out in the afternoon *if* he saw the flamingo on his morning trip out to the island.

I planned to head down to Goose Island State Park the next morning to meet him at 12:30, gambling that he would have found the flamingo in the morning. Late that night before I left, however, I checked my emails and found a message that a flamingo, presumably the same one, had been observed that day at a new location, visible from the fishing pier at Goose Island State Park.

I started off immediately for Goose Island State Park so I could look for the bird from the pier at dawn the next morning, before it was time to go out on the airboat at midday. I arrived there about an hour or so before dawn and snoozed in the car outside the locked gate. When I noticed cars being let in, I drove into the park and down to the fishing pier, where I dozed a bit until it got light enough to see the pier and possibly a bird way out in the water somewhere. I loaded up my binoculars, spotting scope, camera, and bird book and began the trek partway out the amazingly long pier (1,620 feet) that extends across very shallow water into Aransas Bay. I began to scan the tiny islands and rock piles that were filled to overflowing with silhouetted American White Pelicans, Brown Pelicans, White Ibises, Snowy and Great Egrets, Great Blue and Tricolored Herons, and many small shorebirds.

With a delighted shock, I saw it almost immediately—a very long-legged, small-bodied, long-necked, bent-beaked bird silhouetted against the predawn sky. It was quite a ways out, and if I'd been looking for any bird with less distinctive characteristics, I'd never have found it at that distance, but a flamingo has a unique shape. I waited and watched as the sun rose, and despite staring through my telescope more or less into the sun, I began to see a little color on the bird, which got brighter as the sun rose higher. It had quite a nice pink color on its head and upper neck, and in its tail area. Its wings were rather gray and white, features of an immature bird that has not yet attained all of its pink plumage.

Other birders began to arrive, having heard that the flamingo could be seen without booking a boat or getting wet feet. The flamingo, now very cooperative, dozed much of the morning, unaware of the telescopes focused on it by its many admirers. It would awaken periodically, preen a bit, and then wind its neck back up and tuck its head under its wing. Just a couple of times it roused itself enough to walk around, long legs looking like elongated black toothpicks, awkward and unreal. Twice in the next couple of hours, it spread its wings and flew 20 feet or so, showing brilliant pink underwings before it strode back to its sleeping spot amid the white pelicans.

Ruddy Ground-Dove

On January 24, Simone and I were at Big Bend NP searching for new birds for the year, including a Ruddy Ground-Dove reported at Cottonwood Campground. As I approached a recreational vehicle parked near the fence along the river, I saw a small flock of doves on the ground heading into the bushes. As we went farther into the brush, a single small dove flew across the Rio Grande and landed on the pebbly opposite shore. We studied it carefully—black bill, face and breast without scaling, overall gray brown. It was a female Ruddy Ground-Dove. Because we had seen it first on the Texas side of the river, it counted as a Texas big year bird, the only Ruddy Ground-Dove we saw all year.

Mexican (Green) Violet-ear

In June of my Texas big year, things slowed down considerably, but I devoted all of June 3 to my big year after I'd heard that a Green Violet-ear was visiting feeders near San Antonio. After I got permission to visit, I raced down there. Not too long after I arrived, a gorgeous Green Violet-ear was hovering near the feeders. Within a week or so, at least one other Green Violet-ear showed up in Texas.

Green-breasted Mango

Early in my Texas big year, I spent much time in the LRGV. On January 2, we drove into McAllen, where a striking Green-breasted Mango was still in a backyard where it had been reported in early August 2004. It continued to make nearly daily appearances, much to the delight of hundreds of birders.

Green-breasted Mango in McAllen

The sporadic rain got me wet as I tried to figure out where the mango might be perching. I was finally able to view the hummingbird by peering over the backyard fence.

Broad-billed Hummingbird
On January 18, Simone and I headed down to Harris County. After we saw a reported Calliope Hummingbird, we saw a Broad-billed Hummingbird, another stunning bird, at the home of Keith Kingdon.

White-eared Hummingbird
My first stop on June 20, part of a midyear West Texas trip, was at the Eastmans' place in the Davis Mountains, where I knew there had been hummingbird activity, including a White-eared Hummingbird sighting. The Eastmans' home was the epitome of a hummingbird hotspot, with 70-plus feeders. When I arrived the morning of June 20, I saw two Magnificent Hummingbirds, plus Lucifer, Broad-tailed, and Black-chinned Hummingbirds. Over the back railing of their porch, I briefly saw a smallish (compared to the Magnificent Hummingbirds, which also had white face striping) hummingbird with a white blaze on its otherwise blackish face, which then darted away. It wasn't much of a view and I wanted more, but that's what it was—a White-eared Hummingbird.

Mountain Plover
Mountain Plovers are best found in Texas during the winter in large flatland fields. To optimize my chances of seeing a Mountain Plover, I had signed up for a Texas Ornithological Society (TOS) trip to the Granger area northeast of Austin on January 22. I had been on the same trip twice in previous years, and no matter how hopeless the drives up and down the country roads in Williamson and Bell Counties seemed to be every year, we had always found Mountain Plovers and at least a couple of species of longspurs. In 2005, only about five of the plovers were observed at first, but all I needed was one. In my binoculars they looked like featureless buffy stones way out in the field, but once we trained our telescopes on them, we could see that they were quite cute, with white tummies and buffy-brown backs.

Great Black-backed Gull

On March 2, Simone and I went south to Boca Chica to try for a third time for the Great Black-backed Gull that others had seen there. When we got to the Boca Chica beach, we headed south away from the jetty. We drove around piles of driftwood and bottles and other trash on the beach until eventually we turned around without finding our gull. However, when we got back to where we'd begun our drive on the beach, there it was, flying right at us. It was huge and dark, with a big black beak—finally, a Great Black-backed Gull.

    Note: although I did not see a Great Black-backed Gull in Alaska in 2016, I did see one at Utqiagvik in October 2015.

Little Gull

On January 18, since we were in the Houston area, we slipped over to the Quintana jetty, where a Little Gull, rare in Texas, was wintering and was easily found.

Brown Noddy

In the middle of the afternoon on June 21 while in West Texas, I learned that a Brown Noddy had been found all the way across the state, feeding with Laughing Gulls and Black Terns at the end of the south jetties at South Padre Island, where I would most likely need to charter a boat to see it. There had been talk that it could sometimes be seen from either the Boca Chica jetty or the South Padre Island jetty, which sounded less tippy than a little boat in a choppy inlet. I chose the latter jetty, and about 9:00 a.m. on June 22, I lugged my scope, camera, and bird book out on the jetty. I saw a small boat of birders go by and disappear around the end of the Boca Chica jetty and then noticed a flock of birds where I'd last seen their boat. I scanned through the flock and there, flying low over the water, was an all-brown, relatively long-tailed bird among the Black Terns near the end of the Boca Chica jetty. The tail was a bit pointed, and the bird was generally slimmer and more elongated than the Black Terns. It disappeared when a boat passed, and then I noticed it sitting up at the peak of a diamond-shaped rock, where it mostly stayed for the rest of my observation period, leaving only briefly once or twice when a boat went too near. The top of its head viewed through the telescope appeared lighter, but otherwise I didn't notice anything other than a brown color. The beak was quite long and pointy.

Sooty (rare and local) and Bridled (uncommon to rare) Terns

I found these terns on the first pelagic trip of the year on June 17. They are distinguished from each other by differences in their faces, collar color, and underwings.

Red-billed Tropicbird

On the first Texas pelagic trip of the year on June 17, just after the participants had seen the relatively common Masked Boobies, we saw a much rarer and exciting adult Red-billed Tropicbird fly directly over our boat. We got spectacular views, and it was a lifer for many aboard.

Red-billed Tropicbird on Texas pelagic trip

Leach's and Band-rumped Storm-Petrels

I first saw Leach's and Band-rumped Storm-Petrels on the first Gulf of Mexico pelagic trip of the year on June 17. Although both species fly close to the water, their flight patterns differ, as do the shapes of their white rump patches.

Masked Booby

On June 17, we left the dock at South Padre Island at 6:00 a.m. About an hour and a half later, two Masked Boobies were flying around the boat.

Brown Booby

On the afternoon of February 27 as I began my trip back to Fort Worth from a Pineywoods field trip and had gone about 70 miles, I checked my voice messages and heard: "It's a Brown Booby, not a Red-footed." "What is?" was my response, as I had no clue as to what and where "it" was. I finally figured out from the messages and from the posts on Texbirds that a Brown Booby had been found in Port Aransas. There was no question that I had to do an about-face and head back to the southeast, even farther than I had just come. I made it to Port Aransas after dark that day. I rose the next morning before dawn and went over to the marina and beach, the two places the booby had been observed. I wandered back and forth between them but had no luck at first. As it got lighter, increasing numbers of Double-crested Cormorants began to fill the rocks at the marina, punctuated with a few Brown Pelicans. As I was scanning the cormorants with my telescope, all of a sudden at 8:15 a.m., the Brown Booby magically appeared among the cormorants.

Hook-billed Kite

I first saw a Hook-billed Kite on January 4 just up the river from the Salineño overlook, where it had been found the previous day. We saw it coasting through the woods low over our heads.

Common Black-Hawk

On May 10 on the drive down to Big Bend, two Common Black-Hawks were soaring over the hills east of a picnic area along the road. The fat white tail band of each was very visible even when they were high above, but they eventually came low enough for pictures.

Roadside Hawk

On February 4, I went south to San Ygnacio to look for the astounding Roadside Hawk that had recently been discovered, a hawk previously documented only four times in Texas; it is resident from Mexico to northern South America. By the time I arrived in the Valley, it was too dark to look for the hawk, but the next morning long before dawn, I drove over to San Ygnacio. Through the heavy rain my headlights illuminated several parked cars containing sleeping birders who had driven all night to be there. I dozed too until it began to get light, and we all awoke to the rainy day. We forced ourselves to get out and look for the hawk but could not find it at the various spots it had been seen on other days. As far as we could tell, it had slipped over the Rio Grande and gone back to its home south of the border. We hung around, hopeful, though getting wetter and wetter.

I decided to turn my Toyota RAV4 around and sit in the back of it, cross-legged out of the rain with the back door open so I could stare into the trees and continue looking for the hawk without getting any wetter. Just after 4:30, when many of us were thinking about leaving but others from across the state were just arriving, an excited cry went up. The Roadside Hawk had been spotted perched in the distance. A thunder of birders' feet rushed toward a couple of telescopes hastily set up to view the distant hawk. There was much scuffling and agitation over the possibility that the bird would disappear before all got a look, but the wet bird was finally seen by a lot of soaked birders, and at least the latter were very happy.

Zone-tailed Hawk

We saw a Zone-tailed Hawk at San Ygnacio Bird and Butterfly Sanctuary, down the river from Laredo, on January 20 when we were there looking for a reported Blue Bunting and White-collared Seedeaters.

Flammulated Owl

On the evening of May 11, shortly after I heard a Western Screech-Owl calling at Boot Springs in Big Bend NP, two Flammulated Owls started calling, one on either side of me. I'd found one at the same spot two years ago, and I didn't want to disturb them, so I went back to my tent to sleep, very satisfied with the day. The rules of the American Birding Association allow "heard-only" birds to be counted if their identity can be determined from their sounds.

Spotted Owl

On June 21, I arrived at the trailhead for the Devil's Hall Trail in Guadalupe Mountains NP just before 6:00 a.m. and began the trek. I had walked the trail and found Spotted Owls in 2003 and knew that I needed to go over large boulders until the trail forked, and then beyond. I went to the spot where I had seen two immature Spotted Owls in 2003, but there were no owls to be found. I carefully searched each limb and each crevice in the canyon wall but found no owl.

I continued up the trail, over even higher boulders and under overhanging trees. I carefully looked at each tree from all directions. All of a sudden, sitting next to the trunk of a large tree about 20 feet behind me, an adult Spotted Owl magically appeared, quietly regarding my panting, stunned form. The owl never left its perch but just calmly turned its head to follow my departing progress after I took a few quick photos.

Elegant Trogon at Frontera Audubon

Elegant Trogon

As I was walking into Bentsen–Rio Grande Valley State Park on January 14, a birder who had left Frontera Audubon after I had just been there told me an Elegant Trogon had just been seen there. It was too late to race back that day, so I hustled along to look for another reported rarity. The next morning, I was first in line at Frontera Audubon, which opens at 7:00 a.m., and was definitely not the only one eagerly awaiting the opening of the gates. For the next hour and a half, swarms of birders spread out across the grounds. By the time word circulated that the Elegant Trogon had been found again, most of the listers of Texas had arrived, but thankfully the masses didn't scare away the trogon. Not even my excited exclamations, nor others hushing me, scared it away. It not only stayed around that day but remained at Frontera Audubon for over a month, and I saw it again on February 18.

Buff-breasted Flycatcher

There are regular records in Texas for Buff-breasted Flycatchers, but these birds are extraordinarily difficult to locate. On May 14, we found one on a search for Spotted Owl in the Davis Mountains, along with numerous other West Texas birds. I also saw a small family group later in the year in the Davis Mountains.

Social Flycatcher

On January 14 on one of my many trips during 2005 to the LRGV, I went to Bentsen–Rio Grande Valley State Park to try to find another reported rarity. As I joined a small throng of birders, Larry Carpenter beckoned to me to come over and look through his telescope at a Social Flycatcher. I got great looks at it as well as pictures before darkness came, and it was the only time I saw this species in the United States.

Fork-tailed Flycatcher

On September 24, I was in West Texas with Simone. We knew the Davis Mountains Preserve had an open weekend where nature lovers could come and camp, so our plan was to do some more mountain birding. Upon driving late in the day into Fort Davis, where we finally had a cell phone signal, we learned a Fork-tailed Flycatcher had been found at Hornsby Bend in east Austin. We abandoned our plans, packed up our tents, and at about 5:00 p.m. began our cross-state drive of about eight hours. We were unable to find a motel room in Austin because they were full of people who had fled the recent hurricanes (Rita and Katrina). So, we pulled into a McDonald's parking lot in Austin and tried to sleep in the car until first light. When we got to Hornsby Bend, other birders were already there, but no one had yet seen the flycatcher. Shortly after we arrived, however, the Fork-tailed Flycatcher was found near the entrance, hanging out with Scissor-tailed Flycatchers, perching on electrical wires, and periodically flying down to the ground. Because we didn't want to scare the bird, we didn't go very close, so the pictures I got were only passable. The bird itself, however, was wonderful.

Rose-throated Becard

At the beginning of February, I was in the Valley looking for a Rose-throated Becard for a second time. I decided to try for the becard that morning at Sabal Palm Audubon Sanctuary because nearly everyone who had gone there the previous few days had found one or sometimes two becards. After considerable meandering, I found them too, behind the visitor center, one of their reported locations. Although the more spectacular male had also been reported by others, we were very happy with our excellent close-up views of two female Rose-throated Becards that seemed to be aimlessly going from tree to tree, unconcerned about our presence or my camera. Where had they been every other time I'd looked for them?

Yellow-green Vireo

A Yellow-green Vireo in Port O'Connor on April 27 was part of a major vireo presence for a couple of days on the Texas coast. This species is very rare in Texas. It is similar to the common Red-eyed Vireo, with a bright yellow wash above and below.

Black-whiskered Vireo

The vireo excitement began on April 24 with Mike Austin's report of a Black-whiskered Vireo at Sabine Woods. When I had arrived on the evening of the twenty-fifth, it was pouring rain, and the few people who were still there had not seen it. I went back to look for it on the twenty-sixth but did not see it. After birding elsewhere, I found I just couldn't drive north past Houston without going once more to Sabine Woods. On April 28, about three minutes after I arrived, I located the Black-whiskered Vireo in a sapling in the open area just inside the gate. I watched the vireo and got a few pictures before it flew off to the woods and disappeared.

Brown Jay

On January 4, we drove upriver from the Salineño overlook primarily to find a Brown Jay as part our intensive 10-day trip around Texas. I had been nervously glancing at my watch; we had places to go and my plan had been to leave at 11:00, whether the Brown Jays had put in an appearance or not. This deadline came and went, and no Brown Jays appeared. I decided to wait a bit more and nervously wandered off a bit to see what I could see. All of a sudden I noticed big brown birds coming in low from the back of the lot. They were six Brown Jays, four of which were yellow-billed juveniles.

Tamaulipas Crow

Although Tamaulipas Crows were once common residents in the LRGV, by 2005 they were becoming more difficult to find. I saw my first ones on May 2 in a Brownsville subdivision where they had been reported as nesting. To me their dull sound was like someone saying "ahh" for a dentist.

White-throated Thrush

When I was in the LRGV in early January, I saw many rarities. For a few days other birds distracted me but eventually, on January 14, I went back to Frontera Audubon, which was still crawling with rarities and birders. A small crowd of birders was stalking the White-throated Thrush. They finally found it while I was there and we all saw it quite well through my telescope.

Blue Mockingbird

On January 15 at Allen Williams's house in Pharr, the Blue Mockingbird that had been reported in previous years had reappeared, but tailless. After I wandered about his in-town backyard sanctuary, I finally saw the odd-looking bird hopping about on the ground in Allen's front yard without its tail. I'm not sure I would have been able to guess what it was without a clue first.

Dusky-capped Flycatcher

On February 18, I headed slightly west of Brownsville to look for the Dusky-capped Flycatcher that was being mostly heard and not seen near Cannon Road, off US 281. As I walked the dike where it was supposed to be, I was joined by two expert birders who were also looking for the flycatcher. Their expertise was important to me, because it allowed me to be confident about our identification of the calling Dusky-capped Flycatcher that all three of us heard. No sightings, but that's okay—the American Birding Association "allows" heard-only birds to be counted in order to minimize stressing them, which is a particular concern for rarities that are difficult to see. In the past, requiring that a bird be seen for the birder to add it to an official species list caused some birders who wanted to see owls or other hidden or secretive birds to crash through bushes, climb trees or cut them down, play taped bird songs, or take other measures that harassed the birds and destroyed their environment.

Olive Warbler

When I was in Galveston on my route home to Fort Worth, I got a call saying that Sheridan Coffey had found an Olive Warbler in the Davis Mountains. This was a bird I had never observed in Texas and certainly never expected to see during my big year. Of course, I hadn't found it yet, and I was all the way across the state and destined for home, not West Texas. I arrived home at suppertime, stayed for half an hour to say "hi" and repack, and then headed west as far as I could before I collapsed from exhaustion. Before it got too late, I arranged to get into the Davis Mountains Preserve. After overnighting in Big Spring, I arrived at the preserve about 7:30 on May 29 to hunt for the Olive Warbler and found that it was still there. Several birders heard him singing high in the pine trees and saw his bright yellow throat and breast and gray belly. When he turned his head, we could see his grayish eye patch, yellow forehead, and yellow above the eye patch. After we had wandered off to bird other places at the property, we came back and saw the Olive Warbler again, and we also saw it again the next day.

Purple Finch

On January 18, I went to Jesse H. Jones County Park (Houston area) to look for the reported Purple Finches. It was much easier finding them than when I tried in 2003, my first attempt at a Texas big year. Every now and then I was amazed at how different the two years were.

Note: although a single Purple Finch was in Anchorage in 2015, as far as I know none were reported by anyone during my big year in 2016, so it is not on my Alaska big year list.

Cassin's Finch

On February 9, I visited Texline in the northwest corner of the Panhandle, where wintering birds from the north and west sometimes accidentally drift into Texas. Cassin's Finches had been reported recently, and seeing one was my main goal. I drove up and down each street very slowly, window down, listening and looking. I saw American Robins, Cedar Waxwings, Eurasian Collared-Doves, and many House Finches, each of which I studied very carefully before leaving town and driving east. Just barely out of town, a single finchy bird sat on a power line. It had a thin, pointy bill, crisp little stripes on its breast and belly, a face pattern identical to that of the Cassin's Finch female shown in my National Geographic field guide, and a tiny, tinny flight call.

Note: although a single Cassin's Finch was in Anchorage in 2015 (with the single Purple Finch), and one was seen in Palmer during my big year in 2016, I did not see it, so it is not on my Alaska big year list.

Gray-crowned Yellowthroat

I drove south all the way across the state to south of Brownsville, where a Gray-crowned Yellowthroat was being seen. I arrived at Sabal Palm Audubon Sanctuary just before 7:00 a.m. on February 17, and within 10 minutes I heard it singing, but it would not make itself visible. Finally it appeared, singing high in a brushy sapling, which I learned was huisache, a common plant that invades rangeland and pasture in East Texas. This bird is very much sought after by birders, and from a distance it might look more like its more-common cousin, the Common Yellowthroat. The main difference is that this one has a gray cap, olive back, black loral area, no black mask, and a bright yellow throat and tummy. Unlike in 2003, when I wandered back and forth on the trail to keep my eyes on a very flighty Gray-crowned Yellowthroat, this one allowed decent views.

Black-throated Blue Warbler

Black-throated Blue Warblers are uncommon but most years are more easily found in fall than in spring. I had tried to find reported birds but until October 5 had not had any luck. Late in the day Simone and I drove north from Fort Worth to Denton, where one had been reported. I was very dismayed to realize it was getting dark before we got there. We arrived in half light and saw Sue Yost (who had reported it) in her yard looking around, which was not a good sign. She had not found the bird recently. We had only a couple of minutes before complete darkness. We went out in her backyard and gazed up into a tree where a "chip" sound was coming from that was different from the cardinal chips we were hearing. Then Sue spotted a warbler-sized bird, and we all strained to see it with our binoculars. Thank goodness a Black-throated Blue Warbler has a very distinctive white and black and blue pattern, which we were able to see clearly, though briefly.

Rufous-capped Warbler

The plan for January 5 was to go north from the Valley toward San Antonio, where we hoped expert birder Martin Reid was going to produce the Rufous-capped Warbler that he had found late in 2004 while doing bird surveys on a 20,000-acre ranch in Frio County. We followed Martin through the woods on the ranch to the area where he had previously found the Rufous-capped Warbler, along with a Cordilleran Flycatcher. There they both were, unconcerned about our presence, the warbler hopping over and under branches often very near us, searching for insects, and the flycatcher low in the brush, doing the same.

Rufous-capped Warbler in Frio County

Golden-crowned Warbler

Early in the morning on January 15, I hunted for birds at Santa Ana NWR and then went to Los Ebanos Preserve north of Brownsville to hunt for the Golden-crowned Warbler that had been reported. As I arrived in the early afternoon, I joined a couple of dispirited people who had spent the morning unsuccessfully looking for the warbler and were trudging back to try once more. I brightly mentioned I had been seeing every bird I set out to see that day, pretty much right away, and I hoped my luck would hold. They just looked at me crossly and grumbled a bit, not expecting to see the warbler anytime soon. My luck held out. As I babbled on, we approached a trio of birders peering into the bushes. We peered into the bushes too, and there was the Golden-crowned Warbler, hopping about in the shady undergrowth. Sort of a dappled view, but definitely the bird we sought.

Red-faced Warbler

When I arrived in Big Bend NP on August 8 (a date calculated to be close to the usually very brief period for Red-faced Warbler sightings), I immediately went to the Panther Junction Visitor Center to sign up for a Boot Springs campsite for the next night and learned that Mark Lockwood had reported seeing Red-faced Warblers up at Boot Springs the previous day. Was it still around? The next morning I started up the Pinnacles Trail about 6:40 a.m. with my loaded backpack. By 8:00 a.m., Zone-tailed Hawks were flying overhead, Mexican Jays were calling in the distance, and Band-tailed Pigeons were loudly declaring their presence. By the time I arrived at the Boot Springs area a little before 11:00, the sky was darkening, and I could hear thunder in the distance. I hurried to my campsite, scaring up a Whip-poor-will that seemed to like the path. I quickly set up my tent, grabbed my umbrella, binoculars, and camera, and headed to the springs. Just before 1:00, I saw my goal bird, a tiny, flitty, gray and red, Red-faced Warbler in the trees above me. It was near the junction of the Boot Springs Trail and the Juniper Trail and working its way farther up the springs area. I followed it slowly, trying to get a few pictures in the dim light. It joined a couple of Painted Redstarts, and then I lost track of all of them.

Painted Redstart

On May 11 at Boot Springs at the upper end of the Pinnacles Trail at Big Bend NP, I set up my tent and then went birding around the springs. At least one

Painted Redstart, flitting all over and fanning its tail dramatically, greeted me at the springs. The next morning when I emerged from my tent in the early dawn, there was a singing Painted Redstart, a wonderful way to start a day.

Baird's Sparrow

Our first goal out of Alpine on January 6 was the Baird's Sparrow that had been reported south of Marfa in Presidio County. We reached the sparrow spot long before dawn and sat in the car waiting for first light. Eventually we began to hear Eastern Meadowlarks (Lilian's) and to see silhouetted sparrows on the fence wires. These included many Brewer's and Vesper Sparrows, hopping about in the grass along the road and in the grassy wet area in which cattle were also plodding about. The sparrows seemed to ignore the cattle unless it appeared one was about to step on them. Then at the edge of one of the puddles a Baird's Sparrow emerged into my binocular view, with a buffy crown stripe and eye line, two little dark areas on its cheek behind its eye, and a necklace of little streaks on its breast—unlike any sparrow I'd ever seen before.

Henslow's Sparrow near Nacogdoches

Henslow's Sparrow

On February 26, after a day's rest and an unproductive quick trip out of town, it was time to go on the Nacogdoches trip organized by the TOS. Nacogdoches is in East Texas about halfway between Houston and the northern border, the natural headquarters for a Pineywoods bird trip. I had been on this trip in two previous years, and while no one (wisely) promises you any particular species on this trip, I knew there was a good chance of seeing some Pineywoods specialties such as the Red-cockaded Woodpecker and Henslow's and Bachman's Sparrows, as well as some more common but relatively local species. The habitat requirements of these three species are very particular, and sometimes the best places to see them are on private, inaccessible land, so I had decided to maximize my chances of seeing them by joining the experts who had access to this land (Jesse Fagan and Mimi Wolfe).

Following the normal route for this trip, we drove south out of Nacogdoches and wandered around until we came to a piece of private property where Henslow's Sparrows are known to winter. With a bit of vigorous tracking through the field, we kicked up a Henslow's Sparrow fairly quickly, considering how hard it would have been to find on my own. This one had quite a bit of character, and we were able to see it craning its neck from under a small bush, trying to decide whether to make a break for it, which of course it eventually did.

Crimson-collared Grosbeak

The thing that made me realize this year was not going to be just a normal big year, and certainly not a normal calendar year, was the male Crimson-collared Grosbeak at Frontera Audubon eating potato-tree leaves. He had appeared late in 2004 for Howard Laidlaw's big year and stayed around to welcome me to my 2005 big year on January 2. Sometimes he was

Crimson-collared Grosbeak at Frontera Audubon

unbelievably hard to see despite his gorgeous deep red color, but other times he would be hanging on a bent-over leafy branch a foot or so off the ground along a trail, quietly munching leaves. I don't think I'd ever seen a bird just eat leaves, sort of like a koala bear.

Blue Bunting

On January 14, I headed northwest up the Valley to San Ygnacio and Laredo. In Laredo, we tried to find the Blue Buntings and White-collared Seedeaters that had been reported flitting about in the grass and brush under one of the international bridges. At first it appeared that we wouldn't even be able to find the bridge itself. We wandered the streets of Laredo trying to find it and finally came upon a policewoman patrolling on a bicycle. She not only told us where the bridge was but led us to the spot where the birds had been found, but we had no luck with either species.

On January 20, the report of Blue Buntings and White-collared Seedeaters in Laredo pulled us back again. Despite walking all the trails we could find, all we saw there was one of the White-collared Seedeaters and a Nashville Warbler. Simone suggested we try the San Ygnacio Bird and Butterfly Sanctuary down the river from Laredo, where seedeaters are often seen and where a Blue Bunting had been reported, so we headed there. Shortly after we arrived, we were delighted to see a glowing blue male Blue Bunting quietly come down to a water drip and join the seedeaters that were already bathing.

Streak-backed Oriole

In early February, I became aware of a remarkable decision by various bird experts who had viewed photos of a wintering oriole that had been observed on and off at Brazos Bend State Park south of Houston much of the winter. To their astonishment, the woman who had found the oriole was right—it was not just some normal Texas oriole, but a Streak-backed Oriole. This bird had never before been documented in Texas and was very unlikely elsewhere in the United States. The word spread like wildfire in the Texas birding community and beyond, once the experts made their decision.

The oriole was being seen mostly early in the morning in a particular triangular wooded area near Hoots Hollow Foot Trail at the park. By the time I arrived at about 9:30 on the morning of February 11, it had already been found and had disappeared again. A few birders who had missed it were still around, peering up into the brushy tangles and looking down the trails to see whether other birders had their binoculars locked onto a bird. I berated myself for not having left home earlier and wildly tried to look everywhere at once for the oriole. Suddenly, a man came charging down the trail toward a couple of us, saying the oriole had been found again. Birders that I hadn't seen at all emerged from the brush. We all rushed toward the spot where the man had seen the now-disappeared bird, and the excited hunt began at the fresh scent. It took a while, but I spotted the bird hanging in a tallow tree about 15 feet off the ground. Others saw it too as it foraged and then eventually left the area. The Streak-backed Oriole remained in that park for another two-plus weeks and delighted many birders who came from all over Texas and beyond to add this bird to their life list.

Seen Only in Alaska
Common Pochard

Although I had planned to start my Alaska big year in Anchorage, where I live, a rare bird report from Kodiak Island by Rich MacIntosh caused me to change my plans and fly to Kodiak on December 31, 2015, and spend New Year's Eve in a place I had never been or planned as a part of my big year. Therefore, my Alaska big year began at 9:45 on January 1, when Rich MacIntosh arrived at my motel. I followed him through the rain in my rental car to Lake Louise. After the first of many Bald Eagles, the first bird we saw on the lake in the rainy, windy half light appeared to be the much-wanted Common Pochard, but it flew away before we could see it well. When we got around to the south side of the lake, we found what was certainly the pochard swimming with a Common Goldeneye. Although the Common Pochard stayed around for many weeks, with a rare bird you dare not gamble, and it's best to find it as soon as possible.

Tufted Duck

May 15 was the first day of my trip to Adak with Wilderness Birding Adventures. Soon after we were out that day, we came to a lake where there were Greater Scaup and four Tufted Ducks. It was good to see them together, and I realized that even at a distance, the black back of the Tufted Ducks was clearly different from the grayer back of the nearby scaup. For the next four days, we saw Tufted Ducks at least once each day, but I saw no others the rest of the year.

Lesser Sand-Plover on St. Paul Island

Lesser Sand-Plover

On May 22 on St. Paul Island, I had my only sighting of a Lesser Sand-Plover. Someone spotted it hunting for food on an inland mudflat—a small plover, beautiful but unremarkable except for its bright rusty breast band. Lesser Sand-Plovers are generally rare and not expected in the United States, but the most likely spot to find them is western Alaskan islands.

Common Ringed Plover

Common Ringed Plovers are known to nest in small numbers on St. Lawrence Island in Gambell, generally south of the lake. We saw them on each of three days on the Gambell spring trip (May 28, 29, and 30). Because the very similar Semipalmated Plovers were there in greater numbers, each bird had to be examined carefully and preferably heard to be sure of the identification.

Ruff

On the afternoon of our first day in Adak (May 16), we went to Contractors' Marsh, where we heard there were two rarities, and there they appeared: two Ruffs and two to four Common Snipe. We saw the Ruffs again on May 18 and 19. Every time we saw them it was because somebody flushed them suddenly as we walked the marsh, and they always flew off rapidly, landed abruptly, and were not seen until flushed again. It made for multiple quick views and mostly bad photographs, but we did see them.

Curlew Sandpiper

After a whirlwind period of seeing a Northern Wheatear and a Siberian Rubythroat on May 24 on St. Paul Island, I thought the excitement was over and settled down to routine birding. After supper we went to Polovina Point, where earlier in the week we had unsuccessfully searched for a Curlew Sandpiper that was around before we arrived on the island. To my amazement, the bird was out in the kelp-covered puddle below us.

Long-toed Stint

I saw two to four Long-toed Stints each day on St. Paul from May 22 to 24, flying and feeding in the marshes. I was grateful to our leaders, who helped me see the differences between these stints and Least Sandpipers.

Jack Snipe

On September 14 shortly after we arrived on St. Paul Island, the group drove to Rocky Lake, got out and formed a line, walked a few minutes, and flushed the Jack Snipe that had been found before our arrival. I also saw it on September 16 and 22 when we walked marshy areas to try to find it for newly arriving island birders.

Terek Sandpiper

My only two Terek Sandpiper sightings were in 2015 (July 6 and 7) in Anchorage, and on May 27 at Gambell during my big year. The latter bird was found before we arrived, and it was the first bird we sought after we landed in Gambell.

Common Sandpiper

I saw two Common Sandpipers on May 23 on St. Paul, and another on May 27 at Gambell. There are subtle differences between Common and Spotted Sandpipers in plumage and call, and I appreciated having leaders to confirm the identity of these birds.

Common Greenshank

I saw a single Common Greenshank each day from May 22 to 24 on St. Paul, and another at Gambell on June 2. Although it was very similar to a Greater Yellowlegs, the Greenshank was lighter, with greenish, not bright yellow, legs.

Dovekie

Small numbers of Dovekies nest at Gambell. I noted one there on May 28 high on the bluffs.

Arctic Loon
On May 16 on Adak, I saw a single Arctic Loon through the spotting scope. I found one each of the next two days there and observed two more from the Nome-Council Road on June 4.

Short-tailed Albatross
On July 2 on a charter boat trip out of Dutch Harbor, we had been watching one, and then two, Laysan Albatrosses on the water near the boat when the real excitement began. A brown, pink-beaked, immature **Short-tailed Albatross** appeared and landed behind the boat, followed immediately by a black-beaked Black-footed Albatross. We were able to see and photograph all three albatrosses at once.

Brandt's Cormorant
Steve Heinl helped me see my first Brandt's Cormorants at Rotary Beach in Ketchikan on January 7. We saw them again in late February and then in December. A rare wintering bird in Alaska generally found only in Ketchikan, it is distinguished from other cormorants by its bluish and buffy throat.

Northern Pygmy-Owl

White-tailed Eagle
South of the lake at Gambell, a single White-tailed Eagle, first spotted by Aaron Lang, was a very welcome surprise on May 29. It circled from the sea over a mountain bluff, came down once, and then moved out of sight.

Northern Pygmy-Owl
On January 4 as I walked to the end of the Mendenhall Wetlands dike trail in Juneau, I kept scanning for birds, noting a small bird sitting at the top of a spruce tree behind me, a long way back on the trail I had

just walked. On my return, I looked for the small bird, and it was still there. I took a distant photo, and it looked like a small round-headed owl. I love owls, and this was very exciting. I kept taking pictures as I approached. The owl appeared to be hunting and made a couple of short flights from treetop to treetop. I was delighted to identify a Northern Pygmy-Owl, a new bird for the year and for my Alaska state list, the only one I found in my big year.

Eurasian Skylark

On September 23 on St. Paul Island, our van was heading back to the airport because some participants were flying out, when suddenly our leader and driver, Scott Schuette, screeched the van to a halt and yelled "Skylark!" We piled out of the van and amazingly were able to see the Eurasian Skylark, which had flown up from the road. It was flying away from us along the edge of Polovina Lake. It is possible that a mystery bird that had been briefly observed the day before was the same bird.

Siberian Rubythroat

I found a Siberian Rubythroat on Hutchinson Hill on St. Paul on May 24 (my only other Alaska sighting was on June 7, 2015, on St. Paul). Nothing can compare to the startling red throat of this bird.

Red-flanked Bluetail

On September 24 on St. Paul Island, we had two sightings of Red-flanked Bluetail (presumably two different birds), one at the quarry and one along the road past Webster House.

Eyebrowed Thrush

A single Eyebrowed Thrush was found high up a hillside at Gambell on May 31 (first spotted by Barbara Carlson). I had a few traumatic moments before I finally saw what others were excitedly discussing, a small, brownish-drab, robin-shaped bird skulking among the rocks.

Siberian Accentor

On September 7 at Gambell, we had just located a couple of pipits at the south end of the lake when a message came on the radio that a Siberian Accentor had been found in the far boneyard. We were bumpily and rapidly conveyed to the boneyard, where we scrambled up the mountain, only to

Siberian Accentor in Gambell

learn that the bird had disappeared farther up the mountain. We were told we needed to give the bird time to get itself back to the boneyard, so we cooled our heels for an hour or so and then retromped the boneyard but did not find it. We headed off to supper, with plans to reconvene at the boneyard at about 7:30 p.m. By about 7:45, others saw, and then I saw, a Siberian Accentor. Then we discovered there were two of them, which posed for numerous photos on a rocky area just past the far boneyard along the base of the mountain. I saw one each of the next two days.

White Wagtail

I saw White Wagtails from May 27 to 31 at Gambell, where they nest, and from August 31 to September 8, generally flitting and walking around the lake.

Pine Bunting

On November 28, we arrived in Gambell just before 4:00 p.m., past sunset and into twilight. After hurriedly putting our belongings in the lodge, we did a fast walk to look for our goal bird, a Pine Bunting. Clarence Irrigoo Jr., who had originally found it, was at the site, and as we arrived we too saw the Pine Bunting, a very rare bird for the continent. Until it got dark we followed it around as it mostly hopped on the ground, ate wild seeds, and did short flights. Clarence had put out seed in the area, which it visited at least once. The next morning before dawn, we were back out there and so was the Pine Bunting.

Rare in Alaska
Seen in Both States
Wood Duck

TX On Sunday, January 16, I went to a house on Lake Worth in west Fort Worth where a previous tenant had accumulated a humongous yard list. There I heard my first Wood Ducks of the year.

AK I flew into Sitka on the morning of February 25, checked into my motel, and walked less than a block to Swan Lake, where a Wood Duck had been reported. Within three minutes of arriving at the lake, I saw it. As reported, he was hanging out with Mallards out on the lake. A little while later, a woman with a bag of bread crusts walked up and all the Mallards raced over to her. The Wood Duck stayed in the water for a while but then hopped ashore and cautiously approached the Mallard feeding frenzy. Before he reached the bread crumbs, a loud noise nearby scared all the ducks back to the water. I went back to see the Wood Duck one more time before I left Sitka and assumed that would be my last view of it. Surprisingly, the Wood Duck stayed in Sitka, and I was able to see (and photograph) it again in October and November when I returned to Sitka to add other species to my year list.

Wood Duck

Cinnamon Teal

^{TX} In the Ingleside area, I found three Cinnamon Teal (two males) on January 1. They are usually found across the state in West Texas.

^{AK} I was in Juneau in late April to look for migrants. Among the birds of particular interest was a Cinnamon Teal that Gus Van Vliet had reported. On April 30, I drove north to the Eagle Beach area where it had been found. The tide was out, however, and it was difficult to see the ducks. On May 1, I arrived there at high tide, and all the ducks were much closer to the overlook. I looked around the wetland at the other ducks (pintails, wigeons) and geese (Canada Geese and one Snow Goose) and then looked back and saw that the flock of Green-winged Teal had grown, and even better, it now included a male Cinnamon Teal, a very rare bird in Alaska. Even though the Cinnamon Teal was embedded in the flock of Green-winged Teal, its darker cinnamon color made it stand out.

Ruddy Duck

^{TX} In Texas, Ruddy Duck was species number 4 on January 1, and so common and of little note that I did not mention it in my detailed write-up about the day.

^{AK} On June 23, I was wending my way back toward Anchorage from birding in Delta Junction. After checking into a motel in Glennallen, I felt a bit revived, so in the early evening I headed to Kenny Lake, where Ruddy Ducks regularly breed. After a 40-mile drive, I reached Kenny Lake, got out my scope, walked to the lake edge, scanned around, and found two male Ruddy Ducks. There were quite a few other ducks too, some with young, as well as Horned Grebes and their young. Later in the summer I went back to Kenny Lake and saw a single Ruddy Duck (female or immature).

Pied-billed Grebe

^{TX} As with Ruddy Ducks, I first observed Pied-billed Grebes in Texas in Matagorda County on January 1 but did not discuss them further in my big year notes that day. Additional sightings included a family of Pied-billed Grebes at Muleshoe NWR on August 1.

^{AK} On January 6, I headed north of Ketchikan to mostly frozen Ward Lake, where Steve Heinl had told me that a Pied-billed Grebe was wintering in the decreasing area of open water. In my rental car I was decidedly nervous on the icy road, which first went up and then down, down toward the lake. I was

happy to see a few cars by the lake, as I envisioned slipping off the road or being unable to climb back out of the area. I was also very happy to see the Pied-billed Grebe bobbing along in the narrow stretch of water just beyond a small group of ice skaters. I thought this distant view would be it for Pied-billed Grebe for my Alaska big year, but I was able to see one at close range in August at Jim Lake in Palmer, and then multiple birds in Sitka in both October and November at Swan Lake.

Band-tailed Pigeon

^{TX} On May 11, after a quick supper snack, I went back to Boot Springs in Big Bend for an owl-sit at a picnic table. There I saw and heard Band-tailed Pigeons, one of which flew by very close. As it got darker, the pigeons cooed more and more as I waited at the picnic table in the opening near the springs. Early the next morning before daylight I could hear Whip-poor-wills and Western Screech-Owls through my tent walls, and when I came out of my tent in the early dawn, there was a singing Painted Redstart. A wonderful way to start the day. Band-tailed Pigeons were calling in the distance. I heard them again on May 18 at Davis Mountains Preserve and saw them on August 8 in Big Bend NP as I walked the Pinnacles Trail.

^{AK} On the morning of May 2, I flew from Juneau to Ketchikan, and by 8:00

Band-tailed Pigeon in Ketchikan

I was on the road north to a yard where Steve Heinl had told me Band-tailed Pigeons were being fed. As I drove into the yard I saw Band-tailed Pigeons fly away. I decided to wait in my car (in the rain) to see whether they would return and allow a photo. While I waited, a pair of Rufous Hummingbirds came to a feeder, a Northern Flicker called, a Steller's Jay scolded me, and Dark-eyed Juncos hopped on the ground. Eventually Common Ravens landed in a nearby tree and came down to a driveway behind a building, and then I saw the pigeons come back and land out of sight. Finally one of them landed in a tree and let me take its picture. I saw a few of them the next day in the same general area. Ketchikan is one of the few places where this species breeds in Alaska and is one of the most reliable sites to find it.

Sora

[TX] Another nice find among many on the first day of my big year in Texas was a Sora, calmly picking its way along the edge of a spot near Ingleside where I had unsuccessfully looked for a Masked Duck.

[AK] I saw a Sora in Haines on July 15. I first heard it at a very large marsh 15.5 miles away from Haines on Highway 7. Eventually I saw it twice, a tiny bird with a little bright yellow bill, flicking its upturned tail as it picked its way across the mud through the vegetation. It called a couple of times and then went silent. Although I saw it well, it never came out of the vegetation enough to allow a picture.

American Coot

[TX] I found American Coots on January 1 in Matagorda County on the Texas coast, and they were common all year.

[AK] My ultimate goal after I arrived at midday in Ketchikan on February 26 was the American Coot reported near the end of the North Tongass Highway at Knudson Cove Marina. When I arrived, I asked the marina manager, who fed Mallards along with an American Coot at the marina, about the coot. As we spoke, the American Coot appeared near us. Apparently there had been a coot (sometimes two of them) at the marina for three winters. I went back the next day for one more viewing.

Wilson's Phalarope

[TX] On April 21, after exploring the area a bit, we went back to Anahuac NWR, where Wilson's Phalaropes had been reported. A scope scan finally revealed a couple of Wilson's Phalaropes to add to my list. I saw them again in West Texas on August 1 in Gaines County, and in Muleshoe NWR as we searched in vain for reported Red-necked Phalaropes.

[AK] On July 4, Louann Feldmann, Mike Herndon, and I tried to find a Wilson's Phalarope near Goose Bay, where a male had been reported earlier, and where I had looked twice in June. This time we succeeded. At first all we could see were both yellowlegs species, Least Sandpipers, Northern Shovelers, and American Wigeons. We tromped all over, checking out all the big and little lakes in the wetland. Then on our way back we spotted (in the biggest shallow lake) a shorebird that was *not* any of the shorebirds we had spotted earlier. It was a bit smaller than the nearby Lesser Yellowlegs, but much more drab and unmarked. There were no spots or streaks or other evident markings on its breast, which was a soft off-white. Its back was a plain gray brown, as was a light smudge near its eyes and crown. There was a slightly darker area on its wing. Its beak was very thin and its legs were not as long as those of a yellowlegs, but they were yellow. It was walking in the shallow water between and behind clumps of grass about 40–70 feet from us across a portion of the lake. We were not able to see it for long and did not get any photographs. Once it disappeared into the grass clumps we consulted our various apps and found it was essentially identical to the photograph shown for juvenile Wilson's Phalarope in the iBird Pro North America app. In the car as we drove back to Anchorage we looked at all the apps and the bird books again and reached the same conclusion. Neither of the other phalarope species was shown with any plumage that was even close to that of the bird we had seen.

Franklin's Gull

[TX] Franklin's Gull is a common to uncommon migrant in all of Texas. It is particularly common during fall migration in Fort Worth, but I did not have to wait for fall to see it during my Texas big year. Simone and I explored Gene Howe WMA and the Lake Marvin area near Canadian on April 5 and were able to add a Franklin's Gull, floating serenely on a pond at the WMA, before returning home.

[AK] On May 26, I went to the Chester Creek Trail southwest of Westchester Lagoon in Anchorage, where two Franklin's Gulls had been found at Ship Creek a few days earlier and were spotted again along the Chester Creek Trail on May 25. I was pleased to find that the two Franklin's Gulls were still there, far out on the edge of the mudflats initially near a Bonaparte's Gull, allowing a handy comparison of their sizes and back color. I could see the bold white eye crescents of the Franklin's Gulls and the lack of similar crescents on the Bonaparte's Gull. Other local birders came along and confirmed that I was indeed looking at the Franklin's Gulls.

Ring-billed Gull

[TX] On January 3, while I was looking for (and finding) the much rarer Black-legged Kittiwake, I also saw my first Ring-billed Gull of the year flying around the Boca Chica jetty with Herring and Laughing Gulls.

[AK] My North Carolina birding friend Lena and I arrived in Ketchikan early in the morning, were picked up by Steve Heinl, and by about 9:00 were seeing three Ring-billed Gulls amid multitudes of Glaucous-winged, Herring, Mew, and California Gulls. Although there were no adult Ring-billed Gulls with actual bill rings, their size (larger than Mew and smaller than the others) helped me identify them.

Caspian Tern

[TX] On January 3 in the Boca Chica area, I added Caspian Terns as well as numerous other terns and coastal shorebirds to my year list.

[AK] On May 3, Steve Heinl, Andy Piston, and I and birded some sites south of Ketchikan. In addition to the usual species of the area we had a couple of flyover goose flocks, Greater White-fronted and Snow. At one of the usual gull-roost areas, we were surprised to see a Caspian Tern land amid the gulls, a bird that I knew was going to be difficult to find in my Alaska big year. As it turned out, I saw two to six of them during the two days I birded in Gustavus (May 5 and 6), and five at Eagle Beach State Recreation Area north of Juneau on June 15.

Swainson's Hawk

[TX] I first spotted Swainson's Hawk in the Coastal Bend area on March 23, a day when a Glaucous Gull in Corpus Christi dominated my adventures, leaving no room to write about the much more common hawk. I saw a handsome juvenile Swainson's Hawk, with a distinctive moustache, on a fence post on August 31 near Van Horn.

[AK] As Steve Heinl, Louann Feldmann, and I were walking in Hyder on the drizzly afternoon of June 12, we noticed a Common Raven circling high above with a hawk of some kind. We had been bemoaning the lack of raptors, and one appeared over our heads. What was it? After reviewing the shape and markings on the distant hawk, we looked at Steve's pictures showing the typical bicolored wing (my pictures were basically silhouettes) of a Swainson's Hawk, very rare and declining in Alaska.

Western Screech-Owl

TX On May 11, I hiked up to Boot Springs in Big Bend NP with my camping gear. After a quick supper snack, I went near the springs for an owl-sit at a picnic table. Although it was still quite light at about 8:40 p.m., invisible Whip-poor-wills started calling all around me, a flock of Mexican Jays squawked suddenly, and then all was totally silent. The Whip-poor-wills started up again, and then at 9:00, I heard a Western Screech-Owl in the distance. I also saw and heard them later in the year at other spots in Big Bend.

AK After dinner on March 14, with a beautiful sunset in my rearview mirror, I made a 50-mile trip toward Portage, south of Anchorage. I turned into a fish-observing parking lot that led to a campground (not yet open for the year). I packed up my flashlights (two, in case I dropped one), camera, binoculars, and phone and walked the paved road into the camping area. A beautiful half moon in the clear sky meant I did not need either flashlight, even though I stayed until a little after 10:00 p.m. About 9:00, when it was still quite light out, on one of my visual surveys of the silhouetted trees around me I was amazed to see a small Western Screech-Owl, silently silhouetted, staring down from near the top of a deciduous tree very close by. The bird's head was sort of squarish (as opposed to the rounder heads of Boreal and Northern Saw-whet Owls) and had little bumps at the two upper corners—the "ears." I tried to get a picture but as I was fumbling with the camera, the owl silently glided over my head and disappeared. I walked the campground for another hour, mostly listening to the total silence and the quietly flowing water. Only a couple of times did I hear what were probably distant owl calls, but none of them were clear or loud enough to tell me for sure what they were. It is very strange to see, but not hear, an owl at night, an oddly incomplete feeling.

Yellow-bellied Sapsucker

TX I first observed Yellow-bellied Sapsuckers on January 1, and I saw them again many times after that. When I saw them, such as later at Cottonwood Campground in Big Bend on January 6, it was always important to check whether they were their rarer cousin, the Red-naped Sapsucker. I also saw Yellow-bellied Sapsuckers in the Pineywoods area on February 26.

[AK] On August 4, I drove very slowly to Tok from Delta Junction, listening and looking for Yellow-bellied Sapsuckers, which I understood might be in the area. Although I never saw one, while slowly following the pilot car on a long portion of gravel road being resurfaced, I heard the distinctive "churr" call of a Yellow-bellied Sapsucker very close by in the mostly deciduous woods along the road. Because of all the road equipment I could not stop or go back to look for it. Later I heard young sapsuckers somewhere high in another grove of deciduous trees.

Yellow-bellied Flycatcher

[TX] I visited Sabine Woods the morning of August 25 after a long drought on new birds and finally found some new ones, the first of which was a bright Yellow-bellied Flycatcher, along with other already-seen warblers.

[AK] On the afternoon of June 10, our last day in Hyder, it looked as if we weren't going to see anything new for the trip or for my big year, but then we were surprised to hear and then see a Yellow-bellied Flycatcher very close by.

Willow Flycatcher

[TX] By noon on May 2, I was on my way to the Valley to see what migrants might be there. There weren't any new warblers, but it seemed to be flycatcher time, with a calling Willow Flycatcher at the South Padre Island Convention Centre being the first of the new flycatchers the next day.

[AK] On June 9, our first day in Hyder, Willow Flycatcher was my fourth new big year bird (of ten) for the day. One of the best things was it was singing loudly, and not very far away an Alder Flycatcher was also singing loudly, allowing us to be certain of two species that are easily identified and distinguished from each other only by sound. We regularly observed one or two of them each of the days we were in Hyder.

Least Flycatcher

[TX] On January 18, we went to the Quintana Neotropical Bird Sanctuary to see our first Least Flycatcher of the year, a common migrant through the state.

[AK] In Hyder on June 9 and then again on June 10 and 12, we heard and then saw an actively singing Least Flycatcher, a rare bird in Alaska, found primarily in Southeastern Alaska. I was glad to see another one in Juneau, heard first by Gus Van Vliet as we were birding in the Moose Lake area on June 15.

Eastern Phoebe

ᵀˣ Eastern Phoebe is very common in many areas across Texas and can be found all year long there. My first sighting was in Matagorda County in the coastal area on January 1.

ᴬᴷ In Alaska, Eastern Phoebe is casual, and until 2016, I was unaware it had ever been found in the state. On July 12, however, about a month after learning of reports of an Eastern Phoebe reportedly nesting in Nome, I finally had time and energy for a day trip to Nome. Although I was unable to find a car to rent, I eventually found and rented a 15-person van at a normal car rate so I could drive to the culvert under the road in which the phoebes were nesting. When I reached the spot where the phoebe had been reported I quickly saw two Eastern Phoebes going back and forth to a nest, feeding young. I climbed down from the road so I could peer into the culvert and see the messy nest hanging from a pipe running the length of the culvert. I did not stay long, however, because the parents did not seem to appreciate my being there.

Tropical Kingbird

ᵀˣ Tropical Kingbirds, while not rare in Texas, are uncommon and local residents in the LRGV. My first for the year was on May 2 in the same area as a

Tropical Kingbird in Sitka

calling Couch's Kingbird along the Military Highway east of Bentsen–Rio Grande Valley State Park.

^{AK} Matt Goff picked up Louann Feldmann and me on the morning of October 22 after we saw the Wood Duck that had been in Sitka since the previous winter. We spent the morning looking for, but not seeing, the Tropical Kingbird that had been in Sitka at least six days. After lunch, Matt returned to the area while Louann and I looked unsuccessfully for a Swamp Sparrow we thought we might have spotted earlier. Then Matt called us to say he'd found the kingbird. Louann and I drove to his location and saw the Tropical Kingbird perched on overhead lines, flitting about and reperching. I never thought I'd see a named tropical bird in Alaska, but there are previous records.

Eastern Kingbird

[TX] My first Texas sighting of a migrating Eastern Kingbird was on March 18, when Sabine Woods (along with the other coastal hotspots) was filled with Black-and-white, Orange-crowned, and Yellow-rumped Warblers, as well as a newly arrived Yellow-throated Warbler.

[AK] An Eastern Kingbird had been reported in Hyder before we flew there on June 9. After we landed, we wandered around near the seaplane landing spot where dead tree stumps protruded from the long grass. Finally we spotted and photographed the Eastern Kingbird as it perched on some of the stumps.

Cassin's Vireo

[TX] Cassin's Vireo is difficult to find, although not rare, in Texas. While it is uncommon to rare during migration in the Trans-Pecos, Cassin's Vireo is regularly found during fall migration east to the western High Plains. I saw my first one on September 6 in Big Bend as it inspected the bushes along a trail where I was unsuccessfully looking for Hermit Warbler.

[AK] On our trip to Hyder we saw Cassin's Vireo multiple times on June 11 and 12, but in typical vireo fashion it was mostly obscured by branches and leaves. We eventually saw it well, but I was not able to photograph it. I had no other sightings in Alaska.

Red-eyed Vireo

[TX] I first found Red-eyed Vireos on March 18 among the increasing numbers of migrating warblers at Boy Scout Woods at High Island.

^AK^ One of my two main goals in Juneau on June 15 was a Red-eyed Vireo recently reported by Gus Van Vliet. When I reached the site, the Brotherhood Bridge Trail, I found my first Red-eyed Vireo of the year, singing loudly and eventually visible through the dense leaves. Farther along the trail I heard, but did not see, a second singing Red-eyed Vireo. I went back the next day and saw the first bird again before heading home.

American Crow

^TX^ American Crows are very common in Texas, in the east from the coast northward and in north-central Texas. An American Crow in Wharton County was the first bird of my Texas big year as I approached my initial coastal destination on January 1.

^AK^ Hyder is almost the only place in Alaska that American Crows can be found. In the rest of Alaska, there are either Northwestern Crows or no crows at all, as is the case in most of Alaska, where Common Ravens are the only all-black birds. I thought I would see them soon but I had to wait until our second day in Hyder (June 10). Although I saw them daily on the rest of the Hyder trip, the most I saw at any one time was five birds.

Northern Rough-winged Swallow

^TX^ Northern Rough-winged Swallows winter in the LRGV, and I first observed them on January 14 when I was on a trip to see some reported megararities.

^AK^ My only Northern Rough-winged Swallows in 2016 were two on June 10 in Hyder, the best place for them in their limited Southeastern Alaska range.

Mountain Bluebird

^TX^ On January 6 as Simone and I headed to Big Bend from the LRGV, we added Mountain Bluebirds as well as Horned Larks, Roadrunner, Phainopepla, and a lovely Golden Eagle soaring over the nearby hills.

^AK^ I expected my best chance for seeing a Mountain Bluebird would be during spring migration in Juneau. Unfortunately, the bluebirds had migrated through a week earlier than usual, and I missed them. It appeared unlikely that I would see them for the year, because although they do rarely breed in Alaska, their breeding range is very limited. On June 22, on a trip to Delta Junction, I learned a Mountain Bluebird had been found in Chicken a week earlier. After heading east about 125 miles toward Canada, I drove a gravel road 66 miles northeast, past acres and acres of scrawny black spruce blackened by forest fire to Chicken, a small tourist town with a gold-panning and dredging history. Upon arrival, the most obvious birds were Cliff Swallows, which had built nests on and were swarming around and under a big gold dredge. Finally I saw a pair of Mountain Bluebirds hanging around the gold dredge and noticed one of them coming out of a pipe, most likely its nest spot.

Veery

[TX] Although Veeries are beautiful birds, my first for the year, at Sabine Woods on April 18, was overshadowed by the more colorful warblers and other spring migrants, including Blue Grosbeaks, Chestnut-sided, Worm-eating, and Kentucky Warblers, Yellow-billed Cuckoo, and Baltimore Oriole.

[AK] On June 9, the ninth new bird of the Hyder trip was a Veery late in the day after we heard it calling, then singing (very poorly photographed but seen well and heard often). On each of the next three days of the trip, I photographed and audio recorded one or two, and possibly three, Veeries. A Veery is an accidental bird in Alaska, with most records in Hyder.

House Finch

[TX] Although I expected to see my first House Finch in my Fort Worth yard, I first saw one on January 5 in the Brush Country on my whirlwind trip around Texas in 2005. When I went to Texline in the Texas Panhandle on February 9 to look for Cassin's Finch, I first saw the very common House Finches before I left town and found a much rarer Cassin's Finch.

[AK] I was in Juneau on October 17 when I learned from Steve Heinl that a House Finch had appeared the day before in Jerry Koerner's yard, a wonderful Ketchikan hotspot that has produced quite a few wonderful birds over the years and, in particular, was a major help to my Alaska big year. I changed plans and went back to my Juneau motel to look at airline schedules. After some delay due to airline problems, I made my reservation. Steve picked me up the next morning at the ferry dock and we drove immediately to Jerry Koerner's house. Very soon after we arrived, the House Finch joined the 30 or more Dark-eyed Juncos dining on seed in Jerry's yard. The House Finch stayed around about 15 minutes and then departed.

Tennessee Warbler

[TX] We saw our first Tennessee Warbler at Paradise Pond in Port Aransas on April 11 at the same time other migrant species were arriving.

[AK] When I got to Juneau on June 15, one of my two goals was the Tennessee

Tennessee Warbler in Juneau

Magnolia Warbler in Hyder

Warbler that Gus Van Vliet had found on the Moose Lake Trail. After we arrived, all we could find was a Northern Waterthrush, which was trying to sound like a Tennessee Warbler. We explored a bit, returned to the reported location, and found and photographed the singing Tennessee Warbler.

Magnolia Warbler

[TX] I first saw a beautiful black, white, and yellow Magnolia Warbler during spring migration on April 27 in Port O'Connor.

[AK] On June 12 in Hyder, Steve Heinl heard the distant sound of a possible Magnolia Warbler. After all three of us noisily slid down a slope through the underbrush, we saw a single stunning Magnolia Warbler. First I got a view of its distinctive undertail but finally saw the entire bird.

Palm Warbler

[TX] After a couple of days at home resting from early warbler hunting, we saw our first chestnut-capped, tail-wagging Palm Warblers on March 28 on Galveston Island, where they had previously been reported.

[AK] A Palm Warbler was found in Juneau at Rotary Park by Amy Courtney and then again by Gus Van Vliet. I managed to get there on October 16. Not too long after I arrived, Gus found the bird again. It was with a

Yellow-rumped Warbler pal. Both warblers flitted about, often low to the ground, in bushes along the edge of the park pond. I saw two more Palm Warblers on November 7 when I went to Sitka for a Cape May Warbler.

Black-throated Gray Warbler

[TX] I first spotted a Black-throated Gray Warbler on January 6 high in the cottonwoods at Cottonwood Campground at Big Bend. Early on March 15, after a nearly sleepless night in my car, I made the short drive to the upper residential area of the Chisos Basin to conserve my strength for the upcoming climb on the Pinnacles Trail to Boot Springs. A bit bleary eyed as I got out of the car, I was brought abruptly to alertness by energetic cheery birdsong in the tree right above my head. After a bit of peering around in the dim morning light, I located the singer, a Black-throated Gray Warbler, not new for the year, but a great way to start the day. I had never heard one sing before. They were also in the Guadalupe Mountains on August 31.

[AK] On June 12 in Hyder, we were amazed to find one, and possibly two, Black-throated Gray Warblers. We had very good views of a species never previously photographed in Alaska, and reported only once before in the state. It flitted around amid a small flock of Yellow-rumped Warblers and disappeared. We also found it later in the day and spotted it again on June 13.

Spotted Towhee

[TX] I found my first Spotted Towhee as the sun went down on January 6 at Big Bend's Sam Nail Ranch along with a Green-tailed Towhee, just before Simone and I headed to Alpine on our 10-day race around Texas. We saw them again on January 24 as we walked the lower portion of the Pinnacles Trail at Big Bend, and on March 15 as I hiked higher on that trail. Early on the morning of May 12 when I walked from my tent over to Boot Springs, I heard a loud rustling in the leaves just ahead to my left, and my heart stopped. Was it the reported mountain lion? No, it turned out to be just two Spotted Towhees rooting around in the dry leaves.

[AK] Late in 2015 I saw a Facebook post indicating that somewhere in Juneau there was a Spotted Towhee. I tried to follow up on the sighting and then forgot about it until I talked to Gus Van Vliet on a trip to Juneau in early January. He said the towhee was still around and told me which house was hosting the bird. Just before noon on January 5, I found it hanging out with juncos (mostly Oregon Dark-eyed Juncos). I expected it would be my only sighting for the year, but on multiple trips to Ketchikan looking for the Swamp Sparrow, I frequently saw a Spotted Towhee at Herring Cove (December 5 and 9–12).

Swamp Sparrow

TX I saw my first Swamp Sparrow for the year on January 7 in Alpine's Kokernot Park, where we also found a Rock Wren and Black Phoebe. The Swamp Sparrow was my 200th species for the year.

AK Although I spent multiple days in early December sitting in a rental car in Herring Cove (Ketchikan), where others had had good views of a cooperative Swamp Sparrow before I arrived, my Alaskan Swamp Sparrow sighting there was a rather unsatisfactory brief look on December 5, and I later heard periodic sounds of a bird I could not see.

White-throated Sparrow

TX On January 13, after being home a couple of days from my initial 10-day swing around the state, I went to Hagerman NWR, a couple of hours north of Fort Worth, where I was able to find White-throated Sparrows as well as Fox Sparrows and a Winter Wren, bringing the year total to 237.

AK On January 13, I birded with Aaron Lang in Homer at his home and elsewhere. We took a break from a vigil searching for the White-throated Sparrow previously observed in his yard near some brush piles and wandered his driveway to see birds near a neighbor's feeder. When we returned and peered out a window at the same brush pile, our goal bird, his wintering White-throated Sparrow, finally appeared right where he had previously seen it. In October I saw another one briefly in Sitka, flitting about along a brushy roadside.

Rose-breasted Grosbeak

TX On April 17, I was exploring High Island when I saw my first Rose-breasted Grosbeak of the year. Most years, as in 2005, Rose-breasted Grosbeaks are easily found in spring along the Texas coast, particularly at the warbler hotspots of Sabine Woods and High Island, usually in trees filled with warblers.

AK I flew to Ketchikan from Juneau on the morning of July 14 and picked up Steve Heinl. He and Andy Piston had discovered a Rose-breasted Grosbeak four days earlier, and I had been yearning to go to Ketchikan ever since to look for it. I understood that although Rose-breasted Grosbeaks regularly appear in the state, it was not a species I could expect to see in Alaska. We drove to the area where he told me the bird had been singing every time anyone had gone to look for it since its original discovery. When we arrived, there was no sound of a grosbeak. We walked the road, we drove the area, we got out, we listened. There were thrushes, Pacific Wrens, Fox Sparrows, and lots of singing all around us, but no grosbeak. We drove until the road made a sharp uphill turn and then we turned around and drove slowly, listening in the same areas. When we got to where it had originally been found, we were delighted to hear it, and then see it—a beautiful male Rose-breasted Grosbeak. What a wonderful bird to tie the previous big year record for Alaska—number 287.

Black-headed Grosbeak

[TX] Although Black-headed Grosbeaks are most common in the western half of Texas, they migrate through the LRGV and East Texas and can be found there during the winter. I saw my first one on January 15 at Frontera Audubon in the Valley when I was searching for the reported Elegant Trogon.

[AK] Although I saw a Black-headed Grosbeak in Anchorage in 2015, my only Black-headed Grosbeak sightings during my big year were in Hyder on June 10 and 11, two different Black-headed Grosbeaks as proved by photographs of their different orange and black head markings.

Black-headed Grosbeak in Hyder

Western Meadowlark

Western Meadowlark

ᵀˣ Simone and I saw our first Western Meadowlarks on January 5 as we drove west across the Brush Country from south of San Antonio, where we also saw Say's Phoebe, Curve-billed Thrashers, and Cactus Wrens. Western Meadowlarks winter across much of the state and breed in northwest Texas.

ᴬᴷ In January of my Alaska big year I spent quite a bit of time while I was in Juneau looking for the reported Western Meadowlark (sometimes two had been reported). On January 9, I briefly saw one silhouetted bird near the Mendenhall Wetlands, where two of them had been reported sporadically for weeks. It was perched up on a spruce and shortly after being spotted flew down out of sight, never to be found again, despite much looking.

Brewer's Blackbird

ᵀˣ Brewer's Blackbirds winter but do not breed in Texas and are most common in the western portion of the state. My first Brewer's Blackbirds of

2005 were on January 7 along the roadside in the Davis Mountains in West Texas. After that they were sufficiently common that I no longer noted them in my daily bird summaries.

^{AK} In contrast, I have seen only one Brewer's Blackbird in Alaska, and it was very noteworthy. This bird wintered in Hoonah, arriving in the latter part of 2015 and staying into 2016. Getting to Hoonah requires a seaplane trip from Juneau. That was the second unexpected last-minute trip of the year (the first being to Kodiak on January 1). Before my big year began, I kept reading reports that the Brewer's Blackbird was still around, but I waited to make my reservation, sure the bird would disappear before the year began and I would have booked a trip for nothing. But it remained. The Brewer's Blackbird was usually in the company of a Rusty Blackbird. Soon after I arrived both were eating seeds thrown onto a lawn. I added four species to my year list in Hoonah on January 8—both blackbirds plus Golden-crowned and Savannah Sparrows that were enjoying the bird seed as well.

Savannah Sparrow at Izembek NWR

Brown-headed Cowbird

ᵀˣ Brown-headed Cowbirds are common in much of the Lower 48, parasitizing the nests of smaller birds, and generally not a bird sought by birders. That was definitely true in Texas, but of course it did count as another species for my list. My first one for the year was south of San Antonio in Frio County on January 5.

ᴬᴷ In Alaska, however, Brown-headed Cowbird is a desired rarity for Alaskan bird listers. I saw my only Alaskan Brown-headed Cowbird on June 7 in Ketchikan in the very productive yard of Jerry Koerner, where he had previously had a small flock of them.

Bullock's Oriole

ᵀˣ In very dry West Texas on May 10, I wandered the roads and stopped at picnic areas, where there are often trees and sometimes water. That day at one of these areas I saw my first colorful Bullock's Oriole at a dripping faucet outside a rest stop facility.

ᴬᴷ On our second day in Hyder (June 10), we saw and photographed a single Bullock's Oriole, a young male, which disappeared shortly thereafter, never to be seen again.

Rare in Texas
Seen in Both States
Trumpeter Swan

TX On December 28 as I was trying to decide what to do for the last few days of my Texas big year, I had a phone message from Barrett Pierce telling me he knew the location of Trumpeter Swans on some private ponds in the Amarillo area. I immediately headed west and met him in his Amarillo office the next morning. We drove to the ranch where the swans were and slowly drove the roads checking out ponds. When I thought we were not going to find them, we finally saw five distant swans, two adults and three grayish immatures. We stayed well back from them so they would not fly, and then we crept a bit closer through the brush when they dropped their heads down and began to feed among the ducks that were also out there.

Trumpeter Swan

^AK^ For those who live in South-Central and Interior Alaska, it is difficult to realize that Trumpeter Swans are in trouble nationally. During my big year, I found Trumpeter Swans wintering on Kodiak on January 1. By mid-March they were appearing in Homer and Anchorage, filling lakes and marshes, mostly in pairs. Gradually, by early May, most of them departed for more remote areas until the fall, when individuals and family groups reappeared and sometimes stayed for months. My last observations for the year were in mid-November just south of Anchorage. It was not uncommon in October for 10 or more swans, and sometimes over 30, to be spread out in each of the various ponds along the highway between Anchorage and the Portage area some 50 miles away.

Tundra Swan

^TX^ Tundra Swan is included here, although it is variably rare to very rare to irregular across Texas. On January 10, the last day of our big drive around Texas, we went to a wetland in Dickens County in the rolling plains south of the Panhandle where a Tundra Swan had been reported. When we arrived, a single swan was swimming calmly among Mallards, Northern Shovelers, Green-winged Teal, Gadwalls, American Wigeons, and Ring-necked Ducks.

^AK^ On April 4, David Sonneborn found a Tundra Swan at Spenard Crossing. When I arrived the swan was sleeping, with most of its beak tucked out of sight. The little bit I could see did not seem to have any yellow, but when the swan pulled its head out a little more I realized that there was a little bit of yellow on the beak, and the shape of the black around the eye was that of a Tundra Swan and not a Trumpeter Swan. I noted others throughout the summer in Western Alaska (Gambell, Nome) and Northern Alaska (Utqiagvik).

Eurasian Wigeon

^TX^ On November 22, a male Eurasian Wigeon was reported at Muleshoe NWR on the western side of the Panhandle. I was in Corpus Christi at the time, and before I could head west I needed to go back to Fort Worth. Finally, on November 24, Thanksgiving Day, I drove west, arriving at Muleshoe at 3:30 p.m. (369 miles). I went back and forth between the various lakes at the refuge and eventually located the Eurasian Wigeon at dusk at Upper White Lake. Even in the half light, the chestnut head with creamy top and front was very evident, but I knew I'd have to come back the next day to try for pictures.

I was there again on November 25 before it got light. Sandhill Cranes filled the sky, and as the sun gradually illuminated all the ducks on the lake, I relocated the male Eurasian Wigeon hanging out with two American Wigeons on the same lake where I'd found it the night before.

[AK] On March 12, Beluga Slough in Homer was teeming with ducks, mostly Mallards and American Wigeons. A male Northern Shoveler and a distant male Eurasian Wigeon were also at the slough. Our group of birders was able to see both species, and I managed to get a blurry but identifiable picture of the Eurasian Wigeon. I also saw 10–15 Eurasian Wigeons each day in mid-May on Adak.

King Eider

[TX] In April I intended to begin birding in Fort Worth with my North Carolina friend, Lena Gallitano, but the report of a King Eider at Bolivar Flats changed our plans. As part of a growing crowd of eider seekers on April 17, we canvassed the beaches and scanned the waters, but we could not find the eider. We then noticed some other birders down the road and drove toward them to see whether they had found it. On the way Lena spotted a dark lump on a jetty, and we stopped to look. It was the King Eider. Other birders were quickly summoned, and all present got to see and photograph the resting bird. The eider stayed in the Bolivar/Galveston area for weeks, so we needn't have rushed down. But you never know.

[AK] On May 23, when I was on St. Paul Island, I added King Eider as well as Parakeet Auklet, Least Auklet, Horned Puffin, Thick-Billed Murre, Common Sandpiper, Red Phalarope, and Glaucous Gull. I also observed King Eiders at Gambell, Nome, and Utqiagvik until early November.

Surf Scoter, White-winged Scoter, Black Scoter

[TX] None of the three scoters is common in Texas, but Surf Scoter is more common than the other two. Eric Carpenter (who held the Texas big year record in 2003) had made it a major part of his big year in 2003 to find the scoters early in the year. I tried to do the same in early 2005, without success. On November 14, a female White-winged Scoter was reported at Austin's Hornsby Bend. Unfortunately, I was hours away in West Texas at the Guadalupe Mountains when I got the word a little after noon. On November 15, I left Junction at 3:45 a.m. and made tracks for Hornsby Bend. I got there a little before 7:00 a.m., but it was not until a little before 9:00, after having scanned each pond numerous times, that I finally found the female White-winged Scoter diving and floating in the northeast corner of the far northeast pond, gradually drifting toward the center.

As I drove home to Fort Worth, someone found a female Black Scoter where I had just been in Austin, so very early the next morning I went back and saw both scoters.

There was not a Surf Scoter at Hornsby Bend, so I needed to go elsewhere to find one. After hearing of one in Galveston, I went on November 21 and checked out each beach I could get to, working my way down Galveston Island. Near a small jetty across the road from a Holiday Inn, a large dark duck-shaped bird was bobbing in the waves. I did a U-turn, screeched to a halt, grabbed my telescope, and ran down the beach hoping to see the bird again. There it was. I rapidly set up my spotting scope on the sand, focused, and beheld a female Surf Scoter. She gradually drifted down the beach, closer to the jetty. I worked my way out the jetty, sneaking closer to the outer end every time the scoter dove. Finally, I was at the end of the jetty staring down at a very close Surf Scoter.

^{AK} On January 1 at Pasagshak Bay (Kodiak Island), I saw my first Surf Scoters of the year and had later sightings in Ketchikan, Homer, Seward,

Surf Scoter at Petersburg

Juneau, Nome, and Petersburg. I saw my first White-winged Scoters (about 40) in Ketchikan on January 7, and I saw them most months as I wandered around Alaska, with later sightings in Ketchikan as well as Homer, Adak, Gambell, Petersburg, and Juneau. I observed my first Black Scoter on January 1 at Kalsin Pond on Kodiak Island, with later sightings at Homer, Nome, Gambell, Adak, and Petersburg.

Long-tailed Duck

^{TX} On February 16, I learned that a Long-tailed Duck (previously called "Oldsquaw") had been reported at Lake Tawakoni, where I'd just visited. It was seen from a private area, where it was a bit difficult to get near enough to the water to see the bird. When I arrived, I could see the Long-tailed Duck as an interesting dot from the road, but eventually I was able to go closer for a better view. As is often the case with great birds that I worry about missing, I got very close views of this species—two more Long-tailed Ducks at Hagerman NWR in December just before my big year ended.

^{AK} On January 1 on the various small bays off Chiniak Bay (Kodiak Island), I saw my first Long-tailed Ducks of 2016. I also regularly observed Long-tailed Ducks on my trips to Ketchikan, Homer, St. Paul, Gambell, and Utqiagvik.

Long-tailed Jaeger

^{TX} The World Birding Center's last pelagic trip of the year was on Saturday, November 5. Although the waves were high and I was seasick, I saw both a Long-tailed Jaeger and a Pomarine Jaeger, as well as Bridled Terns and Cory's Shearwater.

^{AK} I found my first Long-tailed Jaeger on June 3, flying around over the tundra outside Nome at Coffee Dome on the Kougarok Road, where we also saw multiple Bristle-thighed Curlews. I saw other Long-tailed Jaegers in Utqiagvik and Nome in early July.

Whimbrel

^{TX} On March 18, I birded at Bolivar Flats and then headed to Yacht Basin Road near Rollover Pass, looking for Whimbrels, which are often seen there and were easily found in 2003. There they appeared, two large, stripe-crowned, streak-faced, long-billed shorebirds along with some Willets, a much longer-billed, larger Long-billed Curlew, and a Clapper Rail.

AK On May 6 in Gustavus in the pouring rain, I saw my first two Whimbrels with Nat Drumheller. I observed others in Anchorage, Homer, Nome, and Utqiagvik, all before early July.

Red-necked Phalarope

TX On August 22, Martin Reid called and told me that in addition to Wilson's Phalaropes, a Red-necked Phalarope had been found at Mitchell Lake in south San Antonio. After a short night's sleep, I drove to Mitchell Lake. After looking around at likely spots, we saw the single Red-necked Phalarope, with its distinctive shortish-thin bill, black eye mask, and bold black-and-white back. Red-necked Phalaropes are uncommon to rare fall migrants in the western third of the state, and rare to very rare in most of the rest of the state.

AK On May 9, there were four Red-necked Phalaropes on the west side of Lake Hood in Anchorage. I saw others at Adak, the Kenai Peninsula, St. Paul, Gambell, Nome, and Utqiagvik, with most noted prior to mid-July.

Red Phalarope

TX Red Phalaropes are very rare fall and accidental spring migrants in Texas, with only 42 documented records as of 2014. We were at Lake Meredith in the Panhandle when we learned that a Red Phalarope had been reported at Mitchell Lake in south San Antonio. We raced south. After a brief overnight rest in San Antonio, we met Martin Reid at the lake on the morning of October 11. He drove us into the refuge, and very shortly we were exulting in a very close-up view of a Red Phalarope gently swirling about in the water near the shore of a pond. Although the phalarope could not be seen at times because it was hidden behind shoreline vegetation, we did get very good views.

AK My first Red Phalarope in my Alaska big year was a single brightly colored female on St. Paul Island on May 23. After that I saw them at Nome in June, Dutch Harbor and Utqiagvik in July, each day I was at Gambell in September, and most days when I was on St. Paul Island in September.

Red Phalarope at Gambell

Black-legged Kittiwake

^{TX} I saw a Black-legged Kittiwake, a very rare species in Texas, on day 3 of my Texas big year. I found the previously reported bird sitting on the water close to the shore near Boca Chica beach in the far southeastern corner of the Texas mainland. It was an immature bird with a distinct black hind collar and a black spot behind its eyes. The black slash on its wings turned into a black-and-white *W* (or *M*) on its back when it lifted off from the water to join the much more common Ring-billed, Herring, and Laughing Gulls and other birds flying around the jetty. Later, in July 2005, the Texas Bird Records Committee reevaluated the status of Black-legged Kittiwakes in the state and decided it should be placed on the review list. I therefore wrote up the sighting so it could be officially accepted for my big year.

^{AK} Black-legged Kittiwakes are easily found in most coastal areas of Alaska, especially during the breeding season. I saw the first one of my big year on January 2 on Kodiak. Their wide distribution in space and time in Alaska is shown by my sightings during the year: I saw them in February (Seward), March (Homer), May (Homer, Adak, St. Paul), June (ferry trip from Kodiak to Dutch Harbor), July (Akutan), August (Gambell), September (Gambell, St. Paul), and October (Utqiagvik, Ketchikan). They are particularly common along Homer Spit, sitting on the wood pilings out in the water and swarming over the waves. I also especially enjoyed close views of both immature and adult kittiwakes flying past when we did the Gambell sea watch in September.

Sabine's Gull

^{TX} On September 20, a juvenile Sabine's Gull was reported at Lake Tawakoni in northeast Texas, so I raced over the next day and rapidly scanned every gull group, then settled down to carefully look over every gull again. After half an hour of scanning and checking out each gull and Forster's Tern near and far, I spotted the distinctive wing, tail, and back pattern of a Sabine's Gull flying a couple of hundred feet away. It wandered around the lake for 15 minutes, sometimes fairly close again, landed a couple of times, and then disappeared in the haze to the east. I saw another on the other side of the state at Lake Balmorhea on September 23.

^{AK} I saw two Sabine's Gulls on Nome's Council Road on June 4. I had no other sightings during the year. They nest in coastal areas in Northern and Western Alaska that I did not visit.

Mew Gull

^{TX} Mew Gulls are not easily found in Texas. Toward the end of the year, because I had not yet seen one, I watched bird reports from North Texas and elsewhere. I regularly checked the Fort Worth lakes for them. One had been reported in Dallas at the end of November, but I was unable to find it that day or the next. I also kept checking Lake Worth, where interesting gulls are often found, but all I could find were Ring-billed Gulls. On December 31, I was in West Texas trying to add just one more bird to my year list, but I gave up at midday and headed back to Fort Worth. I drove rather fast, so it was good the traffic police were probably saving their surveillance for later on New Year's Eve. I arrived in Fort Worth about 4:00 p.m., with about an hour of daylight left. I raced to Lake Worth for my last chance for a Mew Gull for the year. Carefully I scanned the growing number of Ring-billed Gulls—and there it was—a Mew Gull. I shook with excitement as I moved the telescope closer and tried to get a decent digiscope picture. The gull was clearly smaller than the Ring-billed Gulls, clearly darker, with a lovely wide white crescent on its wings. Unfortunately its head was under its wing. Then out came its head—and there was a smallish plain yellow bill, with no ring. It was number 522, the last bird for my Texas big year. The next day, New Year's Day, I and many other North Texas birders headed over to Lake Worth and put the Mew Gull on our new year lists.

^{AK} Most gulls leave Alaska in winter, but when they start to return in spring, Mew Gulls arrive in large numbers, particularly in Anchorage. They also winter in some parts of Alaska, so my first Mew Gull for the year was on January 1 in Kodiak. At Westchester Lagoon in Anchorage and at Potter Marsh south of Anchorage in my big year I first noticed them on April 27, when I found them sitting in groups on the still-frozen marsh. The air was loud with their cries. Often the open water between grassy areas and protruding rocks and any type of perch would be crowded with Mew Gulls as they paired up. They were around until early August in the Anchorage area, in reduced numbers as the summer went on, usually some of the most obvious birds over the water. Later in the year, I found them in October in Southeastern Alaska.

California Gull

^{TX} On February 4, I went to Lake Buchanan west of Austin, where both a California Gull and a Pacific Loon had been reported at Llano County Park.

Not being a gull aficionado, I was a bit worried about trying to find the California Gull by myself. I drove to the site and saw some gulls too far away to tell whether there was something other than Ring-billed Gulls. Then for some unknown reason the gulls began drifting my way, some landing on the nearby sandy lake edge and others on an old dock even closer to me. Among the latter were a couple of larger gulls, including adult Herring Gulls, and another gull midway in size. It had a dark eye, was slightly darker than the Herring Gulls, and had red and black spots on its bill. Lots of pictures later, and lots of study of the pictures later, I knew I had it, a California Gull.

[AK] On February 27 in Ketchikan, nearly everywhere along the water were flocks of gulls, often wildly scrambling for herring. Among all the Glaucous-winged Gulls were quite a few Thayer's Gulls and a few California Gulls. I saw them a few more times during the year, always in Ketchikan.

Thayer's/Iceland Gull

[TX] On February 23, Martin Reid called to tell me he'd found an adult Thayer's Gull at a Corpus Christi landfill. It is always best to see gulls in the company of gull experts, so although I had planned to head home, I detoured to the landfill, which was quite close. I was particularly interested in seeing this bird, since a recent bird that I had initially thought was a Thayer's Gull had proved not to be. I rushed to the landfill, and for the next hour or so we worked at relocating the Thayer's Gull. Of course, Martin relocated it, a looming whitish bird among the Ring-billed and Laughing Gulls that predominated.

[AK] On January 7 in late afternoon, in a final attempt for another bird before darkness fell, Steve Heinl and I went to a Ketchikan Safeway store and bought Cheerios to bring in a few gulls. It worked, and among all the Glaucous-winged Gulls that flew in was a single Thayer's Gull. Later sightings were at Homer, Sitka, Gambell, and Utqiagvik.

Glaucous Gull

[TX] On March 23, after wandering around the coast hunting spring migrants, we joined Martin Reid at the Corpus Christi dump, where he had found a Glaucous Gull. Nearly double the size of the surrounding Laughing Gulls and looking like a huge ghost, the Glaucous Gull was a very welcome sight.

[AK] I saw my first Glaucous Gulls on May 23 on St. Paul Island. From spring through September I found them at Gambell, Nome, Utqiagvik, and St. Paul, with increasing numbers at Utqiagvik in October and November.

Red-throated Loon

TX In mid-March I was hunting for warblers when I received a report of at least one Red-throated Loon on the north-central border of Texas at Lake Texoma, visible from Preston Point. At 4:00 a.m. on March 19 I left Port Arthur, where I'd spent the night, and headed north. After seven hours of fast cross-country driving, I arrived at the lake, staying in cell phone contact with Simone, who was driving from elsewhere in Texas. When we both arrived, Common Loons were all we could find for two and a half hours. Finally, there appeared from somewhere a somewhat lighter loon with a thinner, upturned bill. We looked for it over and over for more than an hour, as it was mostly diving and underwater. We had plenty of opportunity to view the Common Loons and compare them with the other busy loon, finally satisfying ourselves as to its identity as a Red-throated Loon.

AK On January 19 in Homer, Aaron Lang and I birded on Homer Spit. As we gradually headed back up the spit, mostly scanning the waters to the west, Aaron finally found a distant Red-throated Loon that I was able to see in my scope. Other sightings were in Ketchikan, Anchorage, Gambell, Nome, and Hyder, with the latest sighting in mid-July (young bird at Nome).

Red-throated Loon in Anchorage

Pacific Loon

^{TX} On February 4, I went to Lake Buchanan west of Austin, where a California Gull and a Pacific Loon had been reported. After finding the California Gull, I scanned the lake with my telescope and located a number of Common Loons without a problem. Then I saw a darker, smaller loon with a smaller, darker bill. After cranking up my telescope magnification, I could barely see a thin, dark "chinstrap" on it, but I couldn't get closer to the bird, which was constantly diving and did not appear inclined to dive its way over toward me. Later it was close enough for me to verify the identifying characteristics of a Pacific Loon.

^{AK} On January 5, three Pacific Loons were diving in the deep water next to the dike trail at the Mendenhall Wetlands in Juneau. I found others in the spring at Ketchikan, Adak, Homer, Gambell, and Nome, with summer sightings in Utqiagvik and fall sightings in Gambell, St. Paul, and Utqiagvik.

Red-breasted Sapsucker

^{TX} In March there was an astounding report of a Red-breasted Sapsucker in West Texas. First sighted by Sheridan Coffey at the Lawrence E. Wood Picnic Area in the Davis Mountains on March 12, this was a bird that had never occurred to me when planning my Texas big year. Its normal range in the United States is Alaska, California, western New Mexico, eastern Arizona, and points south.

Unfortunately, even though this sapsucker was seen by the many other birders who immediately flocked to the picnic area, it looked as if I was not going to be one of those lucky ones. I could not get away from Fort Worth until midday on March 13, and I was sure this astounding bird would be one of those "one (or two)-day wonders" that I would not get to see. Nevertheless I drove west as soon as I could, checked into a motel in Fort Stockton, and anxiously waited for the morning.

When it came, I was on the road at 4:10 a.m. Of course, I arrived at the picnic area before daylight and sat in the car with the window down, freezing, listening for sapsucker tap-taps. I couldn't sit still in the car, so I began to wander around under the trees. In less than a minute after I got out of the car, I heard and saw a sapsucker. Nearly hitting me in the nose as it flew past, the sapsucker landed on the trunk of a nearby pine tree. I had to back up to get the whole bird in my flash pictures, and I could see its amazingly red head and breast in the half light as I flashed away for a solid 15 minutes. The bird, probably as frozen as I was, was in no hurry to go anywhere or do anything. Maybe the flash was warming it or making it feel as if the sun was shining.

Eventually, I got back in the car to warm up and lost track of the bird. I wandered around the picnic area for another hour, but even though I had more pictures of the sapsucker than I could ever need, I could not leave without seeing it once again. As I traversed the picnic area among the trees where I had last seen it, all of a sudden as I glanced back at a tree I'd just passed, there was the sapsucker, behind me about four feet away. It was totally unperturbed and didn't even seem aware of my presence.

[AK] On April 30, we heard a Red-breasted Sapsucker north of Juneau and regularly saw them (until mid-June) when in Juneau, Ketchikan, and Hyder, where they can be found year-round.

Red-breasted Sapsucker in West Texas

Red-breasted Sapsucker in Ketchikan

Northern Shrike

^{TX} On February 9, scattered shrikes were perched on fences and posts as I drove the Panhandle, none of which looked like anything but a Loggerhead Shrike. Near Lake Meredith, I began to look more closely at the shrikes because at least one Northern Shrike had been reported. I finally found it on the west side of the lake, actively hunting from high perches on power lines, with its diagnostic thin eye patch and a hooked beak larger than those of the nearby Loggerhead Shrikes.

^{AK} On January 11 in Anchorage, I got my first big year view of a Northern Shrike, which left the fence where it had first been perched and came across the road to a treetop. There were other Anchorage sightings, as well as in Seward, Kenai, Homer, Nome, Delta Junction, and Juneau.

Varied Thrush

^{TX} On October 22, we were on the boardwalk at the Willows near Sabine Woods. For some reason I turned around at what turned out to be the exact right moment and saw a large thrush-shaped bird fly up from the wet area

beyond the boardwalk and land on an angled trunk leaning over the boardwalk about seven feet away. For a millisecond I thought it was a robin, but it immediately appeared to be significantly chunkier and had very orange wing bars, orange markings on its face, and an orange belly, and it was otherwise brownish gray—a Varied Thrush. It was substantially larger than all of the numerous Hermit Thrushes that were also around.

AK In Alaska Varied Thrushes are very common in many areas, particularly in Southeastern Alaska. I saw three of them in northern Ketchikan on January 7, with other sightings in Anchorage, Juneau, Homer, Hyder, Gambell (end of May), and Sitka.

Red Crossbill

TX On December 27, I heard but did not see a Red Crossbill in the little town of Fabens near El Paso, at a house with many evergreens and singing House

Varied Thrush in Anchorage

Finches. I carefully compared my CD recording of Red Crossbill to another song I was hearing, and it was identical. I checked out all the other songs of finch-type birds and concluded it was an invisible Red Crossbill.

^{AK} On January 1 near Kalsin Bay on Kodiak, we saw a couple of Red Crossbills, and the next day there were some in a Kodiak yard. They were also present in Hyder and Ketchikan in the summer and later in the year.

Snow Bunting

^{TX} Just before Christmas of my Texas big year, a Snow Bunting was reported at an RV park on South Padre Island, over 500 miles south of Fort Worth. On Christmas Day I left home at 3:45 a.m. It was 43 degrees, and I had the whole road to myself. I arrived just before 1:00 p.m., but there were no birders around. Normally such a rarity would have brought them all out, but it was Christmas Day. I wandered around checking out the flocks of grackles and House Sparrows. Then I noticed a woman with a telescope between two trailers at the RV park. She had found the bird, which was calmly eating seeds on the mowed lawn. It was quite sunny and the Snow Bunting seemed drawn to the shadowy area where it was probably a bit more like the climate the bird was used to.

^{AK} My first sighting was on January 1 on Kodiak Island. I also found them in mid-January in Anchorage and Homer, and in the summer I commonly saw them in the west on Adak, St. Paul, and St. Lawrence Islands and at Utqiagvik.

OTHER BIRDS

The following three sections relate to sightings of species that are not rare in the state(s) where they were observed during my big year. Two of these sections list the birds I saw in only one of the two states (Texas only or Alaska only). If I also found them in the second state, they are in a different section: either in one of the previous sections if they are rare in the second state, or in the first section below if they are not rare in either state.

Seen in Both States

Many species were seen in both states and are not particularly rare in either one. Although some of them are found only in low numbers and/or in limited locations in these states, finding these birds during my big years was generally expected and uneventful. For some of these species, however, something of note did happen in my searches, as explained below. For the other birds seen in both states and not rare, the first dates and locations of sightings are given in appendix 1 (as with all species seen during my two big years).

Greater White-fronted Goose

^{TX} I first saw Greater White-fronted Goose on January 1 in Matagorda County on the coast. They winter in the eastern portion of the state and migrate through most of the state except the far west.

^{AK} On the early evening of April 25 as I drove Barley Way near Delta Junction, I came to a field where large numbers of geese were descending, 600 or more Canada Geese and at least 20 Greater White-fronted Geese. I saw more in May in Juneau, Homer, and Kenai, and then in July in Utqiagvik, where there were adults and goslings on the mudflats and water.

Snow Goose

^{TX} I first found Snow Geese on January 1 in Matagorda County. Many more Snow Geese were present on February 9 at Cactus Playa in the Texas Panhandle.

^{AK} On February 28, I saw a single Snow Goose at Sunset Point in Juneau, where it was hanging out with Canada Geese way out across a grassy puddled field. I observed others flying over Ketchikan on May 3

Cackling Goose

^{TX} I first saw Cackling Geese in Texas near Rockport on January 1. They winter in many areas of the state, often with the very similar Canada Geese.

^{AK} On May 1, among many Canada Geese was at least one tiny Cackling Goose at the Mendenhall Wetlands in Juneau. They were also present on Adak and in Gambell and Nome in late spring.

Blue-winged Teal

^{TX} I first saw Blue-winged Teal on January 1 in Matagorda County on the coast. Although they can be found at any time of year, they are less common in summer.

^{AK} In Alaska, while Blue-winged Teal is not rare, it turned out to be difficult to find during my big year. On June 6 I was in Anchorage briefly, just long enough to try to find the Blue-winged Teal reported at Westchester Lagoon. I found it walking slowly in shallow water next to the island, where it was easily viewable. I did not see any others that year.

Canvasback

^{TX} I first saw Canvasbacks on January 10 at Lake Marvin in the northeastern Texas Panhandle.

^{AK} On April 27, I went to Westchester Lagoon in Anchorage and found the reported Canvasbacks, at least five of them far across the lake. I had two other sightings in May in Anchorage and one bird in Sitka in mid-October.

Redhead

^{TX} I saw my first Redheads in Texas on January 16 at a pond in western Tarrant County (where Fort Worth is). A small flock of Redheads was also present on August 1 in West Texas at Muleshoe NWR.

^{AK} My first (and only) Redheads in Alaska were two wintering birds at Buskin Lake on Kodiak Island on January 2.

Greater Scaup

^{TX} I first observed Greater Scaup, rare to uncommon migrants in Texas, on January 11 at a waterway in Fort Worth where a few Greater Scaup often wintered.

^{AK} On January 1 at Pasagshak Bay (Kodiak Island), I saw a huge mixed flock of Gadwalls and Greater Scaup. I found more the next day at Buskin Lake. Later sightings were at Homer, various sites in Southeastern Alaska, and Adak, Gambell, and Nome.

Lesser Scaup

^{TX} I first observed Lesser Scaup, much more common in Texas than Greater Scaup, on January 1 in Matagorda County on the coast.

^{AK} On February 29 at Twin Lakes in Juneau, I went looking for a Lesser Scaup that birders in Juneau had told me I should find there. I saw only one amid the Greater Scaup and Buffleheads there. I found others at Adak, Nome, Ketchikan, and St. Paul Island.

Hooded Merganser

^{TX} I first saw Hooded Mergansers on January 8 in the Texas Panhandle, where they winter and sometimes nest.

^{AK} The first Alaska Hooded Mergansers were two males in the water along the road in Saxman (Ketchikan) on January 7. Other sightings were in Ketchikan in October and Juneau in May and October.

Horned Grebe

ᵀˣ On one of our trips to West Texas in January, we saw a possible Red-necked Grebe at McNary Reservoir just short of El Paso. Unfortunately, even though it seemed to have a yellowish tinge to its beak and was a bit bigger than the surrounding Horned Grebes, we finally concluded it was just a very hefty Horned Grebe, our first sighting for the year, on January 25.

ᴬᴷ On January 1 near Kalsin Bay on Kodiak, I had a close-up view of a Horned Grebe. I later found others in Anchorage, Homer, Seward, Ketchikan, Adak, St. Paul, and Sitka.

Western Grebe

ᵀˣ I first saw Western Grebes in Texas on January 7 along with Clark's Grebes at Balmorhea Lake, a place where both grebes are usually found. They were again present on January 25 at McNary Reservoir just short of El Paso, again with Clark's Grebes.

ᴬᴷ My sightings of Western Grebes in Alaska were limited to Ketchikan in January (beginning on the sixth), February, and May.

Rock Pigeon

ᵀˣ Rock Pigeons are common in Texas, and I first saw them on January 2 in the LRGV.

ᴬᴷ Note: although I often saw Rock Pigeons in Alaska, including flocks that resided on the cliffs near Windy Point south of Anchorage, at the time of my big year, Rock Pigeons were deemed not countable by the Alaska Checklist Committee and therefore do not appear on my big year list.

Eurasian Collared-Dove

ᵀˣ I first found Eurasian Collared-Doves on January 1 in Matagorda County on the coast. On February 9 in the far northwestern Panhandle, I found that they were by far the most common bird in Texline, sitting on buildings and posts and flying around.

ᴬᴷ On January 10, having gotten word of a Eurasian Collared-Dove in south Anchorage, I surveyed the neighborhood spruce trees and finally located the dove hiding on a spruce branch. I saw small numbers of them every month or so in Southeastern Alaska.

Anna's Hummingbird

^{TX} An Anna's Hummingbird was present in Texas on January 7 at a feeder at the Alpine home of Carol Edwards and John Gee. Oddly enough, when I was on my 10-day trip around Texas, I learned from my husband that our wintering Rufous Hummingbird had been joined in the yard by a second, different, "scratchy-sounding" hummingbird. When I was home on January 11, in addition to the Rufous Hummingbird ("Rufie"), just as my husband had described, in the bushes near our porch was a very odd raspy sound. The source was a sort of scruffy, grayish-fronted hummingbird with a couple of dots of pink on its throat and a single dot of pink on its forehead. It was sitting about three and a half feet off the ground and "singing," a young male Anna's Hummingbird. He was totally unafraid of us and rarely moved away when we went into the yard. He had clearly already divided the yard with Rufie, claiming the two hummingbird feeders on the back porch as his own, including the heated feeder, and leaving to Rufie the remaining hummingbird feeders in the yard, away from the porch. He remained a presence in the yard, drawing local birders who had never seen this species in North Texas. When he left about a month later, an apparently very relieved Rufie moved over to the perch the Anna's had favored, a place we'd never observed her before, clearly reveling in his absence and her repossession of the nearby porch hummingbird feeders.

^{AK} My first Anna's Hummingbird (of three for the year) was at the home of Gwen Baluss in Juneau on January 5, the second two days later in Ketchikan, and the third two weeks later in Homer.

Rufous Hummingbird

^{TX} My first Rufous Hummingbird of my big year was present on January 11 in our yard when I returned from my 10-day trek around Texas. She was presumably the same Rufous Hummingbird, "Rufie," that had wintered in our yard the previous four winters (usually leaving in early April, and recorded there until we moved away in 2010). While the story of Rufie starts much earlier than my big year, she was also a large part of my big year. She had first arrived in our yard on Christmas Day 2001, when I was taking out a newly filled hummingbird feeder. She came to the feeders that first day every 15 to 20 minutes until dark. She continued as the days passed. Most of the time, she seemed content to perch on a particular exposed *Photinia* twig, near but not within the cover of dense dark leaves, but would duck into the bush

if a jay called, or a hawk (Cooper's or Sharp-shinned) came through the yard. One of my honeysuckle plants was blooming then and all winter, and sometimes Rufie visited it for a change of pace.

During my Texas big year, in addition to my yard bird, I also saw Rufous Hummingbirds in Rockport on February 23 and at Boot Springs in Big Bend on August 10.

^{AK} In Alaska, a beautiful male Rufous Hummingbird came to the feeder

Rufous Hummingbird, "Rufie"

of Patty Rose in Juneau on May 1. There were later sightings in Ketchikan, Hyder, and Juneau until August 20.

Sandhill Crane

^{TX} I first found Sandhill Cranes in Texas near Rockport on January 1. Later, on January 30, we saw them fly overhead when we were watching Whooping Cranes at Aransas NWR. Sandhill Cranes were also wintering in the Texas Panhandle on February 8.

^{AK} On April 15, I heard at least one Sandhill Crane apparently flying north high overhead in the clouds above Westchester Lagoon in Anchorage. I saw one a couple of days later and regularly throughout the summer, primarily in the Anchorage area where they nest, but also at Gambell, Nome, and Delta Junction.

American Golden-Plover

^{TX} On March 18 after I had birded the beach at Bolivar Flats, a group of seven killdeer-sized birds burst rapidly up from the surrounding grassland and marsh along the road, disappearing into the tall vegetation when they landed a short distance away. My brief look at them made me think of American Golden-Plovers. I could see their light eye line, their overall brown appearance, no black under their wings, no white rump, and a plover-shaped bill. In spite of scanning and rescanning where they'd gone down into the grass, I couldn't see them again. I didn't dare to cross the fence to go look for them. I resignedly put my scope in the car and resumed my drive north, undecided as to whether I should count them. Five minutes later, there was a single bird, silhouetted on top of a small muddy, grassy rise close to the road. There it posed while I photographed it, consulted my field guide, and confirmed that every single feather looked like an American Golden-Plover. However, I could not see its underwings as it calmly stood with its wings pressed tightly against its sides. When it finally flew, I was rewarded by a clinching view of its diagnostic grayish, not black, underwings—an American Golden-Plover.

^{AK} On June 3 at the site where Bristle-thighed Curlews nest on Kougarok Road in Nome, there was an American Golden-Plover. They were common nesting birds in Utqiagvik in early July, and I regularly found chicks.

Semipalmated Plover

^{TX} I first found Semipalmated Plovers on January 18 at Bolivar Flats on the Upper Coast, where they are common winter residents.

AK On May 3, I was in Ketchikan driving back from north of town when I spotted shorebirds at Mud Bight. Among the Least Sandpipers was my first Semipalmated Plover. Others, all seen before July 11, were at Homer, Adak, Gambell, Nome, Utqiagvik, and Anchorage.

Killdeer

TX I saw Killdeer on January 1 in Matagorda County on the coast and regularly thereafter across the state.

AK On February 27, when I birded with Steve Heinl in Ketchikan, our first goal was Killdeer. We found six of them at Mud Bight north of town and later found another one at Bayview Cemetery. I spotted others in Juneau, Kenai, and Anchorage.

Upland Sandpiper

TX I found Upland Sandpipers on March 30 as I patrolled the fields along the road while driving into Liberty. I also saw them in West Texas at Muleshoe NWR on August 1.

AK On June 22, I went south a few miles out of Delta Junction to the area where I had found Sharp-tailed Grouse earlier in the year and was delighted to hear the distinctive wolf whistles of an Upland Sandpiper. The sandpiper called for about 15 minutes from out in the field and then went silent.

Hudsonian Godwit

TX Hudsonian Godwits had been reported around Anahuac NWR, so before going over to Sabine Woods on April 28, I wandered the road near Anahuac and eventually found four Hudsonian Godwits amid dowitchers in the flooded fields.

AK On April 28, there was one Hudsonian Godwit at Westchester Lagoon in Anchorage. Small numbers were present there later in the spring and summer until a larger group (about 25) was found in early August. I saw others in Juneau and Kenai.

Marbled Godwit

TX I added Marbled Godwits to my Texas big year list on a trip to Paradise Pond and the Leonabelle Turnbull Birding Center in Port Aransas on January 31. Although I had rarely found them in north-central Texas, there was one at the Village Creek Drying Beds on August 5.

AK On May 12, I went to Beluga Slough/flats in Homer to search for shorebirds and found a single Marbled Godwit. I saw one other that year, on May 20, at the mouth of the Kasilof River (near Kenai).

Ruddy Turnstone

TX I first saw Ruddy Turnstones on January 1 in Matagorda County on the coast, where they winter.

AK I had distant sightings of Ruddy Turnstones from Adak on May 19, with closer sightings common in September at Gambell and St. Paul.

Red Knot

TX I added wintering Red Knots to my Texas big year list on a trip to Paradise Pond and the Leonabelle Turnbull Birding Center in Port Aransas on January 31.

AK On June 5, we walked across crusty tundra covered with tiny flowers near Nome's Teller Highway, where Red Knots nest. The walk up the gentle incline did not produce any Red Knots, so we turned around and headed back to the road. Eventually we heard the call of a Red Knot in the distance. Our whole group walked in the direction of the call and finally found the bird walking on the tundra.

Sanderling

TX I first saw Sanderlings, regularly found along the Texas coast, on January 3 at Boca Chica Beach in the LRGV.

Red Knots on Texas coast

AK On May 20 at Kasilof Beach (south of Kenai), there were two Sanderlings, and a single bird was present on St. Paul in mid-September.

Dunlin

TX The first Dunlin was present on January 3 at Boca Chica Beach in the LRGV. Dunlins winter in abundance on the coast and migrate through much of the state in spring and fall.

AK On April 1, I was sitting in my car on the side of Freight Dock Road in Homer in pouring rain when a flock of shorebirds burst over the road in front of me, followed shortly by another flock. I immediately guessed "dunlins," but they were gone. I wandered around and then returned to

Sanderling

Mud Bay, where I found a very distant flock of shorebirds bunched closely together, scurrying around at the edge of the mud. The rain had let up, and I scanned the group for a long time. I concluded that most of the 100 or so shorebirds were Rock Sandpipers, but there were definitely 5 to 8 slightly longer-billed shorebirds among them, Dunlins. Later sightings were in Southeastern Alaska, Gambell, St. Paul, Nome, and Utqiagvik (nesting).

Baird's Sandpiper

[TX] We found our first Baird's Sandpiper on March 29 at Anahuac NWR, where there also were new-for-the-year Pectoral Sandpipers.

[AK] Baird's Sandpipers were present at Coffee Dome on Nome's Kougarok Road on June 3. They were also present in Utqiagvik in early July.

Pectoral Sandpiper

[TX] I first found Pectoral Sandpipers on March 29 at Anahuac NWR in the company of Baird's Sandpipers.

[AK] There was a small flock of Pectoral Sandpipers at Anchor Point on May 13. Many were present in the spring and fall at Gambell, and at Nome and Utqiagvik (nesting with young).

Semipalmated Sandpiper

[TX] I first saw Semipalmated Sandpipers, which migrate through Texas, on March 28 in Galveston County on the Upper Coast.

[AK] My first sighting of a Semipalmated Sandpiper was on May 6 in Gustavus. I found others in Juneau, Nome, and Utqiagvik (early July).

Long-billed Dowitcher

[TX] On January 31, we went to Paradise Pond and the Leonabelle Turnbull Birding Center in Port Aransas. Both areas were full of wading birds, ducks, shorebirds, and gulls. The only new-for-the-year birds were Long-billed Dowitchers, identified by the pattern on their sides and breasts and by their flight calls.

[AK] On February 28 in Juneau, Bev Agler, Patty Rose, and I hiked out across the Mendenhall Wetlands, where two Long-billed Dowitchers had been found earlier. Without too much effort we spotted them, feeding side by side along a rivulet. I saw others at Nome, Utqiagvik, Gambell, and St. Paul (latest sighting on September 23).

Wilson's Snipe

^{TX} My first Wilson's Snipe was present in Alpine on January 7. I also saw them on April 2 at the Attwater Prairie Chicken NWR. Wilson's Snipe are common wintering birds and migrants in much of the state.

^{AK} On April 18 along Lake Hood Drive in Anchorage, I heard a definitive Wilson's Snipe calling from a spruce-filled bog. Until December 11 I had regular sightings, primarily in Anchorage but also in Nome, Utqiagvik, and Southeastern Alaska.

Solitary Sandpiper

^{TX} I first saw Solitary a Sandpiper on January 3. Solitary Sandpipers migrate throughout the state and winter along the coast.

^{AK} Solitary Sandpiper was a bird I wasn't quite sure how to locate for my 2016 big year. Having read they nest in Fairbanks, I headed northwest out of Delta Junction to Creamer's Field in Fairbanks on June 23. I went first to the wetland, not quite sure where to look, but there were no sandpipers. I checked one of my bird guide apps and learned I should look in boreal forest wetlands. Then I noticed that Creamer's Field had a trail that went into a boreal forest. I walked on that trail, and on the wet mud near a little bridge I immediately found a Solitary Sandpiper. I saw other Solitary Sandpipers in Anchorage from late July to mid-August.

Pomarine Jaeger

^{TX} I saw a Pomarine Jaeger only once, on November 5, on the last pelagic trip of my Texas big year. Although they have been seen in Texas during every month of the year, they are uncommon migrants and winter residents at sea in the Gulf of Mexico, only rarely seen inland.

^{AK} On June 1 at the Gambell sea watch, I saw a single Pomarine Jaeger. I saw multiple jaegers from the Homer–Dutch Harbor ferry on June 30 and at Utqiagvik in early September.

Parasitic Jaeger

^{TX} I saw a Parasitic Jaeger on my second pelagic trip, on July 29. Parasitic Jaegers are uncommon migrants and winter residents offshore, and even rarer inland.

^{AK} There was a single dark Parasitic Jaeger harassing a tern and then an eagle at Anchor Point on May 13, and I saw other Parasitic Jaegers at Adak, Gambell, Nome, and Utqiagvik, mostly before mid-July.

Double-crested Cormorant

^{TX} I first saw a Double-crested Cormorant on January 1 in Matagorda County on the coast. Unlike the smaller, long-tailed Neotropic Cormorants that are residents in much of southern and eastern Texas, Double-crested Cormorants are migrants through the whole state and just winter residents in coastal areas.

^{AK} I also saw the first Alaskan Double-crested Cormorant, much rarer in Alaska than in Texas, on January 1 on Kodiak, with later sightings in Ketchikan, Homer, Dutch Harbor, and St. Paul.

Great Blue Heron

^{TX} I saw my first Great Blue Heron of the year on January 3 on South Padre Island. Great Blue Herons are common year-round across Texas.

^{AK} I saw a Great Blue Heron in Juneau on January 4. I saw them regularly all year long in Southeastern Alaska but not elsewhere. Because I had become used to the omnipresent Great Blue Herons in Texas, Alaskan wetlands seemed barren without these large blue-gray herons towering over the water and vegetation.

Osprey

^{TX} I saw the first Osprey on January 1 in Matagorda County on the coast. In winter Ospreys are common in many Texas coastal areas, but most of them migrate northward in spring.

^{AK} In Alaska, I saw the first Osprey on May 9, flying over my car and then Lake Hood in Anchorage, carrying a large fish. Other sightings were in Palmer and Anchorage in August. Although range maps show that Ospreys breed across much of Alaska, I have seen them only rarely in my travels across the state.

Bald Eagle

^{TX} I saw the first Texas Bald Eagle on January 1 in Matagorda County on the coast. Bald Eagles are found across much of Texas except the far west, but they only rarely breed in the state.

^{AK} On January 1, on Kodiak Island where there were many eagles, a Bald Eagle was the first bird of my Alaska big year. Bald Eagles are very common in Alaska and I saw them on almost a daily basis when I was bird-watching, including everywhere in Southeastern Alaska and in Homer, Anchorage, and Adak.

Northern Harrier

^{TX} I first saw a Northern Harrier on January 9 as it emerged from a wooded area in the Rita Blanca National Grassland in the Texas Panhandle where we were seeking Long-eared Owls. Northern Harriers winter across much of the state and are particularly commonly seen hunting low over coastal prairies.

^{AK} On March 9, I went to the Matanuska Townsite Road in Palmer (north of Anchorage), where a Northern Harrier had been reported. Almost immediately, a large brown narrow-winged raptor with a white rump flew off across the railroad tracks and disappeared beyond the trees—a Northern Harrier female. Later sightings were at the hawk watch north of Anchorage in April, and in Delta Junction, Juneau, and Homer.

Sharp-shinned Hawk

^{TX} I saw the first Sharp-shinned Hawk, an uncommon winter resident across much of the state, on January 2 in McAllen in the LRGV.

^{AK} On January 2, a long-tailed Sharp-shinned Hawk flew near us near Buskin Lake on Kodiak Island and disappeared into a spruce grove slightly up a nearby hill. I saw others in Anchorage, at the hawk watch north of Anchorage, and in Juneau.

Red-tailed Hawk

^{TX} I saw the first Red-tailed Hawk on January 1 in Matagorda County on the coast. Red-tailed Hawks are common year-round across most of Texas.

^{AK} I went to the hawk watch north of Anchorage on April 8. Red-tailed Hawks (nearly always the dark Harlan's Red-tailed Hawks) and Rough-legged Hawks were the two most common hawks I saw. I also saw Red-tailed Hawks at Delta Junction, Palmer, Ketchikan, and Sitka.

Rough-legged Hawk

^{TX} I first saw Rough-legged Hawks on January 8 along the road north of Lubbock. Later, on February 8, I saw another one in the Texas Panhandle. They are uncommon to rare winter residents in the Panhandle and North Texas, becoming more common in years when there are large numbers of rodents in the grassy fields.

^{AK} At the hawk watch north of Anchorage on April 8, Rough-legged Hawks and Red-tailed Hawks were the two most common hawks I saw. Later sightings of Rough-legged Hawks were at Delta Junction, Gambell, and Nome.

Golden Eagle

^{TX} On January 6, we saw our first Golden Eagle north of Big Bend. Golden Eagles are residents of the Panhandle and West Texas but are only rarely seen in Central and East Texas.

^{AK} Although Golden Eagles were never easily seen around Anchorage, I saw them regularly at the hawk watch about 120 miles north of Anchorage on April 8, and later at Nome.

Great Horned Owl

^{TX} I first saw a Great Horned Owl on January 8 in Dalhart at Lake Rita Blanca in the northern Panhandle, where a single Great Horned Owl sat in a conifer (a place where I'd found Barn Owls in previous years). I saw another on February 8 in the Texas Panhandle. When I was at Sabine Woods on the afternoon of February 12, two Great Horned Owls hooted as I watched my first Prairie Warbler of the year. On August 14, there were two Great Horned Owls sitting on a road in Big Bend, neither of which flew until I was nearly upon them as I drove slowly past. Another mile or so later, there was another Great Horned Owl on the road, which sat while I tried to take a picture of it in the headlights of the car. In about 20 minutes, there was a fourth Great Horned Owl on the road.

^{AK} My first sighting of a Great Horned Owl was in Anchorage on February 13, on the coastal trail where Peter Scully had found it. When I went to try to see it, it did not disappoint me and was firmly and visibly ensconced on a spruce branch snuggled up to the trunk. Although the owl did not budge, it did periodically turn its head and then finally closed its eyes, probably to shut out the sight of my camera below. I heard others in Palmer and Soldotna.

Barred Owl

^{TX} I added a hooting Barred Owl on the outskirts of Liberty to my list for the year on March 30. Barred Owls are found in dense river bottom and upland forests in much of the eastern two-thirds of Texas.

^{AK} Although Barred Owls are not deemed rare in Alaska and may rarely breed in Southeastern Alaska, where they are regularly heard, they can be difficult to see. On the evening of June 8, Steve Heinl, Louann Feldmann, and I searched for Barred Owls, which had been reported calling in the Ward Lake campground north of Ketchikan. I had listened for hours the night before without any luck. It was raining, but we valiantly wandered around the

wet campground, down the trails, on the road—nothing. Finally, after over an hour, having retraced our route without success, we decided to drive farther down Revilla Road to listen in other areas. We had gone only a very short distance in the dark rainy night when Steve spotted a big owl sitting on a road

Great Horned Owl

sign. I did a U-turn and the bird was still there. It flew a short distance to a nearby cliff and perched. In the light of my flashlight we could see it clearly—a black-eyed Barred Owl. While we watched the owl, another distant Barred Owl called, the first we'd heard. We decided it must be a family group, and maybe the owl we were seeing was a young one, unaware that Barred Owls don't usually sit on roadside signs.

Short-eared Owl

Short-eared Owl

TX I saw Short-eared Owls on January 12 in Tarrant County fields just west of Fort Worth, where they could be found on many predawn winter mornings. They also winter in many other areas of Texas except the far northeast, the far west, and the southwest.

AK At about 5:00 p.m. on March 25, I was driving toward the end of Cannery Road in Kenai, where I had been told Short-eared Owls could be found but where I had not previously been able to find one. I was very happy to find my first Short-eared Owl of the year, quite far away but easily identifiable. I saw others in Anchorage, Nome (eight in one day in spring), Gambell, and Juneau.

Northern Flicker

TX I saw my first Northern Flicker on January 3 on South Padre Island, and I saw others on February 26 in the Pineywoods and on March 15 as I hiked the Pinnacles Trail at Big Bend NP.

AK Although Northern Flickers are uncommon in Anchorage, they are relatively easy to find in Southeastern Alaska. My first one was at a suet feeder in the Ketchikan yard of Jerry Koerner on January 7. I saw others in Hyder, Delta Junction, Fairbanks, Haines, and Sitka.

American Kestrel

TX American Kestrel was the eighth bird species for my Texas big year, found on January 1 in Matagorda County on the coast. I also found them wintering

Northern Flicker

in the Texas Panhandle on February 9. American Kestrels winter in much of the state but are uncommon in Texas in summer, being found then in the Panhandle, Northern Plains, and Pineywoods.

AK My first sighting (ever) of an Alaskan American Kestrel was on April 25. About 50 miles south of Delta Junction, it was calling and diving at a Common Raven. I saw others at Delta Junction in June and early August, and one in Juneau in early May. In addition, on a drive to Fairbanks from Delta Junction on June 23, I watched an American Robin attack an American Kestrel.

Peregrine Falcon

TX On January 18, we saw our first Peregrine Falcon at Bolivar Flats on the Upper Coast, streaking by very close and startling not only us, but many shorebirds.

AK Although there were reports of a wintering Peregrine Falcon in Anchorage in early 2016, I saw my first Peregrine Falcon on May 12 on Homer Spit, chasing approximately 25 shorebirds. I saw others at Nome, Utqiagvik, Gambell, and Anchorage (as late as October 15).

Olive-sided Flycatcher

^{TX} I saw the first Olive-sided Flycatcher on May 3 at the South Padre Island Convention Centre. On May 19, I was surprised to find numerous Olive-sided Flycatchers at Guadalupe Mountains NP, since I hadn't realized they bred there. They were calling and fly catching and were very obvious in the taller trees.

^{AK} On June 8, Louann Feldmann and I drove up Brown Mountain north of Ketchikan and saw our first Olive-sided Flycatcher. On August 4, I got a better view and photographs of an Olive-sided Flycatcher southeast of Delta Junction.

Western Wood-Pewee

^{TX} On a drive down to Big Bend on May 10, after we saw two Common Black-Hawks soaring over the hills east of a picnic area along the road, we saw a Western Wood-Pewee flitting about from branch to branch in a large tree. Other Western Wood-Pewee sightings were on May 18 at the Davis Mountains Preserve and August 10 in Big Bend NP.

^{AK} I saw a Western Wood-Pewee at Hyder on June 9 and 11, and another at the Sockeye Burn north of Anchorage on August 12.

Alder Flycatcher

^{TX} My first task in June, after I had spent so much time in coastal Texas looking for spring migrants and in West Texas looking for western birds, was to try to find an Alder Flycatcher before they gave up singing for the nesting season. The large wooded area at Arlington's Legacy Park seemed like a good place to try without going too far from home. On June 1, I parked near a shopping center between the old, western section of the park and the new section and strolled into the western section. As I was about to cross the street to the parking area, I heard the unmistakable call/song of an Alder Flycatcher. Much scanning of the trees revealed a distant unidentifiable bird, but the song was enough. I had it. I hoped for a better view later in the year, and I did have another modest view later.

^{AK} I saw an Alder Flycatcher in Hyder on June 9. Other sightings from June to mid-August were in Anchorage, Delta Junction, Fairbanks, Homer, and Palmer.

Hammond's Flycatcher

^{TX} I saw my first Hammond's Flycatcher on August 31 in the Bowl at the end of a trail in the Guadalupe Mountains. It was working an area along one of the trails, allowing me plenty of time to study it, even though its movements and the shadows kept me from getting a picture of it.

^{AK} On April 26, as I pulled off the road at Tanana Bridge north of Delta Junction, I heard the unmistakable sound of a Hammond's Flycatcher, and slightly south of there at Big Delta State Historical Park I heard another, which I was finally able to see well. I observed them often in Hyder in early June.

Say's Phoebe

^{TX} I first saw Say's Phoebe southwest of San Antonio on January 5. They are residents in the Trans-Pecos and western Panhandle. In winter they can be found eastward to the western Edwards Plateau and down to the southern tip of Texas.

^{AK} On June 4, a Say's Phoebe was flitting about high on the cliffs above the nest of a Gyrfalcon on Council Road in Nome. They breed across the state in central Alaska and are sometimes found in Anchorage. I had a rare sighting of one at our Anchorage house on November 1, 2014, probably on its way south.

Warbling Vireo

^{TX} I saw and heard the first Warbling Vireos on April 19 at Sabine Woods. Although they are mostly migrants through Texas, Warbling Vireos are summer residents in the eastern Panhandle and locally across north-central Texas.

^{AK} I saw and heard Warbling Vireos in Ketchikan on June 8, in Hyder for the next four days, and in Juneau after that. They breed in Southeastern Alaska and are casual in South-Central Alaska and the Bering Sea islands.

Steller's Jay

^{TX} I saw my first Steller's Jay on February 7 in the Bowl at the end of the trail in Guadalupe Mountains NP, and I saw another at the same place on August 31.

^{AK} When I returned to Anchorage on January 3, I saw my first Steller's Jay of the year in my yard, where I saw them most days I was home, as well as in

Steller's Jay eating dried mealworms

Juneau, Ketchikan, and Hyder. Steller's Jay is one of the few wild bird species I have fed on my hand.

Common Raven

TX I first saw Common Ravens on January 6 at Cottonwood Campground at Big Bend. I regularly saw them out west, including on May 18 at the Davis Mountains Preserve.

AK My first Common Raven of the year was on Kodiak Island on January 1. I saw them regularly all year in Anchorage, Juneau, Ketchikan, Delta Junction, Adak, Gambell, Nome, Hyder, Utqiagvik, Sitka, and Petersburg.

Horned Lark

TX On January 6, we saw our first Horned Larks north of Big Bend, and others on February 8 in the Texas Panhandle.

AK On June 5 as we arrived at a site outside Nome where Red Knots were nesting, two Horned Larks flitted away, never to be seen again. There were also two of them south of the lake at Gambell on September 4.

Bank Swallow

^{TX} On February 18, I went to Anzalduas County Park on the Mexican border. Part of the park is a high overlook over the Rio Grande, and swallows of every possible species are often seen there in winter. There, in addition to Barn, Cave, and Rough-winged Swallows, I also saw Bank Swallows, which were difficult to find in Texas, so I was particularly happy to see the little fast-flapping swallows with a brown breast band in with a mix of other swallows.

^{AK} I saw Bank Swallows on Nome's Kougarok Road on June 3, and in Anchorage, Hyder, and Juneau in early June.

Townsend's Solitaire

^{TX} I first saw Townsend's Solitaires on January 8 at Lubbock Cemetery, two of them perched high in a tree. I also saw them on January 24 on a walk along the lower portion of the Pinnacles Trail at Big Bend, and on February 7 as I hiked a trail in Guadalupe Mountains NP.

^{AK} On January 30, I decided to drive south of Anchorage and try for Townsend's Solitaire along the highway near Windy Point where birders had reported them. The trail was completely ice-free, and I clambered over rocks and walked the mostly easy trail farther than before. I did not need to go far, however, because almost immediately I saw a Townsend's Solitaire perched on a spruce, and then it dove down and disappeared. I soon heard a solitaire calling and then two squabbling and singing in the woods not far from my car. Although they were rarely still, I was able to get some photos when they occasionally landed on a branch. I walked a bit farther and then turned around. On the walk back a solitaire flew over my head going downhill. I also saw a very lost Townsend's Solitaire at Gambell at the end of May.

Cedar Waxwing

^{TX} Cedar Waxwings were among the many species I saw on January 1 on Selkirk Island on the Texas coast. I saw more Cedar Waxwings on February 9 in Texline in the far northeastern Panhandle. When I was in Houston on February 11, I saw Cedar Waxwings at the Jesse H. Jones Park & Nature Center, where I looked unsuccessfully for Bohemian Waxwings.

^{AK} After learning that someone had found a Cedar Waxwing in Anchorage on January 16, I drove over and knew I was in the right place because I found a handful of cars parked all together, about six people staring off to the right

Cedar Waxwings

side of the street, and a tripod aimed in the same direction. There next to a bird feeder, and sometimes on it, was my first Cedar Waxwing of the year, and the first one I had ever seen in Alaska. I saw others in Hyder and Sitka.

Lapland Longspur

TX I first saw Lapland Longspurs on January 9 as we headed to Canadian on the eastern side of the Panhandle. They are uncommon to abundant migrants and winter residents in the Panhandle and Northern Plains.

AK On April 16, we heard passing Lapland Longspurs at the hawk watch site north of Anchorage. Eventually a small flock of them landed near us and fed in the roadside grass, periodically flitting a short distance and settling down again. I commonly saw them at Adak, St. Paul, Gambell, Nome, and Utqiagvik.

Lapland Longspur in Nome

Smith's Longspur

[TX] I was registered for and needed to go to Eagle Fest on February 13 at the Rains County Fairgrounds in Emory, east of Lake Tawakoni in North Texas. The goal was to see Smith's Longspurs, almost impossible to find in Texas except in a couple of places where they are quite easy to find. The problem is that most of these places are on private property, inaccessible to most people unless special arrangements are made. I was very glad during my 2005 big year when a trip to one of these private areas was scheduled during Eagle Fest. After our tour bus stopped, we were led to a spot where the longspurs had previously been seen. Even though the grass was very short, we could not find a bird on the ground to scope and identify. We heard a couple of Smith's Longspurs in the air, but where did they go when they landed? Finally, we inched our way close enough to see a couple quite well, and I even got some flight photos that showed the most salient feature, the distinctive white shoulder patch.

^AK^ On June 24, I went to the mile 13 hill on the Denali Highway, a traditional site for Smith's Longspurs, although in recent years it had been a bit sparse. After more than two hours of slow walking up the gentle, flowered slope I reached the top, where all views of the hill were below me or at eye level. I sat on a rock out of the wind and waited and listened. After about 15 minutes a small brown bird flew past just below me, heading east. In another five minutes, it flew back rapidly, low to the grass. I could see it had white outer tail feathers, some white on the wings, and some white patterning on the face. The back-and-forth flights were repeated another 15 minutes later. Periodically I also heard a dry rattle from somewhere. It is likely they were nesting, and possibly what I saw were longspurs flying back and forth to feed young.

MacGillivray's Warbler

^TX^ On the morning of May 18, Carol Edwards took Simone and me into the Davis Mountains Preserve. We drove in as far as allowed, stopping periodically to do short hikes off the road. On one of these hikes, we spotted one of our goal birds, a singing MacGillivray's Warbler high in a tree.

^AK^ I heard MacGillivray's Warblers (up to five), and sometimes saw them, each day in Hyder (June 9 to 13) but didn't observe them elsewhere.

Common Yellowthroat

^TX^ I saw Common Yellowthroats on January 3 on South Padre Island, with later sightings on March 15 at Rio Grande Village at Big Bend just before sunset, on March 29 at Sabine Woods, and on August 31 in the Guadalupe Mountains.

^AK^ A male Common Yellowthroat was singing loudly at Ward Lake in Ketchikan on June 8. I found others in Hyder, Ketchikan, Juneau, and Haines in early and mid-June, and in Juneau and Ketchikan in mid-August.

American Redstart

^TX^ I saw my first American Redstart of the year on February 1 at Sabal Palm Audubon Sanctuary in Brownsville. Although some winter in the Valley and some are summer residents in northeastern Texas, most are migrants through the state.

^AK^ American Redstarts (up to 10) were around each day of our five-day trip to Hyder, beginning on June 9, but I didn't see them elsewhere.

Blackpoll Warbler

TX On April 20, we drove into McFaddin NWR. Although I always think of this refuge as being rather devoid of birds, every time I've gone there, there have been one or two very good finds. This time it was a very tame Blackpoll Warbler in low shrubbery along the road as well as a Palm Warbler on the ground, both of which allowed us to take numerous pictures.

AK On June 3, there was a Blackpoll Warbler on Kougarok Road in Nome. I saw others on the Denali Highway in late June, at Reflections Lake north of Anchorage in mid-July, at my house in Anchorage in early August, and on St. Paul Island in late September.

Townsend's Warbler

TX I first saw Townsend's Warblers on March 15 as I hiked the Pinnacles Trail at Big Bend NP. There were many of them in the Guadalupe Mountains on August 31.

AK Midmorning on May 2, I drove to Ward Lake (Ketchikan) to see what might be around. As I turned onto the road to the lake I heard and then saw my first Townsend's Warbler. I saw them regularly in Southeastern Alaska until mid-July.

Blackpoll Warbler at McFaddin NWR

Wilson's Warbler in Anchorage

Wilson's Warbler

TX I saw my first Wilson's Warbler on January 2 at Frontera Audubon in the LRGV. I saw more on February 1 at Sabal Palm Audubon Sanctuary in Brownsville, another at Boot Springs in Big Bend NP on the morning of May 12 working the branches of a sapling, and others at Boot Springs on August 10.

AK I first saw Wilson's Warbler on May 3 near the Higgins School (north Ketchikan), with later sightings elsewhere (prior to mid-September) in Nome, Anchorage, and Juneau.

American Tree Sparrow

TX On January 9 (day 9 of our 10-day Texas marathon beginning the big year), Simone and I headed toward Texline in the northwest corner of the Panhandle. There we waited for dawn in my car at an abandoned, grass-overgrown yard where I had seen American Tree Sparrows the previous two years. The dawn was spectacular, and when it finally provided enough light to allow us to see, we stepped out of the car into a very frosty morning. Shivering, we wandered around, making pishing sounds to rouse the sparrows from their warm beds somewhere in the grass. Then, there they were, a couple of American Tree Sparrows, along with White-crowned and Savannah Sparrows, popping up into the bushes.

^{AK} On January 18, my day began just after dawn, walking up the hill with Aaron Lang to his house in Homer. From his porch we watched a host

American Tree Sparrow

of White-crowned and Golden-crowned Sparrows, a couple of Lincoln's Sparrows, Dark-eyed Juncos, and my first American Tree Sparrow of the year eating seed near a brush pile in his backyard. I saw others in Nome in spring and on the Denali Highway in summer.

Chipping Sparrow

^{TX} I first saw Chipping Sparrows on January 1 on Selkirk Island as I explored the Texas coast. I saw others on February 7 as I hiked a trail in Guadalupe Mountains NP.

^{AK} On June 9, a Chipping Sparrow was the first species I saw in Hyder. Other than one or two Chipping Sparrows each day in Hyder, the only other sighting was on June 22 in Chicken.

Western Tanager

^{TX} I saw my first Western Tanager on May 10, a singing male lighting up a treetop at Davis Mountains State Park. Other Western Tanager sightings were on May 18 at the Davis Mountains Preserve and in the Guadalupe Mountains on August 31.

^{AK} I saw Western Tanagers (one to three) four of five days in Hyder, beginning on June 9, but I didn't see them elsewhere.

Western Tanager in Hyder

Red-winged Blackbird

^TX Red-winged Blackbirds were present on January 1 in Matagorda County on the coast. They are abundant migrants and residents in much of Texas. In summer their habitat is more restricted to suitable nesting areas, but they are widespread in large flocks during the rest of the year.

^AK On January 29, Aaron Bowman called and said the Red-winged Blackbird female he'd found the day before with some starlings near his Anchorage yard had returned. When I got there the birds had departed, but soon thereafter it was found again, and I was able to see it. I saw others in Ketchikan, Hyder, and Juneau, and at Kenny Lake in addition to Anchorage.

Rusty Blackbird

^TX On the morning of January 28, I went to Buddy (Byron) Stewart Park in Johnson County, where a large flock of Rusty Blackbirds had been reported. This species can usually be found during the winter months at the Village Creek Drying Beds, but they can be hard to locate if off in some untracked corner. Vast puddled areas were spread out along the road into the park, where I easily saw and photographed Rusty Blackbirds.

^AK My first Rusty Blackbird in Alaska was on February 8 in Hoonah, interacting with the much rarer Brewer's Blackbird that was also wintering there. I saw others in Anchorage and Hyder.

Seen Only in Texas

The species in this section are not Alaska birds and I did not see them in Alaska during my Alaska big year. There are very few or no records of these species in Alaska. I found these birds in Texas during my Texas big year. They may be common in Texas, or at least not classified as rare there, although some have limited ranges, may be difficult to find within their range, or may be likely only a few months of the year.

Ross's Goose

I first spotted Ross's Goose on January 1 in Jackson County. I saw many more on February 9 at Cactus Playa in the Panhandle. These white geese with their rounded heads and short bills were always a welcome sight.

Black-bellied Whistling-Duck

Driving north on Highway 77 from Brownsville to Kingsville on January 15, I stopped at most of the many roadside ponds and puddles and saw my first Black-bellied Whistling-Ducks with their bright red bills and reddish legs.

Fulvous Whistling-Duck

I first saw Fulvous Whistling-Duck on January 1 in San Patricio County on the Coastal Bend, a bright golden-brown duck at the edge of a marsh.

Mottled Duck

I first discovered Mottled Duck on January 1 at Paradise Pond in Nueces County. Although Mottled Ducks are very similar to female Mallards, their feathers are a darker brown and their bills lack the black found in the bills of female Mallards.

Plain Chachalaca

I first found Plain Chachalaca on January 2 in the Valley, where despite being numerous and noisy big brown birds, they are often difficult to see.

Northern Bobwhite

On January 13, I did a short North Texas day trip through Jacksboro before dawn, seeing three falling stars on the way to an area in Hardeman County

Northern Bobwhite west of Fort Worth

where a Northern Goshawk had been reported. It was a lovely morning, with a close-up view of four Northern Bobwhite along the road, but no Goshawk. I saw more bobwhite on April 2 at the Attwater Prairie Chicken NWR and heard them in the fields west of Fort Worth during breeding season.

Scaled Quail

Lake Balmorhea was the site of my first Scaled Quail of the year, on February 6. Usually I saw them huddled beneath scattered bushes or running across openings with their "cottontop" crests held high.

Scaled Quail

Gambel's Quail near Ruidosa

Gambel's Quail

On May 16, Simone and I took one of my favorite remote, scenic, and very rough Texas roads, FM 2810 south of Marfa toward Ruidosa. In Ruidosa we stopped to talk to someone working at the shop where we'd been told Gambel's Quail were sometimes fed. There were no quails visible, but we could hear one in the distance. After we drove off, just a little farther down the road a Gambel's Quail was singing on a post, posing for photos on my side of the car.

Montezuma Quail

Montezuma Quail are rare to locally uncommon in Texas, and I have found very few of them in the state. I saw them on May 15 at the home of John Gee and Carol Edwards, where the quails were regular visitors. In the midst of pleasant conversation, not long after we arrived a pair of quails did too, scratching in the dirt like tiny round cartoon chickens.

Ring-necked Pheasant

I first saw a Ring-necked Pheasant on January 8 along the road north of Lubbock. These introduced birds are common across the Panhandle and can usually best be seen on roadsides at dawn or dusk.

Lesser Prairie-Chicken

On January 10, near the end of our 10-day swing around Texas, we tried unsuccessfully to see Lesser Prairie-Chickens in Lipscomb County in the Panhandle, hoping we wouldn't have to come back later in the year. On April 5, we again drove up to Lipscomb County. At first we could only hear Lesser Prairie-Chickens at a distance across the field, but when we drove on another nearby road, we saw two Ferruginous Hawks, one of which was chasing a Lesser Prairie-Chicken. The two hawks settled down on a distant fence to eat something smaller, and then more Lesser Prairie-Chickens started appearing in the nearby field. We estimated that there were at least seven males and four females.

Wild Turkey
We saw Wild Turkeys on January 10 at Lake Marvin in the northeastern Panhandle. They are present year-round in all but some of the far west portions of the state.

Least Grebe
I first found Least Grebe on January 1 in San Patricio County on the Coastal Bend. These tiny thin-billed grebes were always a welcome sight when they emerged from their usual wetland hiding places.

Eared Grebe
On the way north up Highway 77 from Brownsville to Kingsville on January 15, I stopped at most of the many roadside ponds and puddles and saw my first Eared Grebes. While they winter in much of Texas, Eared Grebes nest only in portions of the western Panhandle.

Clark's Grebe
Clark's Grebe was present on January 7 at Balmorhea Lake. I found Clark's Grebes again on January 25 at McNary Reservoir just short of El Paso, along with Western Grebes.

Red-billed Pigeon
On March 2 just before 6:00 a.m. I headed to Salineño to search for Red-billed Pigeons. While the pigeons are regularly present there, they generally fly very rapidly past the view point and are easily missed if you are watching another bird or looking in another direction. Or, even more frustrating for a Texas big year is a sitting bird—in Mexico. I was lucky, and at 7:20, a single Red-billed Pigeon flew by.

Inca Dove
I first noted Inca Dove on January 1 on Selkirk Island in Matagorda County. This tiny lacy-feathered dove is more often heard than seen, cooing its mournful "no hope" calls.

Common Ground-Dove

I first found Common Ground-Dove on January 2 in the Valley. I saw them regularly in South Texas, flitting rapidly away and back down into the brush, often when I was seeking the similar, rare Ruddy Ground-Dove.

White-tipped Dove

I first added White-tipped Dove to my list on January 2 in the Valley. These doves are commonly seen at birding hotspots in the Valley such Santa Ana NWR and Bentsen–Rio Grande Valley State Park, usually feeding at the edges of openings near bird feeders. Their regularly heard call is described in bird guides as similar to "blowing across the top of a bottle."

White-winged Dove

I first found White-winged Doves in the LRGV on January 2. They were regular at our Fort Worth home and were generally there every day I was home.

Mourning Dove

Mourning Dove was my third species for the year on January 1 in Matagorda County on the coast. Mourning Doves are common across all of the Lower 48 states and southern Canada but are only rarely found in Alaska (and not during my big year).

Yellow-billed Cuckoo

I observed the first Yellow-billed Cuckoo of the year at Sabine Woods on April 18. Although their calls are loud and distinctive, it is often difficult to find these slow-moving birds in the bushes and trees where they feed. They nest across the entire state.

Black-billed Cuckoo

On May 1, I went to Sea Rim State Park near Sabine Woods and found multiple cuckoos sneaking about and flying between the low bushes along the beach. One was a Black-billed Cuckoo, hanging out with a Yellow-billed Cuckoo so I could easily compare wing and bill colors. There was another Black-billed Cuckoo at Packery Channel the next day. Although they migrate across Texas, they are difficult to find even during migration and only rarely breed in North Texas.

Greater Roadrunner in South Texas

Greater Roadrunner

On January 6, we saw our first Greater Roadrunner north of Big Bend. Later sightings were on March 15 at Rio Grande Village in Big Bend just before sunset, and on the Boy Scout Ranch Road on August 14, when I saw at least nine individuals. Although found across the state, they are often difficult to locate.

Groove-billed Ani

I observed a Groove-billed Ani on January 3 on a trip to Sabal Palm Audubon Sanctuary. These fat-billed black birds lurk in the South Texas brush and are difficult to see, even though their liquid calls reveal their presence.

Lesser Nighthawk

On January 15 at Santa Ana NWR in the late morning, a Lesser Nighthawk was perched in a tree. I found them regularly in the Trans-Pecos later in the year, often diving low and fluttering over the dry brushy landscape at dawn and dusk.

Common Nighthawk

I observed the first Common Nighthawk of the year on April 19 as I drove to High Island. Although they are often seen flying during the daytime, one of my favorite nighttime sounds is Common Nighthawks booming during courtship.

Common Pauraque

Late on January 14 after birding during the day at Bentsen–Rio Grande Valley State Park, I walked into the park to find a Common Pauraque. One was very obliging, landing near me on the road close to the park entrance, where I viewed it by flashlight. I also heard them on March 1 at Bentsen–Rio Grande Valley State Park. A drive after dusk on September 17 at Laguna Atascosa NWR produced at least 67 Common Pauraques on the road.

Common Poorwill

On the evening of May 13, two other birders in the area and I went over to Davis Mountains State Park at dusk. As we drove the scenic drive, we spooked up a Poorwill that had been sitting on the road.

Chuck-will's-widow

The first Chuck-will's-widow of the year flew off the road as we drove into another birder's yard in Galveston on the evening of March 27. These large nightjars are regularly found on the Texas coast during migration and nest in the northeastern part of the state.

Eastern Whip-poor-will

A trip to Sabine Woods on March 29 produced a perched, well-observed Whip-poor-will plus eight warbler species, a young male Indigo Bunting, a Wood Thrush, and a calling Fish Crow.

Note: Mexican Whip-poor-will, which is now classified as a species, was not a separate species in 2005. Thus, while I did see it, I am not counting it as part of my Texas big year. Early on the morning of May 12, before daylight, I could hear Whip-poor-wills and Western Screech-Owls through my tent walls in Big Bend NP.

Chimney Swift
On March 23, after hunting warblers in Port Aransas, we stopped at Blucher Park in Corpus Christi and saw our first soaring Chimney Swifts before checking for gulls at the Corpus Christi dump.

White-throated Swift
I first noticed White-throated Swifts in Val Verde County west of San Antonio on January 5. I also saw them in the Guadalupe Mountains on August 31. They are found only in the far western portions of the state.

Magnificent Hummingbird
On June 20, I found two Magnificent Hummingbirds, plus Lucifer, Broad-tailed, and Black-chinned Hummingbirds and a rare to very rare White-eared Hummingbird together at feeders in the Davis Mountains. This large, dark, mostly green hummingbird with a purple crown is aptly named, and a highlight when it comes to feeders in the mountains of West Texas.

Blue-throated Hummingbird
On May 11, above my head and above the Painted Redstarts I was watching at Boot Springs in Big Bend, a couple of Blue-throated Hummingbirds metallically called, hard to find in spite of their loudness until they sallied out from their branch. I saw them again on August 10 at the same site.

Lucifer Hummingbird
On May 21, my husband and I drove from Fort Davis to the home of Carolyn Ohl in the Christmas Mountains. She had very graciously set up chairs for visiting birders so we could face the flowers visited by hummingbirds. After a Black-chinned Hummingbird riveted our attention to the flowers, there was a series of very brief appearances by a male Lucifer Hummingbird, which was chased off by the very aggressive Black-chinned Hummingbird each time it appeared. Finally, the Lucifer Hummingbird was able to sneak to a flower for long enough that we could see him well, particularly his head with its down-curved bill, purplish throat, and white line behind the eye. I saw another one on June 20 in the Davis Mountains, and another on August 10 at Sam Nail Ranch in Big Bend NP, which immediately zoomed away across the dessert.

Ruby-throated Hummingbird

On March 22, we headed south to look for spring migrants at Paradise Pond in Port Aransas and found our first Ruby-throated Hummingbird, as well as new warblers and vireos for the year. During spring migration on the Texas coast, these hummingbirds often fill the air with the sound of their humming wings and their chips and chatters as they dart around the trees, chase each other, and feed at blossoms.

Black-chinned Hummingbird

My first Black-chinned Hummingbird of the year was actively feeding in the mesquites around Cottonwood Campground at Big Bend NP on March 16. Another was aggressively chasing away my first Lucifer Hummingbird on May 21 in the Christmas Mountains, and another was in the Davis Mountains on June 20.

Broad-tailed Hummingbird

The first Broad-tailed Hummingbird was present on May 14 in the Davis Mountains, and I found another there on June 20. The rosy-red throats of the males help distinguish them from the more common Ruby-throated Hummingbirds.

Allen's Hummingbird

On February 23, Simone and I went to the Rockport yard of Susan Beree and saw a male Allen's Hummingbird along with Rufous and Buff-bellied Hummingbirds. While female Allen's and Rufous Hummingbirds are indistinguishable from one another, male Allen's Hummingbirds have a solid green, rather than rufous, back.

Calliope Hummingbird

On January 18, Simone and I headed down to Harris County to see a Calliope Hummingbird at the home of Ron and Marcia Braun. It was a stunning tiny bird with bright red throat streaks and was easily found.

Buff-bellied Hummingbird

I first observed Buff-bellied Hummingbirds on January 2 in the Valley. In addition to many sightings in the Valley, where it is common, there was also a Buff-bellied Hummingbird in Rockport on February 23.

Yellow Rail

On April 2, I overheard someone at Attwater Prairie Chicken NWR talking about going over to Anahuac NWR later in the day to join the Yellow Rail walk being led by David Sarkozi the next day. While I was planning to go later in April when my birding friend from North Carolina, Lena Gallitano, came to visit, my nervousness about possibly missing this hard-to-find bird made me decide to go on this Yellow Rail walk too. At 4:00 the next morning I was at Anahuac, rubber boots on, camera ready. I had done this walk other years and knew I was in for heavy-duty exertion. Over half an hour later, we had found four Yellow Rails, and yes, I had fallen more than once (but I was not the first to fall, which is counted as a necessary sacrifice to bring out the rails). On April 17 when I went back, a large group of people had gathered because the rail walks were ending for the year. Not only were the rails still around, but as I recall the final count for the day was nine Yellow Rails.

Black Rail

I added Black Rails to my year list on March 28 at Galveston Island State Park, where Simone and I were delighted to hear the characteristic "ki-ki-krrr" sounds of not one, not two, but three Black Rails, all carrying on at the same time in a corner bordered by road on two sides. Of course we could not see the rails at all, even though they were probably less than three feet from us. The size and shape of little mice, these dark black birds are usually impossible to see unless lured from their sedgy habitats. We had another close invisible encounter with another Black Rail on a different road in the park.

Clapper Rail

I first heard and saw a Clapper Rail on January 3 on South Padre Island. Later sightings included Yacht Basin Road near Rollover Pass on March 18. This species is commonly heard calling loudly at dawn and dusk in the Texas coastal marshes but is less frequently viewed.

King Rail

I first spotted a King Rail on March 29 on what was supposed to be a quick drive through McFaddin NWR, just down the road from Sabine Woods. The rail slowly emerged from the wet roadside vegetation and brought the car to a screeching halt. After thorough study of the bird, I confirmed its identity.

Virginia Rail

I found my first Virginia Rail on January 3 on South Padre Island. Between two invisible Black Rail finds in Galveston on March 28, we had an actual encounter with a visible Virginia Rail. It was lying in the road, stunned by something but alive, and seemed to be gradually coming around. Simone picked it up to move it off the road, but I got a couple of quick pictures before she set it gently down out of harm's way.

Purple Gallinule

On April 17 after my North Carolina friend and I did a Yellow Rail walk at Anahuac NWR, there was just enough time for us to find a Purple Gallinule before darkness fell. It is always startling and unforgettable to find this plump purple-green bird with a red-and-yellow bill and yellow legs and feet climbing marshy vegetation or walking across a lawn.

Purple Gallinule and chick at Anahuac NWR

Common Gallinule (Moorhen)

I first saw Common Gallinules on January 1 in Matagorda County on the Coastal Bend. Although not as brightly colored as Purple Gallinules, the darker Common Gallinules are noisier and more easily found in East Texas.

Whooping Crane

On January 30, Simone and I drove south from Fort Worth to Aransas NWR to look for Whooping Cranes. We drove to the observation tower, climbed the stairs, and there they were—three of them easily identified through the telescope and distinguished from the more numerous Great Egrets by their large size and their bustle. I always felt it was a wonderful perk to live in a state where the world's Whooping Cranes winter.

Whooping Cranes at Aransas NWR

Black-necked Stilt

I first observed Black-necked Stilts on January 3 on South Padre Island. Black-necked Stilts, found all along the Texas Gulf Coast, are striking, unmistakable black-and-white birds with long, gangly red legs and thin, straight bills.

American Avocet

I first saw American Avocets on January 18 at Bolivar Flats on the Upper Coast. Although with their black-and-white bodies they are somewhat similar to stilts in winter, avocets have long gray legs and upturned bills, and during breeding season they have bright rusty heads and necks.

American Oystercatcher

I first noticed American Oystercatchers on January 18 at Bolivar Flats on the Upper Coast. Unlike the all-black, red-billed Black Oystercatchers found along the Alaskan coast, American Oystercatchers are black and white. In Texas they are found only along the Gulf Coast.

Snowy Plover

Snowy Plover was present on January 3 at Boca Chica Beach in the LRGV. The pale Snowy Plover is declining in the United States, with various populations threatened by such factors as beach degradation, development, and pollution.

Piping Plover

I first observed Piping Plovers on January 3 on South Padre Island. Piping Plovers are even more endangered than Snowy Plovers, as their nesting and wintering ranges have decreased because of development, artificial adjustment of water levels in inland lakes and rivers, and other human activities that cause them to abandon their nests or be displaced.

Wilson's Plover

I first found Wilson's Plover on March 18. There were two at Bolivar Beach among the many other plovers (Semipalmated, Piping, and Black-bellied Plovers) and other shorebirds. While superficially similar to the other small plovers, Wilson's Plover is larger and has a longer, heavier black bill. Although not endangered, this mostly coastal species is also declining.

Long-billed Curlews

I first spotted Long-billed Curlews on January 3 at Boca Chica Beach in the LRGV. I also saw them at Yacht Basin Road near Rollover Pass on March 18 in a search for Whimbrels.

Stilt Sandpiper

On March 6, we drove north of the Valley to try for more shorebirds and found Stilt Sandpipers near San Benito at the edge of a small roadside lake. When found in spring, they are distinctive, with darkly barred underparts, a dark cap, and bright rusty ear patches.

White-rumped Sandpiper

I first found White-rumped Sandpiper on April 11 in Nueces County in the Coastal Bend. Unlike nearly all other small shorebirds, White-rumped Sandpipers have entirely white rumps without a dark central area, best seen when they fly.

Buff-breasted Sandpiper

I went to Attwater Prairie Chicken NWR on April 2 even though I knew I could not count the Attwater/Greater Prairie-Chickens there, as there was no evidence that any were wild birds. Along the road in the refuge were two Buff-breasted Sandpipers. I also saw a couple along the road in Chambers County on April 18.

American Woodcock

On the evening of January 28, I tried for woodcocks on Western Oaks Road in Fort Worth, where I had tried earlier without success. Finally, at about 6:15 p.m., I heard an American Woodcock descending high above me, twittering all the while, but just a couple of times. I didn't hear any "peents," however. The next morning while it was still dark I returned to the area and drove out and heard the typical woodcock "peent" call.

Willet

I first saw Willets on January 3 at Boca Chica Beach in the LRGV. I also found them near Rollover Pass on March 18. Willets, with their bold black-and-white wing pattern and noisy calls, can be found year-round on the Texas Gulf Coast.

Laughing Gull

I first identified Laughing Gull on January 3 at Boca Chica Beach in the LRGV. For people like me who often have difficulty identifying gulls, the distinctive black hood and red bills of adult Laughing Gulls are a welcome sight along the Gulf of Mexico.

Lesser Black-backed Gull

I first observed Lesser Black-backed Gull on January 18 at the Quintana jetty, where we had gone to see the reported Little Gull. These gulls winter from September to April along the Texas coast.

Least Tern

On March 18, I went to the Bolivar Flats Houston Audubon Sanctuary, where among the zillions of American Avocets and sandpipers and plovers (Semipalmated, Piping, Black-bellied, and Wilson's Plovers), which were on the "already-seen" list, were yellow-billed Least Terns beginning to stake out nest sites on the beach.

Least Terns on the Texas coast

Gull-billed Tern
A Gull-billed Tern was flying on January 3 at Boca Chica Beach in the LRGV. They are usually seen flying low over coastal beaches and marshes.

Black Tern
On April 22, we explored the jetty out of Sabine Pass. As we wandered around looking for the jetty and a reported booby (not found), we saw our first Black Terns on their migration through Texas.

Common Tern
On March 6 at Laguna Atascosa, shorebird species that we had already seen were plentiful. We were also able to add an adult Common Tern to our year lists, with its bright red bill and characteristic black wedge shape on its upper wing.

Forster's Tern
I first spotted Forster's Tern on January 3 at Boca Chica Beach at the southern tip of Texas. Forster's Terns are common coastal residents, often seen hovering and then diving into the water. Some fly north in spring and breed at inland lakes.

Royal Tern
I first observed Royal Tern, with its large orange-red bill, on January 1 in Nueces County in the Coastal Bend, and I saw it throughout the year along the coast.

Sandwich Tern
I first saw Sandwich Tern on January 3 at Boca Chica Beach. I regularly observed the unique yellow-tipped black bill of Sandwich Terns throughout the year when I scanned flocks of gulls and terns sitting on the beach.

Black Skimmer
I first saw a Black Skimmer on January 3 at the South Padre Island Convention Centre. When they are not flying low over the water hunting for small fish with their lower mandible skimming the surface, large flocks of Black Skimmers often sit together on the beach sand, with their huge black-tipped red bills pointing in the same direction.

Cory's and Audubon's Shearwaters

I spotted Cory's and Audubon's Shearwaters on the first Gulf of Mexico pelagic trip of the year, on June 17. Both species are uncommon but are increasingly found off the Texas coast.

Wood Stork

On May 26, after having been in West Texas for a while, I saw that Wood Storks had very recently been reported at Brazoria NWR. I went east and drove south along Bolivar Flats, took the ferry to Galveston, and zigzagged down to the refuge. There, as advertised, was a small flock of Wood Storks at the edge of Olney Pond among the Roseate Spoonbills, White and White-faced Ibises, Tricolored and Great Blue Herons, and Great Egrets.

Magnificent Frigatebird

On April 27, I decided to go to Port Aransas, where a Black-throated Blue Warbler had been reported. Although I did not see the warbler, I did see a Magnificent Frigatebird on the ferry ride to Port Aransas.

Magnificent Frigatebird on a Texas pelagic trip

Northern Gannet

I added Northern Gannet to my Texas year list on a trip to Paradise Pond and the Leonabelle Turnbull Birding Center in Port Aransas on January 30. Northern Gannets are found along the coast in winter, with large numbers sometimes observed offshore.

Neotropic Cormorant

I first saw a Neotropic Cormorant on January 3 on a trip to Sabal Palm Audubon Sanctuary. This slender, long-tailed cormorant is resident along the coast and in the LRGV and also occurs inland in the summer.

Anhinga

Anhingas were flying over the road as I approached the LRGV on January 14. Although some Anhingas can be found at any time of year in much of the eastern half of Texas, most of these snake-necked birds migrate northward into Texas in late winter and are summer residents along the coast and in Brush Country.

American White and Brown Pelicans

I first saw American White and Brown Pelicans on January 1 in Calhoun and Aransas Counties, respectively, on the Coastal Bend. In the Northern Plains, where coastal Brown Pelicans are extremely rare, it is not uncommon to see huge migrating flocks of American White Pelicans slowly swirling high overhead.

American White Pelicans along the Texas coast

Brown Pelican preening on the Texas coast

American Bittern

The first sighting of an American Bittern was on March 7 at Padre Island National Seashore while we were hunting for a Masked Duck. On March 29 at Anahuac NWR, an American Bittern was stalking deliberately, ignoring all passersby.

Least Bittern

I first spotted a Least Bittern on January 3 on South Padre Island. On April 21, we got excellent views of a Least Bittern perched high in some reeds right next to the road at Sabine Woods. On July 20, I was very happy to find a nest of three baby birds midway up in the cattails along the boardwalk at the Port Aransas Leonabelle Turnbull Birding Center. They were the typical birds only a mother bird could love, with spiky yellowish feathers sticking out in every direction, but even in their ugliness they were pretty cute. Every time I

Least Bittern

moved at all, there was an immediate, very bittern-like straight-up pointing of their beaks. If I stayed still, they would relax and walk around in the cattails, holding on with their large feet without falling, even with little support. I came back on July 28 to see them again.

Great Egret

I saw the first Great Egrets of the year on January 1 on the coast. By March 28, some of the trees in the rookeries at Smith Oaks were filled with pink Roseate Spoonbills balancing on the branches and white breeding-plumed Great Egrets snuggling up to each other.

Snowy Egret

I first noticed a Snowy Egret on January 1 in Matagorda County on the coast. The medium-sized, totally white egret is easily distinguished from other US egrets by its size and by its black legs with bright yellow feet. It is year-round on the coast, and most breeding occurs in the eastern half of the state.

Snowy Egret

Little Blue Heron

I first found Little Blue Heron on January 3 at the South Padre Island Convention Centre. Although this slender slate-gray heron is limited mostly to the eastern third of the state as a summer resident, small numbers also winter along the coast.

Tricolored Heron

I saw Tricolored Heron on January 1 in Matagorda County on the coast. It is found mostly on the coast and can be distinguished from other herons by its blue-gray back and wings, patches of rust-colored feathers, and white belly.

Reddish Egret

I first observed Reddish Egret on January 3 in Cameron County in the LRGV. Reddish Egrets are well known for their erratic feeding behavior in shallow coastal ponds as they charge around with wings spread.

Cattle Egret

On the way north from Brownsville to Kingsville on Highway 77 on January 15, I saw my first Cattle Egrets of the year at the many roadside ponds and puddles. They can be found across much of the state, usually eating insects in fields with cattle and horses.

Green Heron

I first observed Green Heron on March 7 in Nueces County on the Coastal Bend. They winter along the coast and breed in wetland habitats across most of the state.

Black-crowned Night-Heron

I saw Black-crowned Night-Herons near the Upper Coast as the last new bird on January 1. Later sightings were on March 15 at Rio Grande Village in Big Bend just before sunset. In summer they are found across the state.

Black-crowned Night-Heron

Yellow-crowned Night-Heron

On March 22, we headed south to look for spring migrants at Paradise Pond in Port Aransas and while there found our first Yellow-crowned Night-Heron. Yellow-crowned Night-Herons breed in the eastern half of Texas.

White Ibis

I first easily saw White Ibis on January 1 in Matagorda County on the coast, where they are year-round residents.

Glossy Ibis

On April 17, when we were looking at the rare (for Texas) King Eider at Bolivar Flats, other birders were looking at a Glossy Ibis, which we added to our lists too. Glossy Ibis, very similar to the much more common White-faced Ibis, is found only rarely on the Texas coast.

White-faced Ibis

I first found White-faced Ibis on January 1 in Matagorda County on the coast, where it resides all year long. Its white "face" is really a thin line of white feathers around its eye, with red facial skin between the eye and bill.

Roseate Spoonbill

I saw the first Roseate Spoonbill of the year on January 1 at the Leonabelle Turnbull Birding Center in Port Aransas. By March 28, some of the trees

Roseate Spoonbill at Boy Scout Woods, Texas

in the rookeries at Smith Oaks were glowing pink and white with Roseate Spoonbills and Great Egrets.

Black and Turkey Vultures

I saw both Black and Turkey Vultures on January 1 in Matagorda County on the coast. Although both species are large and black, they can be distinguished by the red head of the Turkey Vulture and the white patches at the wing ends of the black-headed Black Vulture.

Swallow-tailed Kite

On May 1, I drove to Liberty, one of the few spots in Texas where black-and-white Swallow-tailed Kites are often found, but only during the breeding season. After driving the neighborhood streets for about 15 minutes, I found my goal Swallow-tailed Kites, two of them, swooping low across a lake at the edge of the neighborhood.

White-tailed Kite in South Texas

Mississippi Kite along the Texas coast

White-tailed Kite (once called Black-shouldered Kite)
I first observed White-tailed Kite on January 3 in Cameron County in the LRGV. They occur year-round in South Texas and along the coast.

Mississippi Kite
I first saw one of my favorite species, the Mississippi Kite, on April 10 at our first visit to the Kreische Brewery State Historic Site in La Grange. I also saw

them on May 1 in Liberty shortly before I saw Swallow-tailed Kites for the year. In early August I found more than 40 in North Texas as they gathered prior to migrating south.

Cooper's Hawk

Cooper's Hawk was another species I first found in Matagorda County during my whirlwind birding on the coast on January 1. I saw another on February 8 in the Panhandle.

Harris's Hawk

Harris's Hawk was present on January 3 at Sabal Palm Audubon Sanctuary. When I went to South Texas I was always glad to see these fairly common dark brown birds with their distinctive rusty shoulders, leggings, and underwings and long black tail with white at the base and tip.

Harris's Hawks along the Texas coast

White-tailed Hawk

A White-tailed Hawk was flying along the road on January 1 in Matagorda County on the coast. Although it has similar rusty shoulders, the dark gray (not brown) back, white underparts and leggings, and nearly all-white tail with just a narrow black band help distinguish this uncommon coastal hawk from Harris's Hawk.

Gray Hawk

My first Gray Hawk of the year was perched on a post on January 6 at Cottonwood Campground in Big Bend. On February 18, while I was listening to a Northern Beardless-Tyrannulet at Anzalduas County Park in the LRGV, a Gray Hawk flew by. The range of Gray Hawks in Texas is limited to Big Bend and the LRGV, and in my experience they are often difficult to find there.

Gray Hawk at Big Bend

Red-shouldered Hawk

I first saw Red-shouldered Hawk on January 4 at Salineño in the LRGV. Unlike other Texas hawks that have red shoulders (Harris's, White-tailed), the Red-shouldered Hawk lives in moist woodlands and has a dark spotted back and barred rusty underparts.

Broad-winged Hawk

We saw our first Broad-winged Hawk in a Galveston yard on March 28, where it appeared to have been waiting for birds to come to drink at a pond. In fall migration, Broad-winged Hawks were swirling in large kettles overhead at the Hazel Bazemore Hawk Watch in Corpus Christi.

Ferruginous Hawk

Ferruginous Hawks were present on January 8 along the road north of Lubbock. Later, on February 8, I saw them again in the Panhandle. These hawks regularly winter in the Panhandle and eastward across parts of North

Ferruginous Hawk

Texas, and they can be there in large numbers in years when many rodents are present.

Barn Owl

I went to Anahuac NWR on February 12 rather than going directly home from a bird chase in Houston. In 2003 I had confirmed that Barn Owls fly around the buildings and lights at Anahuac NWR in the predawn, so I thought I'd try in 2005. This particular morning there was a major predawn gathering of fishermen. As I stood off to the side and tried to see or hear an owl, all I could hear was loud laughter, motors running, toilets flushing, and feet walking on the gravel driveway. Just before I concluded that it was totally hopeless to even try for a Barn Owl in all the cacophony, I heard an owl and saw two shadowy forms of the right size fly by. I wrote down a tentative Barn Owl, needing a better view to be certain. My next stop was Sabine Woods, a bit north of Anahuac near Port Arthur. Not too long after I got to Sabine Woods, I was very pleased to see a Barn Owl, an avian ghost, leave one of the trees on the west side of the main wooded area. I counted it that day.

On February 17 at dusk, I saw one fly across the road ahead of me as I entered Brownsville. The next day, after adding Dusky-capped Flycatcher to

Barn Owl

my year list near Cannon Road off US 281, I hung around, still hoping for a view of the flycatcher. Instead, I suddenly heard the raucous cries of Green Jays, and a large whitish bird flew across a deep ditch pursued by the jays—another Barn Owl. The owl lowered itself into some bushes down the right-of-way, and I took a few distant photos without moving. Since the road out of the area took me past the owl, I inched my car in that direction, allowing increasingly better pictures of this unique bird with its pale body and heart-shaped face. The owl stayed put as I drove by, even though one of the Green Jays was still giving it a hard time.

Eastern Screech-Owl

My first sighting of an Eastern Screech-Owl, peering out of a nest box, was on January 4 just upriver from the Salineño overlook. Ten days later when I was back in the LRGV, multiple Eastern Screech-Owls serenaded me as I took a late evening bird walk at Bentsen–Rio Grande Valley State Park.

Ferruginous Pygmy-Owl

By September I had not yet seen a Ferruginous Pygmy-Owl. I scheduled a visit to El Canelo, a ranch north of Raymondville, which traditionally had a pair of them. The male of the known pair had recently died, but I learned the female was still around. I arrived at El Canelo early on the morning of September 28. Within a minute of my arrival, I was hearing the calling female Ferruginous Pygmy-Owl, and after a couple more minutes of searching, I was staring up into the staring-down face of a Ferruginous Pygmy-Owl. She flew across the lawn to another set of trees, and I wandered off to see what else was around. When I returned to the house, she was back in the original tree, and the light was much better for photographs.

Ferruginous Pygmy-Owl

Elf Owl

On May 10, I drove to the K-Bar Ranch road at Big Bend NP just before dusk to check for Elf Owls in holes in a pole where I'd seen one two years earlier.

Elf Owl in South Texas

Amazingly, after I'd been there only a few minutes in waning light, a tiny round owl head poked out of the same hole as in 2003, and its bright yellow eyes looked around. Then the owl disappeared back into the hole.

On May 16, I was back out west driving down to Ruidoso looking for Gambel's Quail when I noticed what seemed to be little round sparrows sitting on a distant line next to a power pole. When I stopped to check them with binoculars, however, the birds turned out to be two tiny owls. After inching the car forward, I got a good enough view to see that they were Elf Owls. The fact that they were out in broad daylight and were slightly scruffy in appearance led us to believe they were probably immature birds, very lovable ones, too. Eventually, they both flew down into the brush beneath the pole where they had been sitting, presumably to go hunting. In any case, they disappeared, and I drove on.

Burrowing Owl

Burrowing Owl

On April 4, Simone and I headed west to look for Lesser Prairie-Chickens, among other things. We wandered a bit around the Panhandle and saw our first Burrowing Owls of the year in Briscoe County.

Long-eared Owl

On January 9, we went to Unit 18 of the Rita Blanca National Grassland in the Panhandle, where Howard Laidlaw had reported Long-eared Owls toward the end of his 2004 Texas big year. The road out to Unit 18 was muddy and very slippery. I was a nervous wreck as I inched along the road toward the driveway into the unit, fearing a gooey slide into a ditch. The tires were thickly coated with slippery mud and showed little inclination to go where I aimed them, but we finally got to the driveway. We walked the long rutted driveway from the road because I was worried about getting stuck. Once at the unit, we peered into the isolated stand of deciduous brush and trees and tried to figure out where a Long-eared Owl could possibly hide in the open branches. At first, there did not appear to be a single bird anywhere. Then we saw something fly back farther into the brush. We could not see what it was. It, or perhaps they, kept eluding us, no matter where we looked. We finally split up, one on each side of the little stand of trees, hoping that at least one of us could figure out what was eluding us. That did it. All of a sudden, we could see five different Long-eared Owls eerily flying around and through the trees in the winter light. Two of them flew out from the woods and back in, and the others perched deep in the dense branches. A Northern Harrier joined the melee, and I managed to get a few quick pictures before they all disappeared back into the woods. We backed off from the disturbance we had caused, mission accomplished for that day.

Ringed Kingfisher

I first found Ringed Kingfisher on January 3 on a trip to Sabal Palm Audubon Sanctuary. This large kingfisher is one of three kingfisher species regularly present in the LRGV, and it is the only one with a completely rust-colored belly.

Green Kingfisher

I spotted Green Kingfisher on January 4 at Saliñeno in the LRGV. The tiny Green Kingfisher is shorter than a robin and often difficult to see as it sits on a low branch along a river.

Red-headed Woodpecker

I saw the first Red-headed Woodpecker of my big year on February 26 on a trip to the Pineywoods that included a TOS field trip to the Nacogdoches area. They are year-round residents in the eastern half of Texas.

Acorn Woodpecker

I first saw Acorn Woodpecker in Fort Davis on January 7. This bold black-and-white western woodpecker is found in only a few areas in West Texas.

Golden-fronted Woodpecker

I first observed Golden-fronted Woodpecker on January 2 at Frontera Audubon in the LRGV. While the Golden-fronted Woodpecker has a small

Acorn Woodpecker in Fort Davis

yellow area above its bill, the gold nape is a much better identifying feature. The primary range of this species is south of the Texas border, with its only US range extending north from Mexico across Central Texas. Its eastern range overlaps that of the very similar Red-bellied Woodpecker, which has a red crown and nape.

Red-bellied Woodpecker

A Red-bellied Woodpecker was present on January 10 near Lake Marvin in the northeastern Panhandle. Another sighting was on February 26 in the Pineywoods in the Nacogdoches area. They reside in the northeast quarter of the state.

Williamson's Sapsucker

On December 10, after wandering around the Lawrence E. Wood Picnic Area for a while, I met Mark Lockwood, who had volunteered to try to help me find a Williamson's Sapsucker at the Davis Mountains Preserve, a bird I should have already found for the year but had not been able to find. It was certainly a day for sapsuckers, with Red-naped Sapsuckers everywhere. With Mark's help I began to get a bit better at distinguishing Red-naped from Yellow-bellied Sapsuckers, since I had so many to study. Although we often stopped and listened for a "tap-tap" as we drove up and then back down the mountain road, we could not find our goal bird. It was beginning to look pretty grim as we neared the visitor center again, when all of a sudden a lovely dark male Williamson's Sapsucker flew to a tall pine near us.

Red-naped Sapsucker

I first found a very cooperative Red-naped Sapsucker on January 7, tapping gently on the tree trunks at the Lawrence E. Wood Picnic Area in the Davis Mountains, known for its wintering sapsuckers. One of my main goals there was Williamson's Sapsucker, which turned out to be one of my nemesis species for most of the year.

Ladder-backed Woodpecker

I first saw Ladder-backed Woodpecker on January 3 on a trip to Sabal Palm Audubon Sanctuary. I observed others on February 7 as I hiked a trail in Guadalupe Mountains NP. On August 8 in Big Bend NP, I saw a young Ladder-backed Woodpecker begging from its parent.

Red-cockaded Woodpecker

My first view of this Pineywoods specialty was on February 27 on a TOS field trip to the Nacogdoches area. The red "cockade" is a tiny, mostly invisible tuft of red over each distinctive white cheek patch.

Pileated Woodpecker

I saw my first Pileated Woodpecker for the year on February 26 on a TOS trip to the Nacogdoches area in the woodpecker-rich Pineywoods. This noisy, mostly black woodpecker is more than twice the size of any other Texas woodpecker. Its red crest reminds me of Woody Woodpecker every time I see it.

Prairie Falcon

I first found Prairie Falcon on January 9 as we headed to Canadian on the eastern side of the Panhandle. While Prairie Falcons are mostly only winter residents of West Texas, they breed in the mountains of the western Trans-Pecos.

Monk Parakeet

On February 4, when taking a break from wandering all over Texas, I remembered the Monk Parakeet colony in Fort Worth and immediately drove there to see them so I wouldn't inadvertently forget to see them later in the year.

Green Parakeet

I'd missed Green Parakeets in my earlier visits to the Valley, so I made more effort when I was there on February 17, hanging out in McAllen at dusk at spots traditionally favored by the parakeets as they return to their nighttime roosts. At 5:31 p.m. at the intersection of Tenth and Dove Streets in McAllen, a flock of Green Parakeets flew in.

Red-crowned Parrot

I saw my first Red-crowned Parrot on January 15 at Frontera Audubon in the Valley when I was there to find the reported Elegant Trogon. While common in urban areas in their limited LRGV range, Red-crowned Parrots are endangered in Mexico.

Northern Beardless-Tyrannulet

Anzalduas County Park often hosts the Northern Beardless-Tyrannulet, known as the tiny flycatcher with a name longer than it is. I went there on February 18 and walked around the grounds of the park listening for its loud calls. After watching a gorgeous adult Gray Hawk fly by, I finally heard the Northern Beardless-Tyrannulet and tracked it down to a tree near where I'd seen it the previous year.

Eastern Wood-Pewee

An Eastern Wood-Pewee was calling at Sabine Woods on April 19 when East Texas migration was going strong. This flycatcher migrates across East Texas, with some breeding in northeast Texas.

Acadian Flycatcher

I first observed Acadian Flycatcher at Sabine Woods on April 19. It has a range similar to that of the Eastern Wood-Pewee and can be located there by its percussive "piz-za" call.

Gray Flycatcher

I first found Gray Flycatcher on March 14 in Brewster County in the Trans-Pecos, which is the only place this drab gray flycatcher is reliably found in Texas.

Dusky Flycatcher

On May 18, after a long, wearying climb in the Davis Mountains Preserve, we found our goal bird, a Dusky Flycatcher previously found by others, nesting in a scrubby area just below the peak toward which we had climbed.

Cordilleran Flycatcher

My first Cordilleran Flycatcher sighting was in Frio County south of San Antonio on January 5. Other sightings were on May 18 at the Davis Mountains Preserve and August 10 at Big Bend NP.

Black Phoebe

I first saw Black Phoebe in Alpine on January 7. I also regularly spotted it in riverside areas in the LRGV, such as at Anzalduas County Park.

Vermilion Flycatcher

I first noted Vermilion Flycatcher in Laredo on January 4. I also saw them just before sunset on March 15 at Rio Grande Village in Big Bend. At Big Bend the brilliant red and brown male and his faded-brown and white mate are usual features of the campgrounds as they sit on and flit between picnic tables and branches.

Vermilion Flycatcher

Ash-throated Flycatcher

On March 2, after seeing my first Red-billed Pigeons for the year at Salineño, I went over to Falcon State Park and saw my first Ash-throated Flycatcher for the year. Other Ash-throated Flycatchers were present on May 18 at the Davis Mountains Preserve.

Great Crested Flycatcher

I first saw a Great Crested Flycatcher on March 28 in Galveston County on the Upper Coast. Because the loud "wheep" of this eastern flycatcher was common where I grew up in Wisconsin, I was always delighted when I first heard it each spring in Texas.

Brown-crested Flycatcher

I saw and photographed a Brown-crested Flycatcher on May 2 in Kenedy County in the LRGV. This bird, similar in appearance to the Great Crested Flycatcher but with a distinctive whistle and a very different call, is a common summer resident in the LRGV.

Great Kiskadee

I first found Great Kiskadee on January 2 in the Valley, where they are very common. They are unmistakable with their bright yellow breast, rust-colored wings, and bold black-and-white faces as they fly from tree to tree and call loudly.

Couch's Kingbird

I first saw Couch's Kingbird on January 2 in the Valley, where they sometimes winter. More usually they are summer residents in the LRGV and other South Texas counties, where their "breeer" and "kip" can be heard in the trees and brush.

Cassin's Kingbird

On May 10 at Davis Mountains State Park, I saw my first Cassin's Kingbirds for the year. They are ubiquitous in summer in some portions of far west Texas.

Western Kingbird

On April 11, we went to Paradise Pond and the Leonabelle Turnbull Birding Center in Port Aransas after seeing a Masked Duck and saw our first Western

Kingbirds of the year. Western Kingbirds are found in summer in most of Texas except the northeast.

Scissor-tailed Flycatcher

On the way down to the Valley on March 5, I saw my first Scissor-tailed Flycatcher of the year in the median of the road in Brooks County just before we reached the Valley. On April 21, we found a pair of nesting Scissor-tailed Flycatchers on our drive out of Anahuac NWR. They are found across most of Texas in the summer, flashing their streaming tail feathers and salmon underparts as they fly from treetops and fence lines. They are the symbol of the Texas Ornithological Society, and I always felt they should have been the Texas state bird as well.

Scissor-tailed Flycatcher

Loggerhead Shrike

I saw my first Loggerhead Shrike in Matagorda County on the coast in the rush of new species for the year on January 1. Later, on February 8, I saw them again in the Panhandle, where they are common in winter, often onfusing the search for the rarer wintering Northern Shrike.

Black-capped Vireo

On May 2, I found my first Black-capped Vireo for the year at Balcones Canyonlands northeast of Austin, a reliable place for this rare species.

White-eyed Vireo

I first found White-eyed Vireo in Frio County south of San Antonio on January 5. Although White-eyed Vireos are often difficult to locate in their thick brushy habitats, their loud song lets you know they are present.

Bell's Vireo

On May 7, I participated in the Fort Worth Audubon Spring Count, during which our count group heard and saw my first Bell's Vireo for the year. I regularly heard and saw them in the dry brush of Big Bend NP and once found one of their nests.

Gray Vireo

On May 19, Simone and I drove to Guadalupe Mountains NP to see what we could find along the McKittrick Canyon Trail. After we ogled and photographed a rattlesnake in the road (from inside the car), we drove into the park and found a Gray Vireo singing along the road in the scrubby brush. It perched long enough for a few pictures, and then we drove on to begin our hike.

Hutton's Vireo

I first spotted Hutton's Vireo on March 15 as I hiked the Pinnacles Trail at Big Bend NP. Other sightings were on May 18 at the Davis Mountains Preserve and August 10 at Big Bend.

Yellow-throated Vireo

On March 22, we headed south to look for spring migrants at Paradise Pond in Port Aransas and found our first Yellow-throated Vireo of the year.

Although similar to Pine Warbler in appearance, the Yellow-throated Vireo is distinctive in its much brighter yellow spectacles, slow movement, and slow burry phrases.

Blue-headed Vireo

The first Blue-headed Vireo was present on January 3 at Sabal Palm Audubon Sanctuary. Blue-headed Vireos winter in the eastern two-thirds of the state and then migrate north.

Plumbeous Vireo

I first saw Plumbeous Vireo on May 14 in the Davis Mountains, where we were searching for, and not finding, Spotted Owls. I found the vireo to be very common in the Guadalupe Mountains on May 19.

Philadelphia Vireo

A Philadelphia Vireo was singing at the Willows near Sabine Woods on April 26, one of three new vireos in as many days. Philadelphia Vireos are found in Texas only during migration.

Plumbeous Vireo in the Guadalupe Mountains

Green Jay

I first saw Green Jay on January 3 on a trip to Sabal Palm Audubon Sanctuary in the Valley. One reason bird-watchers go to the LRGV is to see this stunning, noisy, green, blue, black, and yellow bird that is not regularly found anywhere else in the United States (shown on cover).

Blue Jay

I first observed Blue Jay on January 1 in Matagorda County on the coast. This crested black, blue, and white jay is the most common jay in the eastern two-thirds of Texas but is rare in South Texas.

Woodhouse's (Western) Scrub-Jay

I first saw Woodhouse's Scrub-Jay in Alpine on January 7. Scrub-Jays are common residents of the Edwards Plateau north of Big Bend.

Mexican Jay

I first heard Mexican Jays on January 24 on a walk along the lower portion of the Pinnacles Trail at Big Bend, the only area of the state where they are regularly found.

Fish Crow

On March 29, a calling Fish Crow at Sabine Woods, difficult to identify without its call, was the first of the year. Their Texas range, limited to the northeastern part of the state, is at the western edge of their national range, which extends across the southeastern United States and overlaps the range of the nearly identical American Crow.

Chihuahuan Raven

I first found Chihuahuan Raven on January 3 on a trip to Sabal Palm Audubon Sanctuary. It is found in the dry, scrubby grasslands of West Texas. If seen at close range, it can sometimes be distinguished from Common Ravens where their ranges overlap by its neck feathers with white bases. Otherwise its slightly higher croak is the best clue to its identity.

Purple Martins and Cave Swallows

I first found Purple Martins and Cave Swallows on a drive to the LRGV on January 31. Purple Martins are common in much of the eastern United States, often nesting in nest boxes. During fall migration, they gather in huge roosts of thousands of martins, one of which I accidentally found at a shopping center near our house in Fort Worth when I went on an evening walk. Cliff Swallows can be found in much of Texas in the summer and usually nest under bridges and overpasses, and in limestone caves in the south.

Carolina Chickadee

I first saw Carolina Chickadee on January 1 in Matagorda County on the coast. It is a common resident in the eastern half of Texas. North of Texas this chickadee could easily be confused with Black-capped Chickadee, but there is only one documented record of the latter species in Texas.

Mountain Chickadee

Guadalupe Mountains NP, at the Bowl at the end of the trail, was the location of my first sighting of a Mountain Chickadee on February 7. Other Mountain Chickadee sightings were on May 18 at the Davis Mountains Preserve and in the Guadalupe Mountains on August 31.

Juniper Titmouse

In mid-November (between scoter searches), I walked a couple of different trails in the Guadalupe Mountains, and finally, on November 18, a little flock of chickadees materialized, in the midst of which I heard the distinctive sounds of a Juniper Titmouse. I saw it fly past me to a dense juniper. It was the right color and size. After this brief sighting, it flew through the junipers and disappeared, not to be found again.

Tufted Titmouse

I first saw Tufted Titmouse on January 18 in Harris County on the Upper Coast. Both Tufted and Black-crested Titmice reside in Fort Worth, one of the areas where the two species overlap. The Tufted is found primarily in the eastern third of Texas north of the central coast, and the Black-crested is a common resident of much of the western two-thirds of the state, including the southern coast and the Valley.

Black-crested Titmouse

I first saw Black-crested Titmouse on January 2 in the Valley. Other Black-crested Titmouse sightings included those on May 18 at the Davis Mountains Preserve.

Verdin

Verdin was present in Laredo on January 4. This small gray bird with its pointed bill might be mistaken for a warbler except for its size, bright yellow head, and chestnut shoulder patches. It is usually found in dense thorny scrub in West and South Texas.

Bushtit

On March 14 on the way south to Big Bend NP, I added Bushtits to the year list, little nonstop birds that are often remarkably hard to find despite their large, moving flocks and incessant chatter. I found other Bushtits on May 18 at the Davis Mountains Preserve.

White-breasted Nuthatch

I first saw White-breasted Nuthatch in Alpine on January 7. Later sightings included those on March 15 as I hiked the Pinnacles Trail at Big Bend NP and on May 18 at the Davis Mountains Preserve.

Pygmy Nuthatch

On October 20, we made an early start up the trail to the Bowl in the Guadalupe Mountains, where there were Pine Siskins, Mountain Chickadees, Red-breasted and White-breasted Nuthatches, Bushtits, a very high flock of overflying Sandhill Cranes, Common Ravens, a Red-naped Sapsucker, and finally, three Pygmy Nuthatches. As with most birds that are initially hard to find, I saw them again later in the year.

Brown-headed Nuthatch

I saw many Brown-headed Nuthatches on February 26 in the Pineywoods on a TOS field trip. This nuthatch is very similar to the Pygmy Nuthatch but is found in northeastern Texas, all the way across the state from the western Pygmy Nuthatch.

Rock Wren

I first spotted Rock Wren in Alpine on January 7. I saw others on February 7 as I hiked a trail in Guadalupe Mountains NP. While Rock Wrens and Canyon Wrens both occur in West Texas, Canyon Wrens are usually found only in canyons and Rock Wrens can be found in any rocky or scrubby habitat, including canyons. Rock Wrens have a spotted, dark brown back and streaked, off-white breast.

Canyon Wren
I added Canyon Wren to my year list on February 7 as I hiked back down the mountain on a trail in Guadalupe Mountains NP. Unlike Rock Wren, Canyon Wren has a cinnamon belly contrasting with a white throat and breast, and it can easily be distinguished from the duller Rock Wren.

House Wren
I first found House Wren on January 2 in Hidalgo County in the LRGV. House Wrens winter in South Texas and migrate through the state, with a summer presence in the Panhandle and at high altitudes in West Texas.

Winter Wren
I first saw Winter Wren on January 13 in Grayson County in the Northern Plains. They winter in East Texas, migrating north in early spring. They do not go as far as Alaska, where the very similar Pacific Wren is found. In fact, Winter Wrens and Pacific Wrens were once grouped together as the same species.

Sedge Wren
I first spotted Sedge Wren on March 28 when we went to Galveston Island to search for the reported Palm Warblers. In addition to Palm Warblers, we found noisy Sedge Wrens, one of which seemed shyly interested in having its picture taken for a while, as it came closer and closer and then finally disappeared into what were probably sedges.

Marsh Wren
I saw my first Marsh Wren of the year at the Willows near Sabine Woods on February 12. As I walked the boardwalk there, my pishing sounds brought out a Marsh Wren just enough so I could see the dark cap and dark back with heavy markings.

Carolina Wren
I first saw Carolina Wren on January 1 in Matagorda County on the coast. The loud, cheerful "teakettle" song of the rusty and buff Carolina Wren is common across much of the eastern two-thirds of Texas.

Bewick's Wren
I first found Bewick's Wren on January 4 just upriver from the Salineño overlook, and again on February 7 as I hiked a trail in Guadalupe Mountains NP.

Although found in much of the state, it is common only in the western two-thirds. It is similar to the Carolina Wren but more slender, with a longer tail and all-white underparts.

Cactus Wren
I first observed Cactus Wren southwest of San Antonio on January 5. Well named, it lives in the cactus country of West Texas and nests in cactus and thorny bushes.

Blue-gray Gnatcatcher
I first saw Blue-gray Gnatcatcher on January 2 in Hidalgo County in the LRGV, where they winter. These small blue-gray, mockingbird-shaped birds breed across much of Texas.

Black-tailed Gnatcatcher
I first spotted Black-tailed Gnatcatcher on January 6 at Cottonwood Campground in Big Bend. The small Texas range of the Black-tailed Gnatcatcher overlaps that of the similar Blue-gray Gnatcatcher in far west Texas (Trans-Pecos down to the LRGV). The raspy call, white spots on the graduated tail feathers, and black cap with contrasting white eye ring of the breeding male Black-tailed Gnatcatcher help identify this species.

Western Bluebird in Fort Davis

Eastern Bluebird
I first saw Eastern Bluebird on January 1 in Matagorda County on the coast. Some Eastern Bluebirds winter in South Texas. This species migrates across the entire state and commonly breeds in the eastern half of the state and in the eastern Panhandle.

Western Bluebird
I first found Western Bluebird in Fort Davis on January 7. Both Eastern and Western Bluebirds have

a blue back and an orange breast. The male Western Bluebird's purple-blue throat and the female's brownish-gray throat allow them to be distinguished from Eastern Bluebirds, which are also found in the West Texas mountain habitat of the Western Bluebird.

Wood Thrush
The first bright reddish-brown Wood Thrush of the year was at Sabine Woods on March 29, when warblers (eight species) and our first Indigo Bunting of the year were also present.

Clay-colored Thrush
I saw my first Clay-colored Thrush on January 2 at Frontera Audubon in Hidalgo County in the LRGV, and another on February 1 at Sabal Palm Audubon Sanctuary in Brownsville. While Clay-colored Thrushes had a very limited range in South Texas when I moved there in 2000, their population has now expanded into many riparian woodlands and urban habitats in the Valley, and wandering birds have been found far north of there.

Gray Catbird
Gray Catbirds were present on January 18 at the Quintana Neotropical Bird Sanctuary. They regularly winter in coastal sanctuaries, and as spring migration begins their numbers increase and they are often one of the most common species, mewing loudly from the bushes and darting across paths. They breed in the northeastern part of the state.

Curve-billed Thrasher
I first saw a Curve-billed Thrasher southwest of San Antonio on January 5. Curve-billed Thrashers are residents of the western half of Texas, the lower coast, and the LRGV. They have a curved bill similar to that of the Crissal Thrasher, which has an overlapping range in the Trans-Pecos, but they lack the rufous undertail patch of the Crissal.

Brown Thrasher
I first found a Brown Thrasher on January 18 at the Quintana Neotropical Bird Sanctuary. Their range extends across northeastern Texas to the eastern Panhandle.

Curve-billed Thrasher in the LRGV

Long-billed Thrasher in the Valley

Long-billed Thrasher

I first saw a Long-billed Thrasher, a resident of southern and coastal Texas, on January 2 in the Valley. Their heavily streaked underparts are similar to those of Brown Thrashers and different from those of Curve-billed and Crissal Thrashers. Brown Thrashers have shorter bills than the long, curved bills of Long-billed, Curve-billed, and Crissal Thrashers.

Crissal Thrasher

On January 26, we spotted two Crissal Thrashers posing for us on brush on the way out of Monahans Sandhills State Park between Monahans and Odessa. Later sightings were on March 15 as I hiked the Pinnacles Trail at Big Bend NP, and on August 12 one was perched at Dugout Wells in Big Bend NP.

Sage Thrasher

On a drive south from Van Horn to Pecos, we got excellent views of our first Sage Thrasher of the year on January 26. On February 8, I saw them again in the Panhandle. Typically I saw them one at a time on the prairie on a winter day, a drab gray bird on a fence wire or a branch.

Northern Mockingbird

I first observed Northern Mockingbird, the Texas state bird, on January 1 in Matagorda County on the coast. Mockingbirds are vocal and omnipresent across most of Texas. In our Fort Worth yard, I heard mockingbirds imitating meadowlarks, bobwhites, and many different human-made sounds.

Phainopepla

On January 6, we saw our first Phainopepla north of Big Bend. The shiny black crested males with conspicuous white wing patches and their gray mates are found in far west Texas, primarily in the Trans-Pecos.

House Sparrow

I first saw House Sparrow on January 1 in Matagorda County on the coast. This introduced bird is found all across the Lower 48 and much of Canada, but only infrequently if at all in Alaska.

Sprague's Pipit

I saw my first Sprague's Pipit on January 22 in the Granger area

Phainopepla north of Big Bend

northeast of Austin when I went to look for Mountain Plovers. This buffy bug-eyed pipit winters in East Texas.

Lesser Goldfinch

I first found Lesser Goldfinch in Fort Davis on January 7. Although their sounds are similar to those of the American Goldfinch, Lesser Goldfinches are somewhat smaller. The males have a black rather than a yellow back, and both sexes have a white wing patch at the base of their primaries not found in American Goldfinches.

American Goldfinch

I first saw American Goldfinch on January 1 in Matagorda County on the coast. Each winter we were in Texas, American Goldfinches came regularly to our yard for Niger seed. Sometimes there were over a hundred of them clinging to feeders and fighting to get to the seed.

Chestnut-collared Longspur

I first located Chestnut-collared Longspur on January 6 in Presidio County in the Trans-Pecos. All four longspur species winter in Texas, all but Smith's Longspur being found in West Texas. In some years there are mixed flocks of longspurs just west of Fort Worth in North Texas, but usually they are farther west.

McCown's Longspur

I first observed McCown's Longspur on January 9 as we drove to Unit 18 of the Rita Blanca National Grassland in the Panhandle, and again on January 22 in the Granger area northeast of Austin when I went there to look for Mountain Plovers.

Ovenbird

I first spotted Ovenbird on January 14 under bushes at Frontera Audubon in Hidalgo County in the LRGV. During spring migration at Upper Coast hotspots, I also saw this olive warbler with its black-bordered orange crown slowly walking along the forest floor.

Worm-eating Warbler

I first found Worm-eating Warblers on April 18 at Sabine Woods on their spring migration through the state. These stripe-headed buffy warblers were usually quietly working their way through the trees, poking at dead leaves looking for food, and sometimes eating worms.

Golden-winged Warbler

Golden-winged Warbler was one of 14 migrating warbler species in and around Sabine Woods on April 28. Its neat black throat and ear patch, bright yellow crown, and large yellow wing patch give the Golden-winged Warbler a dapper appearance.

Blue-winged Warbler

Our first migrating Blue-winged Warbler was at the Leonabelle Turnbull Birding Center in Port Aransas on April 11. Blue-winged Warblers are bright yellow, with a distinct black eye line, blue-gray wings, and white wing bars.

Black-and-white Warbler

I saw my first wintering Black-and-white Warbler on January 2 at McAllen in the LRGV. There was another at the Willows near Sabine Woods on February 12. Unlike other warblers, they usually climb tree trunks and work their way out branches, sometimes uttering their thin, repetitive, squeaky songs.

Black-and-white Warbler near Sabine Woods

Prothonotary Warbler at Sabine Woods

Prothonotary Warbler

On March 30, Prothonotary Warblers were singing in Liberty yards as we drove through town. I also found them on April 19 at Sabine Woods, one of the 11 warbler species I saw that day. With their bright yellow bodies and blue-gray wings, they are generally similar to Blue-winged Warblers; however, they are larger and have no wing bars or eye line.

Swainson's Warbler

On May 1, I drove to Richland Creek WMA south of Fort Worth, where some migrating eastern warblers stop to nest. A Northern Waterthrush, Northern Parula, Nashville Warbler, and finally, a Swainson's Warbler were all singing loudly as I drove through the WMA. I had put on boots when I arrived at the WMA, thinking I'd need to splash into the wet woodlands to find the Swainson's Warbler, but there it appeared, singing loudly, easily photographed from my dry spot on the pavement.

Nashville Warbler

I first noticed Nashville Warbler on January 20 in Laredo. More usually Nashville Warblers are found during migration. They are identified by their bold white eye ring on a gray head, and by their olive-green back and yellow underparts.

Mourning Warbler

On August 25, I found a Mourning Warbler bathing in the ground-level birdbath at Sabine Woods. They are uncommon migrants in the eastern half of Texas. It is often difficult to find this olive-backed bird in the dense vegetation it prefers.

Kentucky Warbler

I first saw Kentucky Warblers on April 18 at Sabine Woods. They are unmistakable when observed on migration through Texas, with their bold yellow spectacles and underparts, black crown and face pattern, and olive back, as they walk along the damp forest floor.

Hooded Warbler

On March 22, we headed south to look for spring migrants at Paradise Pond in Port Aransas and found our first Hooded Warbler of the year. Hooded Warblers were also present at Sabine Woods on March 29, flitting through low brush and between bushes, their tails often flicking, with distinctive black hoods surrounding their yellow faces.

Hooded Warbler

Cerulean Warbler

On April 26, I counted 15 species of warbler, the new one for the year being a Cerulean Warbler at Sabine Woods. Cerulean Warblers are vulnerable, with estimates of up to 75 percent decline in the last 40 years because their eastern US habitat is threatened. They are uncommon to rare on migration in East Texas. The male is the only warbler with a bright blue back, white wing bars, and streaked white underparts. The female has a bluish crown, greenish back, and pale yellow throat.

Bay-breasted Warbler

On April 25, Bay-breasted Warblers had clearly just arrived at Sabine Woods and filled the tree branches as I stood in the heavy rain to watch them. Even with poor visibility, the bright, dark rusty crown and breast, black face, and buffy neck patches of the male Bay-breasted Warbler are unmistakable.

Blackburnian Warbler

On April 22 at Sabine Woods, we found a brilliant male Blackburnian Warbler, the only warbler I have ever mistaken for an oriole as it darted through high leafy branches, its bright orange face all that I could see in my brief glimpse.

Bay-breasted Warbler at Sabine Woods

Chestnut-sided Warbler

I first noted Chestnut-sided Warblers on April 18 at Sabine Woods along with other new warblers for the year, Worm-eating and Kentucky Warblers. The chestnut sides of the male are the most useful field mark, with identity confirmed by its bright yellow crown and black whisker and eye line.

Pine Warbler

I first found wintering Pine Warblers on January 1 at Selkirk Island on the coast. There was also one at the Willows near Sabine Woods on February 12, and I saw many of them on the February 26 field trip to the Nacogdoches area in the Pineywoods. Pine Warbler is one of the few warblers that is a common year-round East Texas resident, with breeding of this olive and yellow warbler occurring in the far northeastern part of the state.

Yellow-throated Warbler

My first Yellow-throated Warbler, on March 18 at Sabine Woods, was especially photogenic as it peered out through the willow catkins. I saw another on March 29, also at Sabine Woods. This yellow-throated black, white, and gray warbler, found only in northeastern Texas and the Pineywoods, is very similar in appearance to Grace's Warbler, which is found in West Texas, primarily in the mountains of the Trans-Pecos.

Pine Warbler at Sabine Woods

Yellow-throated Warbler at Sabine Woods

Prairie Warbler

I went to Sabine Woods on February 12, where I found a reported Prairie Warbler. In winter, this bright yellow warbler, with its yellow eye patch and eyebrow and black face pattern and side streaking, was most welcome. We saw one again at Sabine Woods on March 29. Although many migrate through the state, some also breed in northeastern Texas and a few winter along the coast and in the LRGV.

Black-throated Green Warbler

I first found Black-throated Green Warblers on January 3 on a trip to Sabal Palm Audubon Sanctuary. Other sightings were on March 22 (Paradise Pond) and March 29 (Sabine Woods). Some Black-throated Green Warblers winter in the LRGV and along the lower coast, but most sightings are during migration in the eastern half of Texas. Usually their bright yellow face and black throat distinguish them from other warblers in their range, except in the Hill Country, where Golden-cheeked Warblers with these same features are found. The eye line of the Golden-cheeked Warbler and the male's black back help separate them.

Black-throated Green Warbler at Sabine Woods

Canada Warbler

Although it often seemed as if migrating Canada Warblers were more difficult to find in spring, we found our first one on April 11 at the Leonabelle Turnbull Birding Center in Port Aransas. Canada Warblers migrate through the eastern half of Texas. No other warbler has the necklace (black in males, gray yellow in females) of a Canada Warbler. Both sexes are dark blue gray above, without wing bars, and have a bold white eye ring.

Louisiana Waterthrush

Louisiana Waterthrush was present on February 11 at the Jesse H. Jones Park & Nature Center, moving about in flooded brush. As spring migration ramped up, I also found them at Paradise Pond in Port Aransas on March 22, sometimes in the presence of a very similar Northern Waterthrush.

Northern Parula

On March 18, when I went to Boy Scout Woods at High Island to look for early migrants, I saw my first Northern Parula of the year. Others appeared at Paradise Pond in Port Aransas (March 22) and Sabine Woods (March 29). Northern Parula is a migrant through Texas, but some breed in East Texas and a few winter in the LRGV.

Tropical Parula

I went to Frontera Audubon on February 18, where in addition to the rare (but already on my year list) Crimson-collared Grosbeak and Elegant Trogon still present, I saw my first Tropical Parula of the year. Tropical Parula, a rare to uncommon resident of the LRGV and coastal areas just north of the Valley, is very similar to Northern Parula, with a blue-gray back, yellow throat and breast, and white wing bars, but it lacks the broken white eye ring of the latter.

Yellow-breasted Chat

Yellow-breasted Chat was my 400th species for my Texas big year, first found on April 11 in Nueces County in the Coastal Bend. These chats are closer to the size of towhees than to the smaller size of most warbler species. Their white spectacles, dark lores, and bright yellow undersides are also distinctive.

Golden-cheeked Warbler

Golden-cheeked Warbler

Golden-cheeked Warblers are found only in Mexico and Texas and in no other part of the United States. Simone and I began the official warbler season by going over to Meridian State Park on April 9, where the expected Golden-cheeked Warblers were singing noisily, though they were somewhat difficult to spot.

Colima Warbler

Before dawn on May 11 after some hours on the Pinnacles Trail at Big Bend NP, I heard and saw Colima Warblers at the somewhat higher elevations and at Boot Springs. They are listed as threatened. They breed only in the Chisos Mountains of Big Bend NP and in Mexico. They are mostly brownish green (back) and gray (underneath and face), with a white eye ring. The brightest color is a bright yellow rump and vent, and there is a small splash of rusty color on top of the head that may be difficult to see.

Lucy's Warbler

On May 10, I went to Cottonwood Campground in Big Bend NP to look for Lucy's Warbler, which in Texas is usually found only right next to the Rio Grande at the west end of the park. The bird was fairly easy to find, singing in a small bush to the left of the gate as I entered the campground, but it vanished shortly thereafter.

Virginia's Warbler

Although my goal at Cottonwood Campground in Big Bend on March 16 was the tiny grayish, yellowish- or rust-rumped Lucy's Warbler, I found a larger yellow-vented, yellow-breasted Virginia's Warbler with a bold white eye ring, the first of the year. Virginia's Warbler is an uncommon to rare migrant and summer resident in West Texas, breeding at upper elevations of the Davis and Guadalupe Mountains.

Grace's Warbler

My first Grace's Warbler of the year was present on May 14 in the Davis Mountains. I saw others in the Guadalupe Mountains on August 31. The high elevations of these two mountain areas are the only locations where Grace's Warblers nest in Texas.

White-collared Seedeater

We first tried to find seedeaters on January 4 in Laredo, where they had been reported, but we were unsuccessful. We were pulled back to Laredo on January 20 by more reports of seedeaters and Blue Buntings. We finally saw a White-collared Seedeater. These tiny birds are uncommon to rare residents along the Rio Grande north of the Valley. Males are black and off-white, while females are brown and buffy, the only noteworthy feature of the female being the thick, curved bill.

Olive Sparrow

I first found Olive Sparrow in Texas on January 3 on a trip to Sabal Palm Audubon Sanctuary. I saw another while looking for (but not finding) a reported Flame-colored Tanager in the Valley in Hidalgo County on March 1. Olive Sparrows are common in many South Texas brush areas.

Olive Sparrow in South Texas

Green-tailed Towhee

I first saw Green-tailed Towhee in Texas on January 6 at Sam Nail Ranch in Big Bend just as the sun went down. The Green-tailed Towhee is a West Texas migrant and winter resident, being found only infrequently during the summer in the Davis and Guadalupe Mountains.

Eastern Towhee

On February 12, I went to Sabine Woods to look for a reported Eastern Towhee. After seeing a Barn Owl leave one of the trees on the west side of the main wooded area, I wandered the trails making little pishing sounds, and as I had hoped, the reported bird that had lured me to Sabine Woods popped up to be added to my count.

Rufous-crowned Sparrow

On January 24, we walked the lower portion of the Pinnacles Trail at Big Bend, where we saw our first Rufous-crowned Sparrows. Other Rufous-crowned Sparrows were present on February 7 as I hiked a trail in Guadalupe Mountains NP. This species is found on dry, rocky slopes in West Texas.

Canyon Towhee

I first found Canyon Towhee in Alpine on January 7. I saw others on February 7 as I hiked a trail in Guadalupe Mountains NP and on March 15 as I hiked the Pinnacles Trail at Big Bend NP. Canyon Towhees, with their reddish crowns, pale gray-brown backs, and white belly patch, are year-round residents of West Texas from the Trans-Pecos north to the Panhandle.

Botteri's Sparrow

I found Botteri's Sparrows after a bit of intensive looking in Cameron County in the LRGV on May 2. The secretive, drab Botteri's Sparrow is very similar to Cassin's Sparrow, both of which are found in the LRGV and along the southern coast of Texas. Learning what it sounds like is the best way to find and identify it.

Cassin's Sparrow

I first spotted Cassin's Sparrow on January 7 on a drive from the Davis Mountains to Balmorhea Lake in West Texas. The Texas range of the Cassin's Sparrow extends from the LRGV to the Panhandle and west to the state line. To find it, it is best to know the song and watch for its singing display flights, when the white tips on the rounded tail are visible.

Bachman's Sparrow

I first saw Bachman's Sparrow on a TOS Pineywoods field trip on February 27 as it sang in the Nacogdoches area. It resides in grassy open pine and oak forests. This is another sparrow best found by listening for its single whistle followed by a trill.

Clay-colored Sparrow

I found Clay-colored Sparrow on January 6 at Cottonwood Campground at Big Bend. Clay-colored Sparrows winter in South Texas and migrated through our Fort Worth yard in spring each year, usually staying for a few days. We called them our "little buzzers" as they sang nonstop from the bushes and trees.

Brewer's Sparrow

On January 6, we saw our first Brewer's Sparrows when we were looking for Baird's Sparrows southwest of San Antonio and north of Big Bend. Brewer's

Sparrows winter in the Trans-Pecos and migrate through West Texas. They are quite similar to Clay-colored Sparrows but have a different song and head pattern.

Field Sparrow

I first saw Field Sparrow on January 10 in the northeastern Panhandle. They winter across much of Texas and have multiple isolated breeding populations in the state. Their whistled song gradually speeds up to a trill.

Black-chinned Sparrow

On May 13, I made a quick trip to Boy Scout Ranch Road off US 17 north of Fort Davis. The water holes and relatively lush vegetation along the road generally make it a hotspot for whatever is passing through. This time, the highlight was a singing Black-chinned Sparrow, partway up a mountain about halfway down the road. They were also present in the Guadalupe Mountains on August 31.

Vesper Sparrow

On January 6, we saw our first Vesper Sparrows when we were looking for Baird's Sparrows southwest of San Antonio and north of Big Bend. Vesper Sparrows, migrants and winter residents in Texas, can be identified by their white outer tail feathers, white eye ring, and dark ear patch outlined below by white.

Lark Sparrow

I first found Lark Sparrow on January 5 in Frio County south of San Antonio. Lark Sparrow is not just a "little brown job." Although it does have a typical sparrow-like brown and black back, its head has a bright rust and white pattern, and it has a black spot on its whitish breast. It also has large white corners on its dark tail. It migrates across and breeds in much of the state.

Black-throated Sparrow

On January 24 on the way into Big Bend NP, we saw our first Black-throated Sparrows. This species, which breeds in much of South and southwest Texas, is another easily identified sparrow, with a large black throat and breast patch, black ear patches, contrasting eyebrows, white moustache, and white belly.

Black-throated Sparrow

Sagebrush Sparrow

I first located Sagebrush Sparrow on January 7 in Brewster County in the Trans-Pecos. Most Sagebrush Sparrows (classified as Sage Sparrow when I did my big year), appear in far west Texas as migrants, but some breed there locally.

Lark Bunting

I first found Lark Buntings on January 6 in Presidio County in West Texas in the area where I saw my only Baird's Sparrow of the year. They were also quite numerous at Big Bend NP in early August. During breeding season the black male with white wing patches is unmistakable.

Grasshopper Sparrow

I first observed Grasshopper Sparrow at Attwater Prairie Chicken NWR on April 2. They breed in much of the state and winter in South Texas but are often difficult to find. They can be identified by their buffy unstreaked underparts, white central crown stripe, and buzzy songs.

Le Conte's Sparrow

On February 13, just after seeing Smith's Longspurs at Eagle Fest east of Dallas, we also had great views of a Le Conte's Sparrow on the ground. It nearly hit me as it flew in and landed almost at my feet.

Nelson's Sparrow

On April 17, we birded around Bolivar Flats, adding Nelson's Sparrow (known then as Nelson's Sharp-tailed Sparrow) before heading to High Island for some serious warblering. Unless they are well seen, the similar Nelson's and Le Conte's Sparrows are often difficult to identify in the field. The latter species has a white central crown stripe (not gray), chestnut streaks on the nape (not a streakless nape), and straw-colored back streaks (not white or gray).

Seaside Sparrow

On January 18, we saw many Seaside Sparrows at Anahuac NWR on the Upper Coast, their dark, big-billed forms popping up and down out in the marshes.

Harris's Sparrow

I first saw Harris's Sparrow on January 10 in the northeastern Panhandle. Harris's Sparrow is a large, handsome sparrow with a bold black crown, throat, and breast. It is a common wintering bird in many areas of North Texas east of the eastern Panhandle, and it is the icon of the Fort Worth Audubon Society.

Harris's Sparrow

Hepatic Tanager

I discovered my first Hepatic Tanager of the year on May 14 in the Davis Mountains, where we were searching for Spotted Owls. Other Hepatic Tanager sightings were on May 18 at the Davis Mountains Preserve and in the Guadalupe Mountains on August 31. Although the bright red adult male might be mistaken for a male Summer Tanager, the Hepatic Tanager male has a dark gray rather than a yellow bill, a grayish cheek patch, and grayish red on its body. The females of both species are usually a very similar yellow green but do differ in bill color.

Summer Tanager

I first spotted Summer Tanager on January 2 at Frontera Audubon in the LRGV. The range of Summer Tanagers overlaps with that of Hepatic Tanagers in the Trans-Pecos but extends beyond that across much of the state.

Scarlet Tanager

On April 17, the newly arrived migrants at Boy Scout Woods (High Island) included a spectacular male Scarlet Tanager. In some years the number of brilliant red migrating Scarlet Tanagers decorating the trees along the coast is unbelievable to those who have not seen it.

Northern Cardinal

I first saw Northern Cardinal on January 1 in Matagorda County on the coast. Northern Cardinals are common across almost all of the state. In winter in our Fort Worth yard, the numbers increased dramatically, with up to six bright red males and six buffy and red females coming to our feeders at sunset when they were most active.

Scarlet Tanager at Sabine Woods

Pyrrhuloxia in South Texas

Pyrrhuloxia

I first found Pyrrhuloxia in Frio County south of San Antonio on January 5. They are found in the southwestern half of Texas, where their range overlaps that of Northern Cardinal. Until you become familiar with them, it is possible to confuse the female Northern Cardinal with the grayer Pyrrhuloxia.

Blue Grosbeak

On April 18, my friend Lena and I drove from Winnie to my favorite East Texas warbler area, Sabine Woods. Essentially all the warblers and other spring migrants that we'd seen elsewhere were also at Sabine Woods, plus the first Blue Grosbeaks. Blue Grosbeaks can be found across most of Texas in the summer, often singing loudly from the tops of bushes and fences.

Blue Grosbeak at Sabine Woods

Lazuli Bunting

On August 20, when I came back down after a very rainy, scary day up in the Davis Mountains, I heard that other birders who had not climbed the mountains that day had found Lazuli Buntings behind the building at the preserve. I obtained permission to stay a bit longer and wandered around before it got dark. In the tall seeded grasses were many birds, primarily Lesser Goldfinches and Painted Buntings. As I was about to give up, I saw a bird periodically popping up above the grasses before it dove back out of sight. It was a Lazuli Bunting, probably a young male (or maybe a female), with a blue rump, orangey breast, brownish back, and whitish wing bars.

Indigo Bunting

I first noticed a young male Indigo Bunting at Sabine Woods on March 29 in the company of eight warbler species (Common Yellowthroat, Northern Parula, and Yellow-throated, Yellow-rumped, Hooded, Prairie, Black-and-White, and Black-throated Green Warblers). During spring migration on the coast, the small, all-blue, Indigo Bunting male could sometimes be found in the same bush as the larger, mostly blue, Blue Grosbeak male with his rust-colored wing bars, and the multicolored Painted Bunting male.

Varied Bunting

Midmorning on May 12, there was a dark purple-blue male Varied Bunting singing from a bush at the Sam Nail Ranch at Big Bend NP. On August 11, there was a family of Varied Buntings visiting the meager windmill water drip at the same site.

Painted Bunting

Painted Bunting showed up on April 19 at Sabine Woods. On August 8 at Big Bend NP, young and adult Painted Buntings were drinking thirstily from a roadside puddle. In the birding world, there are very few little birds as spectacularly flashy as the male Painted Bunting, with his purple-blue head, yellow-green back, and red breast, rump, and eye ring. It is sometimes difficult to remember to also appreciate the beauty of the bright green and yellow-green female.

Painted Bunting at Sabine Woods

Dickcissel
On April 22, we explored the jetty out of Sabine Pass and found our first Dickcissel of the year. The Dickcissel was named for its song, which sounds like a hidden insect calling from a weedy field rather than a bird. In spite of his bold black bib, white and yellow belly, and chestnut wing patch, the male Dickcissel is often difficult to see even when he perches on top of a weed and sings.

Bobolink
When we were at Sabine Woods on April 19, we heard that there were Bobolinks down the road between Sabine Woods and the Willows. We hastened down there, and near the sign to Sea Rim State Park next to the road were a couple of breeding-plumage male Bobolinks pausing on their migration through the state.

Eastern Meadowlark
On January 6, we were looking for Baird's Sparrows southwest of San Antonio and north of Big Bend when we heard, and then saw, Eastern Meadowlarks (Lilian's) along with silhouetted sparrows on the fence wires.

Dickcissel at Sabine Pass

Both Eastern and Western Meadowlarks winter in Fort Worth and are not singing then, requiring birders interested in identifying them to learn the detailed plumage differences and/or different calls of the two species when they fly. When they start singing in spring, the simpler whistled song of the Eastern Meadowlark can be distinguished from the more melodic burble of the Western Meadowlark.

Yellow-headed Blackbird

We found two Yellow-headed Blackbirds on January 9 as we headed to Canadian on the eastern side of the Panhandle. I saw more on April 22 at Sabine Pass, a bit east of their usual migration route, which is in the western half of the state. There are small breeding colonies in the Panhandle.

Common Grackle

I first saw Common Grackle on January 1 in Matagorda County on the coast. I learned soon after moving to Texas that all three grackle species can be found along some coastal areas, such as north of Rockport, allowing birders to hone their skills in grackle identification. Common Grackle is less common than Great-tailed Grackle in much of the state and is not generally found in the far west.

Boat-tailed Grackle

On February 12, I went to the Willows, a forest of willows where there used to be a boardwalk along the road between Sabine Woods near where TX 87 ends. I knew that at least one Boat-tailed Grackle could usually be found there, and one was present. Their usual range is limited to coastal prairies, especially the Upper Coast, within 30 miles of the Gulf of Mexico.

Great-tailed Grackle

Great-tailed Grackle, a bird found across much of the state and very common in North and East Texas (obnoxiously so in the view of many people), was the seventh bird for my Texas big year on January 1, observed in Matagorda County on the coast.

Bronzed Cowbird

I first saw Bronzed Cowbird on January 1 in Matagorda County. Bronzed Cowbirds, with their bright red eyes, can be found in summer in much of the southern and southwestern part of the state but have a more limited South Texas range in winter.

Orchard Oriole

On April 11, we headed to Paradise Pond and the Leonabelle Turnbull Birding Center in Port Aransas after finally seeing a Masked Duck. Orchard Orioles had arrived, as had Western Kingbirds, Tennessee, Blue-winged, and Canada Warblers, Yellow-breasted Chat, and Northern Waterthrushes. Orchard Orioles, our only oriole species in which the male is chestnut and black and not orange or yellow and black, is a summer resident in the northeastern two-thirds of the state.

Hooded Oriole

I first observed Hooded Oriole on January 4 just upriver from the Salineño overlook along the Rio Grande, where they breed. Male Hooded Orioles have a black throat patch, black wings with white wing bars, and a yellow to orange body.

Altamira Oriole

I first found Altamira Oriole on January 3 on a trip to Sabal Palm Audubon Sanctuary. Its range in the United States is limited to the LRGV and northward along the river to northern Zapata County. It can be distinguished from the other orange orioles in South Texas by its larger size (about two inches longer), thicker-based bill, thin black throat patch, and the adult's orange shoulder patch.

Audubon's Oriole

I first saw Audubon's Oriole on January 4 near the Salineño overlook. This black-headed yellow oriole is found in South Texas Brush Country.

Baltimore Oriole

I first spotted Baltimore Oriole on April 18 at Sabine Woods. Baltimore Orioles migrate through the eastern half of the state. Some of them stop in North Texas or the eastern Panhandle to breed.

Scott's Oriole

On May 10 in the Chisos Basin area of Big Bend NP, a lovely male Scott's Oriole posed for me atop a yucca plant. Scott's Oriole males are yellow with a black head, back, throat, and breast. They breed in the Trans-Pecos east to the center of the state.

Altamira Oriole in the LRGV

Seen Only in Alaska

The species in this section are not Texas birds and I did not find them in Texas during my Texas big year. There are very few or no records of them in Texas. I saw them in Alaska in my Alaska big year. They may be common in Alaska, or at least they are not classified as rare there, although some have limited ranges, may be difficult to find, or may be likely in only a few months of the year.

Emperor Goose

On January 1 when I was on Kodiak Island, I found that Emperor Geese were common wintering birds there. I also saw small fly-by flocks at Gambell in spring and fall. Because their winter range is mainly in the remote Aleutian Islands, an Emperor Goose in Anchorage in early 2017 drew birders from all over the state.

Emperor Goose

Brant

I saw fly-by Brant during sea watches at Gambell on May 29, and they were present at Utqiagvik and St. Paul in summer and fall. Brant are small, dark geese with black bellies (the form found in Alaska) that winter on the Aleutian Islands and breed on northern and northwestern coastal areas and islands.

Steller's Eider

On January 1 at Pasagshak Bay (Kodiak Island), I saw the first Steller's Eiders of the year. I also found them at Homer, Gambell, and Utqiagvik. Steller's Eiders have white heads with small greenish ear tufts and a black throat and eye patch. Most Steller's Eiders breed in Siberia, with only small populations in coastal Western and Northern Alaska. They winter in the Aleutian Islands and to a lesser extent in South-Central Alaska.

Spectacled Eider

On June 4, there was a single Spectacled Eider male on Council Road in Nome in a shallow pond. Multiple Spectacled Eiders were present in early July in Utqiagvik, and I saw one there in early November.

Common Eider

Beginning on May 16, I observed nearly 200 Common Eiders each day in mid-May on Adak, with smaller numbers each day at Gambell and Nome in

Steller's Eiders at Kodiak Island

spring, and increasing numbers in Utqiagvik in October and November. This species is common in summer but declining in many coastal areas. In winter it is found in the Bering Sea and various bays and inlets. It can be distinguished from other eiders by its sloping forehead and feathers extending out on the bill to the nostrils, and by the male's black crown and forehead.

Harlequin Duck

The first Harlequin Ducks were on Kodiak on January 1. Wintering Harlequin Ducks were present at Ketchikan, Hoonah, Homer, Seward, and Sitka. In spring I saw them at Adak, St. Paul, Gambell, and Nome, with similar observations in the fall. Harlequin Ducks are small sea and river ducks. The male is dark gray with white face and neck patches and a cinnamon side. The female and young male are dark brown with white spots on the side of the head and near the bill.

Barrow's Goldeneye

On January 1 there were both Barrow's and Common Goldeneyes in the various small bays on Kodiak Island. Later sightings include locations in Southeastern Alaska, Adak, St. Paul, and Anchorage. In South-Central Alaska in summer and the Aleutian Islands in winter where the two goldeneye species overlap, Barrow's Goldeneye may be distinguished by its more oval face and steep forehead. The male has a white crescent on each side of its otherwise dark face, compared to the white spot of the Common Goldeneye.

Barrow's Goldeneye at Seward

Common Goldeneye females in Anchorage

Ruffed Grouse

On April 26, at least five displaying male Ruffed Grouse could be heard (but not seen) near Bolio Lake south of Delta Junction, spaced out along both sides of the road. In Hyder (June 10 to 13) we not only heard, but also saw, a Ruffed Grouse while it was drumming, and we saw another one fly into a tree and perch.

Spruce Grouse

On January 11, we tried for a bird that Aaron Bowman had noticed recently off Campbell Airstrip Road in Anchorage—a Spruce Grouse male apparently on territory. After walking the very icy, hilly trail, Aaron, his son, Louann Feldman, and I finally got to where he had previously found the grouse. It was totally quiet, with the only birds being Common Ravens high in the sky heading to their nighttime resting spots. We walked around a trail intersection but found nothing. While we were standing at the intersection, I suddenly noticed a Spruce Grouse strolling down the trail toward us. The grouse got within a couple of feet, circled around, pecked at my walking stick that was lying on the ground, and repeatedly approached us, clucking all the while. After we had taken many pictures, we decided to leave, at which point the grouse started attacking Louann's legs as she led us up the trail. After we had gone about 15 feet, we were out of the grouse's territory, and he just watched us leave. We saw others south of Kenai and at the Sockeye Burn north of Anchorage.

Ruffed Grouse in Hyder

Spruce Grouse in Anchorage

Sharp-tailed Grouse near Delta Junction

Sooty Grouse

On April 30, as we stood in the rain near a bog north of Juneau, we heard the very low hoots of a distant Sooty Grouse. Others were heard (but not seen) until mid-June in Gustavus, Hyder, and Ketchikan. I understand that if you take a tram to high elevations above Juneau in summer, you can see Sooty Grouse chicks and their mothers, but I have not yet done so.

Sharp-tailed Grouse

On April 25 on Barley Way (southeast of Delta Junction), there were three Sharp-tailed Grouse near the road. The next day I went to a lek just south of Delta Junction and found six of them still on the lek, four of which would periodically engage in little cockfights and then relax between bouts. One of them did a little pirouette and then started pecking at the ground. On June 22, when I stopped on Barley Way, a single female came out of the brush and clucked her way around my car.

Willow Ptarmigan

On February 16, Louann Feldmann and I climbed in the mountainous area at the end of Arctic Valley Road in Anchorage. At the top of the mountain slope ahead of us was a narrow sunny area, where she spotted the first Willow Ptarmigan, the state bird of Alaska. As we scanned the area, we could see at least 40 ptarmigan walking around on the snow and sitting in the willows.

Willow Ptarmigan in Nome

As we approached, the ptarmigan moved away from us, never allowing us to come too close. Whenever any of them flew, we could see they had black on their tails and were not the rarer White-tailed Ptarmigan.

Rock Ptarmigan
On May 15 on Adak as our two trucks caravanned along the mostly dirt roads, we scared up some Rock Ptarmigans. They were a daily sighting for the next four days, and I also found them in early June in Nome.

White-tailed Ptarmigan
As promised by owner Bob Bird, Vino, a Brittany spaniel, was the "star of the show." After staying overnight in a campground near Summit Lake (between Anchorage and Kenai), we met Bob about 6:30 a.m. on August 27 to begin a hike. While we worked our way up the gentle 2.5-mile climb, Vino bounded across the hills along the trail. Near where we had been told we would likely find White-tailed Ptarmigan, Vino went on point and held it until we got closer. When he was verbally released he bounded toward the White-tailed Ptarmigan, which flushed as Vino approached. We saw about seven birds,

Red-necked Grebe in Anchorage

much grayer than Willow Ptarmigan at this time of year, with white outer tail feathers visible in flight.

Red-necked Grebe
I saw my first Red-necked Grebe on January 1 on Kodiak Island. They breed in Anchorage and I regularly found them there between April 9 and August 16 (e.g., at Westchester Lagoon), and I also saw them in Ketchikan, Juneau, Homer, Nome, and St. Paul (September 19).

Black Swift
I spotted three to four high-flying Black Swifts on June 10, 12, and 14 in Hyder, the only likely place to see them in Alaska.

Vaux's Swift
On April 30 over the river at Brotherhood Bridge in Juneau, two twittering gray-brown Vaux's Swifts were arcing high and back down. I tried to follow them with my camera, but they moved too fast and then disappeared

completely. I saw others in Ketchikan (early May and June) and Hyder (early June).

Note: although I am still convinced that one of the swifts I saw in San Antonio on October 11 was a Vaux's Swift, the Texas Bird Records Committee did not accept it, and it is therefore not on my big year list or my life list for Texas.

Black Oystercatcher

On January 2 at the Trident Basin floatplane facility in Kodiak, there was a flock of 17 Black Oystercatchers. I observed others later at Sitka and Adak, and on the ferry trip from Homer to Dutch Harbor.

Pacific Golden-Plover

I saw my first Pacific Golden-Plover on May 12 at Mud Bay in Homer. I observed others at Adak and Nome in spring and St. Paul and Gambell (spring and fall). Although Pacific Golden-Plover is very similar to American Golden-Plover, with which it overlaps in Alaska, Pacific Golden-Plover has more white along the side of the male, a thicker bill, and longer legs.

Black Oystercatcher seen from ferry on trip to Dutch Harbor

Bristle-thighed Curlew

I saw Bristle-thighed Curlews on June 3 at their well-known breeding area in Nome (Coffee Dome on Kougarok Road). After seeing one Whimbrel, we heard and then saw in flight and on the ground multiple Bristle-thighed Curlews, similar to but distinct in call and appearance from the Whimbrel.

Bar-tailed Godwit

On May 16, we found Bar-tailed Godwits at Clam Lagoon on Adak Island, with sightings there of 12–25 godwits each subsequent day of our trip. There was also one on St. Paul a few days later. Bar-tailed Godwits are found primarily in summer in far western Alaska.

Black Turnstone

I first saw Black Turnstones on January 1 on Kodiak Island. Others were present in Ketchikan and Nome in spring, in Anchorage in July, and in Sitka and Kodiak in November. This black-and-white shorebird can be found on migration and in summer in South-Central, Western, and Southwestern Alaska.

Bar-tailed Godwits on Adak Island

Surfbird

I found Surfbirds on January 1 on Kodiak Island. I saw others in Ketchikan and Homer in May, in Nome in June, and on Kodiak Island in November. While they are dark gray and white in winter, in breeding plumage their backs are black, white, and rusty colored.

Sharp-tailed Sandpiper

I saw a Sharp-tailed Sandpiper on September 3 at Gambell. It was difficult to find because it stayed in the vegetation in the corner of the marsh. I also saw them most days on St. Paul Island between September 14 and 25. Sharp-tailed Sandpipers, similar in size and markings to Pectoral Sandpipers but without the prominent breast streaking, migrate through Western Alaska, where they are much more commonly present in fall than in spring.

Red-necked Stint

I saw a single Red-necked Stint at Gambell on May 29, and another on June 4 at Nome. Red-necked Stints are rare migrants in Northern, Southwestern, and Western Alaska and sometimes breed there. The rufous color on a breeding Red-necked Stint's neck and upper breast can be pale or very bright.

Rock Sandpiper

I first noticed Rock Sandpipers on January 1 on Kodiak Island. Others were present in Homer during the winter, in Juneau, Adak, and St. Paul in the spring, and in Gambell and St. Paul in September. Breeding Rock Sandpipers, with their distinctive black lower breast patches, are common along the coast

Sharp-tailed Sandpiper on St. Paul Island

in Western and Southwestern Alaska. The feathers on their crowns and back are black with chestnut edges.

Common Snipe

Although very unlikely in the rest of Alaska, Common Snipe are regular enough on Western Alaskan islands such as Adak that they are not deemed rare in Alaska. There were two to four Common Snipe at Contractors' Marsh on Adak on May 16 and for the next three days, and one more was present on May 23 on St. Paul Island.

Gray-tailed Tattler

On August 31, I went with Wilderness Birding Adventures to Gambell. We arrived in early afternoon and started loading our luggage on the cart, but when we heard that a rare bird had recently been located, we changed plans, unloaded the cart, and were transported to Troutman Lake near the airport, where a Gray-tailed Tattler was casually wandering along the pebbly shoreline. I saw another one on September 16 on St. Paul Island.

Wandering Tattler

On May 12, I found nine Wandering Tattlers just beyond a large dock at the end of Freight Dock Road in Homer. I saw others at Adak and Nome (spring), and St. Paul (spring and fall).

Wandering Tattler at Homer

Wood Sandpiper

I first observed a Wood Sandpiper on St. Paul on May 22 and each of the next three days, with another single sighting at Gambell on May 29. Wood Sandpipers, although not common, are regularly found during migration in Western and Southwestern Alaska. They are rare enough that I always found it necessary to consult a field guide to be sure which uncommon medium-sized shorebird I was seeing.

Common Murre

I observed Common Murres on the water on January 1 along Kalsin Bay on Kodiak Island. Although there had been a big die-off the previous winter, I still saw them quite commonly during the year in Southeastern Alaska, Homer, Adak, St. Paul, and Gambell and on the ferry trip between Homer and Dutch Harbor in late June.

Thick-billed Murre

I first observed Thick-billed Murres on St. Paul on May 23 and also found them at Gambell in late May and early September, and in late June on the ferry trip from Homer to Dutch Harbor. They are very similar to Common Murres and nest on the same cliffs on St. Paul Island, but they can be

Thick-billed Murres on St. Paul Island

Black Guillemot at Utqiagvik

distinguished by the Thick-billed Murre's darker black upper parts (not sooty gray brown), black throat into which a white point extends from the breast (not a rounded white area), and usually a white line on the bottom of the upper mandible.

Black Guillemot
I spotted 15 Black Guillemots on the Gambell sea watch on May 28, with similar numbers most days at the same location during the rest of my spring trip and on November 29, plus two birds sitting on rocks at the edge of a gravel parking area at Utqiagvik on July 8. Where the ranges of Black and Pigeon Guillemot overlap in Western and Northern Alaska, they can be distinguished in all plumages by the color of the underwings, which is mostly white in the Black Guillemot and dusky gray in the Pigeon Guillemot.

Pigeon Guillemot
On January 2 at the Trident Basin floatplane facility in Kodiak, I saw my first Pigeon Guillemot. I saw others at Homer, Ketchikan, and Seward in winter, at Adak, St. Paul, and Gambell in spring, on the ferry trip between Homer and Dutch Harbor in late June, and at Gambell in early September.

Marbled Murrelet

Marbled Murrelets were numerous on January 6 in Ketchikan, mostly flying swiftly low over the water. Other sightings were at Homer and Adak, and on the ferry trip between Homer and Dutch Harbor.

Kittlitz's Murrelet

Four Kittlitz's Murrelets were present with Marbled Murrelets on Adak on May 16. I saw a couple of Kittlitz's Murrelets each of two other days there, and in early July I found them on the ferry trip from Homer to Dutch Harbor.

Ancient Murrelet

I spotted a single Ancient Murrelet from Adak on May 16. I observed 25 to 50 each subsequent day on Adak. I saw a couple in late May (St. Paul), about 30 near Dutch Harbor in early July, and a couple in Gambell in early September. The white streaks on the black head and nape of the Ancient Murrelet are thought by some to give it an "ancient" look.

Cassin's Auklet

On June 30, just after we left Kodiak on the ferry trip from Homer to Dutch Harbor, we saw at least three gray Cassin's Auklets flying away from the boat. Six others were present on July 2 near Dutch Harbor.

Parakeet Auklet

Nesting Parakeet Auklets were present on St. Paul on May 23–25, with other Parakeet Auklets seen at Gambell May 28–29 and September 4–5, and on the ferry from Homer to Dutch Harbor on June 30. The black Parakeet Auklet's large orange-red bill superficially resembles that of some parakeets.

Least Auklet

Least Auklets were nesting on May 23–25 on St. Paul, with others present in spring in Gambell and near Dutch Harbor, and in September in Gambell. The adjective "cute" is particularly apt in describing the tiny (just over six inches), plump Least Auklets hopping from rock to rock on St. Paul Island, sometimes only a few feet away from us.

Whiskered Auklet

Although we saw our first distant Whiskered Auklets from the ferry on July 1 as we approached Dutch Harbor, it wasn't until the charter boat trip out of Dutch Harbor the next day that we saw multitudes of them, conservatively estimated at 5,000. The Whiskered Auklet has three white facial plumes: one extends downward from the base of its red and yellow bill, one extends backward from its eye, and the third extends from its bill upward over its head. A slender black crest curls forward over its bill.

Crested Auklet

On January 1 on a rough side road along Kalsin Bay (Kodiak Island), we saw a few Crested Auklets fly by. Others were present on St. Paul Island, at Gambell, and on the ferry trip from Homer to Dutch Harbor in late June. Like the Whiskered Auklet, the Crested Auklet has a black crest curving forward over its beak, and in breeding plumage there is a single white plume behind its eye. It is larger than the Whiskered Auklet and has a sooty rather than a pale belly.

Horned Puffin

Rhinoceros Auklet

On May 13 and 14, there was a single Rhinoceros Auklet at Anchor Point (between Kenai and Homer). At the end of June I observed two from the ferry between Homer and Dutch Harbor. Rhinoceros Auklets are large, mostly blackish-brown birds with heavy yellow bills. They have two white facial plumes and a pale yellow horn at the base of the bill in breeding plumage.

Horned Puffin

I first saw Horned Puffins on May 23 on St. Paul, with other spring sightings at Gambell and Dutch Harbor, and September sightings at St. Paul and Gambell. The breeding adults of both puffin species have orange and yellow bills and white faces surrounded by black. Black underparts and creamy tufts extending off the back of the head distinguish Tufted Puffins from Horned Puffins, which are white underneath. They also have a tiny "horn" protruding upward from their eyes.

Tufted Puffin

I spotted distant Tufted Puffins on May 17 from Adak. Nesting puffins were present in late May and early June on St. Paul and Gambell, with other sightings in late June on the ferry from Homer to Dutch Harbor, and in September on St. Paul and Gambell.

Red-legged Kittiwake

I first observed nesting Red-legged Kittiwakes on St. Paul Island on May 22 and then each day of the spring trip, with more sightings there in September. The bright red legs of these small gulls are especially noticeable on birds sitting on the cliffs of St. Paul but are visible even when the kittiwakes are resting on sandbars and when they are flying.

Ross's Gull

Ross's Gulls are usually present only in early October, migrating generally eastward off the north coast. On October 8, after I had been in Utqiagvik for a couple of days, I finally saw the first Ross's Gull at about 2:00 p.m., and a couple of small flocks after that for a total of about 15. The next day, we birded from dawn until just after 2:00 p.m., when the first Ross's Gulls appeared. Even then there were only a few small groups of Ross's Gulls (total of about 35), mostly quite

Red-legged Kittiwake on St. Paul Island

a distance offshore. Other years when I went to Utqiagvik in early October, there were many more Ross's Gulls each day, sometimes over 1,000.

Slaty-backed Gull

A single Slaty-backed Gull was present on St. Paul on May 22 and 23 and was periodically seen there from September 17 to 22. I also saw them on May 31 and September 2 in Gambell, and on October 9 in Utqiagvik.

Glaucous-winged Gull

I saw my first Glaucous-winged Gulls of the year on January 1 in various small bays off Chiniak Bay on Kodiak Island. They were commonly present in Southeastern Alaska, the Kenai Peninsula, Anchorage, Adak, St. Paul, and Gambell. In Anchorage, many of the large gulls are confusing hybrids (Glaucous-winged × Herring Gulls).

Aleutian Tern

On May 13 at Anchor Point north of Homer, a distant Aleutian Tern was my first sighting. I also saw them daily in mid-May on Adak Island, as well as in Nome in early June. Although Aleutian Terns have a distinctive white forehead and darker wings than the much more common Arctic Terns, these two species are often more easily distinguished by the high squeaky twitters of Aleutian Terns compared to the raucous screeches of Arctic Terns.

Arctic Tern

On April 24, there were about eight Arctic Terns at Westchester Lagoon in Anchorage. I regularly found them in Anchorage, where they nest, until late July, and also saw them in Southeastern Alaska, Utqiagvik, and Nome.

Yellow-billed Loon

On January 19, I was birding with Aaron Lang in Homer when he found a Yellow-billed Loon that immediately disappeared, although we searched the water for nearly half an hour. As we drove back up the spit, pulled over, and scanned again, Aaron saw what appeared to be a Yellow-billed Loon. We got out of the car, and it popped up quite near us. We both saw the Yellow-billed Loon before it dove again. When it reappeared farther out near a Common Loon, I was able to get a few distant photographs. It was bird species number 100 for the year. Later sightings were at Gambell (spring and fall) and St. Paul (fall).

Spotting Birds in Texas and Alaska | 259

Laysan Albatross

On May 16 from a high overlook on Adak, we saw at least six Laysan Albatrosses far out over the water, and another one a couple of days later. I also saw eight of them on a charter boat trip near Dutch Harbor in early July, an amazing trip with three species of albatross all in view at one time on the water behind the boat.

Black-footed Albatross

We saw Black-footed Albatrosses on June 29, the first day of the ferry trip from Homer to Dutch Harbor, and also saw four of them a couple of days later near Dutch Harbor in the company of Laysan Albatrosses and a single Short-tailed Albatross. I also observed them later in the summer on the Gulf of Alaska ferry trip.

Northern Fulmar

Large numbers of Northern Fulmars were intermixed with Short-tailed Shearwaters on May 16 offshore of Adak Island. Later in May, they were at their nesting cliffs on St. Paul, with smaller numbers at Gambell in spring and fall, and huge numbers near Dutch Harbor in early July.

Short-tailed Shearwater

On May 16 on Adak Island at a high overlook at an old Loran station, we saw streams of probably thousands of distant Short-tailed Shearwaters. They were also near Dutch Harbor in July, and offshore in late summer and fall from Gambell, St. Paul, and Utqiagvik.

Sooty Shearwater

On June 29, early on the first day of the ferry trip from Homer to Dutch Harbor, we saw many Sooty Shearwaters. Although the ranges of Sooty and Short-tailed Shearwaters overlap in the waters south of Alaska, careful observation of their underwing coloration and their head shape at close range assists in identification.

Fork-tailed Storm-Petrel

We saw four Fork-tailed Storm-Petrels on the first day of the ferry trip from Homer to Dutch Harbor (June 29). The light gray plumage of Fork-tailed

Storm-Petrels gliding and flapping low over the water made their identification easy.

Red-faced Cormorant
Two Red-faced Cormorants were present on Adak on May 18. I saw nesting birds on St. Paul in late May and in September. The range of Red-faced Cormorants is limited to the Pribilof and Aleutian Islands and South-Central Alaska. The more common Pelagic Cormorant also has red around its eyes in some plumages, but the red is less extensive than on the red face of the Red-faced Cormorant, which also has a distinctive, partly yellow bill.

Pelagic Cormorant
On January 2 at the Trident Basin floatplane facility in Kodiak, there was a handful of Pelagic Cormorants. Later sightings of this most common of the Alaska cormorants were in Ketchikan, Homer, Seward, Adak, Gambell, and St. Paul.

Northern Goshawk
On January 30, as I approached the end of the boardwalk at Potter Marsh south of Anchorage, I saw a bird-shaped lump in a tree silhouetted against the snowy slopes. It looked like a large raptor. My heart started to pound as I realized it was a goshawk-shaped raptor. My scope was in the car, so rather than risk the bird leaving as I raced back to get it, I cranked up the magnification on my camera and fired off a zillion photos. It was a Northern Goshawk, a young bird. After I watched for a while, the goshawk dove downward and disappeared. I saw others later at the hawk watch north of Anchorage in April, and in Homer and Juneau.

Note: in North Texas a Northern Goshawk was reported in early January, and I tried to find it on January 12, without success.

Snowy Owl
I saw my first Snowy Owl in Utqiagvik on July 5, and one or two each of the next two days. Later, on November 5, I saw a Snowy Owl at Point Barrow.

Northern Hawk Owl
On January 11, past Point Woronzof in Anchorage, Louann and I had a treetop view of a Northern Hawk Owl that was wintering there. We later

Northern Hawk Owl at Delta Junction

came back and got a slightly closer view, but not as close as in the previous December. I later saw Northern Hawk Owls in Delta Junction and Kenai.

Great Gray Owl

As my big year progressed, there would be regular reports of a Great Gray Owl in Kenai (south of Anchorage). I almost always drove down there to try to find it, without success, until October 2. Even then, I only heard it on two evenings, and on the second evening saw it briefly drop down from a spruce branch and disappear. Thanks to Toby and Laura Burke.

Boreal Owl

Boreal Owl has always been a nemesis bird for me; I didn't find it at all during my ABA big year across the continental United States and Canada, so the three sightings in 2016 were particularly rewarding for me.

On January 23, I learned that Aaron Bowman had located a Boreal Owl at Spenard Crossing in Anchorage. It was very well hidden high in a dense portion of a spruce and mostly invisible. We circled the tree trying to see it better but could see only glimpses of some of its feathers.

On February 12, I was in Anchorage at Campbell Creek Estuary Natural Area when magpies suddenly began calling raucously in the distance and Steller's Jays headed west through the woods toward the racket. As I approached, I could see the jays and magpies darting into and out of a dense area quite close to the ground. The terrain between me and the action was covered with fallen logs and included a short but steep hill. When I reached the top of the slope and looked around, I was astounded to see a Boreal Owl at eye level about 15 feet from me. The owl turned its head periodically as the jays and magpies approached, and then it stopped to preen when they left for a while. Only rarely did it look in my direction, and then it opened only one eye. Eventually the magpies returned to make more noise and then they, and I, withdrew, leaving the owl where we had found it.

Boreal Owl

On February 23 at Spenard Crossing, I again heard a huge outcry by Steller's Jays and Black-billed Magpies far down a trail. I ran the icy path toward the sounds and there met another woman running toward me from the other direction. Together we climbed over branches and uneven crunchy snow toward a leaning dead spruce propped against a trunk where all the noisy action seemed to be centered. The jays and magpies were going crazy with agitation but all we could see was a dense tangle of dead spruce branches around a very dark area. We circled the tree and with concentrated peering, we finally saw a well-hidden Boreal Owl.

Northern Saw-whet Owl

I saw a Northern Saw-whet Owl thanks to Peter Scully, who showed me the very hidden one he somehow found along a coastal trail in Anchorage on February 6. While I have heard their little toots in the predawn hours each spring in Anchorage, including from our house, this is the only one I have actually seen in Alaska.

Northern Saw-whet Owl

American Three-toed Woodpecker in Anchorage

American Three-toed Woodpecker

On January 11, Aaron Bowman led Louann Feldmann and me to a small Anchorage park near the junction of Lake Otis Parkway and Tudor Road, where he had found an American Three-Toed Woodpecker. On exactly the same spruce where he had previously seen the bird, we heard tapping and spotted the American Three-toed Woodpecker. I saw another one at the Sockeye Burn north of Anchorage later in the summer.

Black-backed Woodpecker

On January 28, I visited the Sockeye Burn north of Anchorage for the first time, looking for woodpeckers. I saw very few birds as I drove the roads and then walked along Randal Road. On my return walk westward to the car, I suddenly heard a quiet, irregular tapping and saw a male Black-backed

Woodpecker diligently working its way up a very black trunk. He got about 20 feet above the ground and then flew down toward the base of another burned trunk. I saw another one later in the summer at the same site. There was also a single Black-backed Woodpecker at Hyder in early June.

Gyrfalcon

Soon after we arrived on Adak on May 15, a low-flying Gyrfalcon came out of nowhere and flew away across the hills and disappeared. We saw a couple of them the next day, four of them in Nome (including two at a nest) in early June, and in September there was one in Gambell and one on St. Paul.

Pacific-Slope Flycatcher

Many Pacific-slope Flycatchers were calling at Ward Lake (Ketchikan) on June 7, only a few of which I could find. I heard and sometimes saw others at Hyder the next week, in Juneau and Ketchikan the week after that, and in Ketchikan and Haines in mid-July.

Canada (Gray) Jay

On January 14, I was near my Anchorage neighborhood when I noticed a perched bird on a tall spruce along the road. There was traffic, so I could not stop. I made a U-turn and pulled off onto the edge of the road. I could not get out of the car to get a better look because of traffic, so I drove past the bird, pulled onto another side street, and walked back toward the bird, taking more pictures as I approached. Finally, I was sure that it was a Canada Jay. I saw others during the year, mostly in Anchorage but also at the Sockeye Burn and Delta Junction north of Anchorage and in Homer.

Canada Jay in Anchorage

Black-billed Magpie

In great contrast to Texas, in Alaska, especially around Anchorage, Black-billed Magpies are a very, very common bird. I saw my first one on January

1 in Kodiak. After that I saw them almost every day I was in Anchorage, and multiple times each month all year long. In my Anchorage yard, it was rare to have a day without them, and as many as five to eight magpies were often present at any one time. They were also present in Juneau, Homer, Palmer, Seward, and the Kenai Peninsula.

Note: although I didn't find the Black-billed Magpie during my Texas big year, I tried. Texas had only four documented records of Black-billed Magpie as of 2014 (TOS Handbook), although they are more numerous in Oklahoma. Someone reported a Black-billed Magpie west of Fort Worth in late summer 2005 near Lake Kemp. My trip was disrupted before dawn by a deer crashing out of the surrounding woods into my car. Birding was modest, but there was no sign of any magpies.

Northwestern Crow

I first observed a couple of Northwestern Crows on January 1 along Kalsin Bay. I saw them regularly in Southeastern Alaska all year. Although Northwestern Crows are only rarely found in the city of Anchorage, they come as far north as Girdwood in the southern part of the Anchorage borough. There are no other crows in Alaska except for American Crows, which are found only in Hyder in mainland Southeastern Alaska at the Alaska-Canada border.

Black-capped Chickadee

On January 1 near Kalsin Bay on Kodiak, we saw a Black-capped Chickadee at a bird feeder. Black-capped Chickadees were regular visitors to my Anchorage feeders and I often saw and heard them elsewhere during the year on the Kenai Peninsula and north at the Sockeye Burn.

Chestnut-backed Chickadee

I first observed Chestnut-backed Chickadee in Juneau on January 5 at some feeders, and I often heard it in the rain forests of Southeastern Alaska in 2016.

Boreal Chickadee

I saw and heard most of the year's Boreal Chickadees in Anchorage all year long. I noticed the first on January 10. Others were present on the Kenai Peninsula and at Delta Junction.

Pacific Wren on Kodiak Island

Pacific Wren

A chattery Pacific Wren on January 2 on Kodiak was the last bird (number 52) of my first trip of my big year. I found others in Southeastern Alaska, where they are common in the rain forests, and on Adak and St. Paul. Although they were previously rare in Anchorage, the number of Pacific Wren sightings in the area is increasing.

American Dipper

I found my first American Dipper in Ketchikan Creek on January 7 in Ketchikan. I also spotted them in the winter in Anchorage when they came to the few open-water areas. Two dippers were singing and chasing each other near Portage on March 14.

American Dipper in Anchorage

Arctic Warbler

I saw Arctic Warblers, common summer migrants and breeders in Western Alaska and parts of the Interior, on each of the three main Nome roads beginning on June 3, on the Denali Highway in late June, and in Gambell in early September.

Bluethroat

We first saw Bluethroats on Nome's Kougarok Road on June 3. A single wounded bird was present at Gambell in early September. The bright blue, rusty orange, and black throat of the breeding male is unmistakable. Although they are rare to locally uncommon in Northern and Western Alaska, it is usually possible to find at least one in Nome in summer.

Northern Wheatear

On May 24 on St. Paul Island, as we did a sweep of Hutchinson Hill, someone called out a Northern Wheatear. I looked around, saw it, and then had no time for a picture because of other rarity sightings. We also saw them in

Nome on June 3 and 5, and in Gambell in late August. This little gray, black, and white bird is regularly found in rocky upland and alpine areas in Western Alaska and is also found in the Chugach Mountains of Anchorage.

Bohemian Waxwing

My first Alaskan Bohemian Waxwings were in large flocks in Anchorage on January 10, the first day of the year I spent much time there. They were around through March and then returned in mid-November.

Note: although I did not see any Bohemian Waxwings during my Texas big year, they were reported at a park just north of Houston on February 11. I was in Houston anyway, so I headed across town to the Jesse H. Jones Park & Nature Center to look for waxwings. It turned out to be a problem to find even the more common Cedar Waxwings in the park, but I checked out nearly every trail in the attempt. Finally, after a ranger told me that there were waxwings in a neighborhood near the park, I left and saw Cedar Waxwings, but no Bohemians.

Bohemian Waxwings

Eastern Yellow Wagtail

A single Eastern Yellow Wagtail was present on Nome's Kougarok Road on June 3, and another on Nome's Council Road on July 12. Eastern Yellow Wagtails nest in the western half of Alaska.

Red-throated Pipit

I found four Red-throated Pipits, rare and local migrants and breeders in far western Alaska, in a wet marsh at Gambell on June 1. I saw single pipits at Gambell on August 31 and September 7, and on St. Paul on September 22.

Brambling

Between the time I made plans to go to Homer and my arrival on January 18, Aaron Lang learned of a Brambling coming to feeders in Homer. When my much-delayed plane got to Homer, it appeared we had time to check for the Brambling before it got too dark. When we got to the site, we sat by the homeowners' back window overlooking the area, and a flock of juncos and a Brambling soon arrived. Although the lighting was a bit low, both Aaron and I were able to get a couple of photographs before the birds flitted off and it got dark. Another Brambling was present on St. Paul Island on May 23, and there was a flock of five Bramblings there on September 24.

Gray-crowned Rosy-Finch

On January 18, as I was driving down the Homer Spit and staring at a flock of Glaucous-winged and Mew Gulls, a small bird flitted over my head. My first thought was it must be a Song Sparrow (one of which I had just seen toward the beginning of the spit), but more little birds followed, my first Gray-crowned Rosy-Finches of the year, feeding among the small plants along the spit. I observed many others during the year on Adak and on St. Paul Island, where they nest.

Pine Grosbeak

I saw the first Alaska Pine Grosbeak at feeders in Kodiak on January 2. When I got back to Anchorage the next day, six of them were coming to my feeders. They were in Anchorage (usually at my feeders) every month of the year except August and September and were also present in Seward, Palmer, and Hyder.

White-winged Crossbill

White-winged Crossbills were numerous the winter before my big year (2014–2015) but were basically nowhere in Alaska the first four months of my big year. On May 2, having heard that a White-winged Crossbill was being seen at Jerry Koerner's house in Ketchikan, I spent two hours there, but the crossbill did not show. The next day I was there about 5:30 a.m. and watched about 15 species hopping, singing, eating, and entertaining me. Just before 7:00 a.m. as I was preparing to leave, a very red bird flew into the very pink cherry blossoms. It was the White-winged Crossbill, which then dove to the ground behind the flowering bushes and disappeared. I didn't dare leave the shelter of the porch for fear I would scare all the birds, so I waited impatiently. The crossbill finally hopped into view, eating seeds. There were later sightings of White-winged Crossbills in Juneau, Anchorage, Delta Junction, and Kenai.

Common Redpoll

I saw my first Common Redpolls on January 5 along the dike trail at the Mendenhall Wetlands in Juneau, where they were feeding off low vegetation. I found them every month of the year, often at our Anchorage feeders, especially in winter. Other sightings were in Homer, Kenai, Seward, Palmer, Nome, Utqiagvik, Gambell, and St. Paul.

Hoary Redpoll

On January 12 at our Anchorage feeders, about 20 Pine Grosbeaks were joined by a large flock of about 40 redpolls, as well as Black-capped Chickadees and Dark-eyed Juncos. I scanned them carefully, and one of them was a Hoary Redpoll with classic Hoary features—white unmarked rump, white nearly unmarked sides, and pale back. They were also present at Nome in spring, St. Paul in September, and Utqiagvik in October.

McKay's Bunting

On November 28, Laura Keene and I flew from Anchorage to Gambell, with a stop in Nome of more than three hours. In Nome, we hired a cab and went looking for McKay's Buntings. We checked a spot in town, added seed to the place where these buntings had been present in past years, and waited. Nothing. We then went to Round the Clock Road, another place for them, and soon saw a flock of about 30 buntings, many of which were very white—McKay's Buntings. Because we did not get good photos of any of the lightest buntings, I was glad I had another trip scheduled to Nome.

On December 1, Louann Feldmann and I flew to Nome, where we saw McKay's Buntings at a feeder site near the Nome-Teller Road. We watched the McKay's as well as Snow Buntings until it was too dark to see details. The next day we went back and waited to see whether the buntings would return. Shortly afterward (still predawn, at 10:30 a.m.), a few McKay's Buntings came in, mostly perching on the electric lines. Then a flock of about 30 buntings, mostly Snow Buntings, came down and then flew up to the lines and were replaced by another flock of 10 buntings (all but two were McKay's). When we left to go see the sunrise at about 11:00 a.m., all 40 buntings were on the lines above the seeds.

Golden-crowned Sparrow

My first Golden-crowned Sparrow was in Hoonah on January 8. I periodically saw others around the state from early May through September, including in Southeastern Alaska, Anchorage, Nome, Gambell, St. Paul, and Kodiak.

McKay's Bunting

7
AN OUTRAGEOUS IDEA

When I started planning what to write about in this book, as I compared the two states and my two big years it occurred to me that someone with an even greater big year obsession than mine might consider doing a *simultaneous* big year in Texas and Alaska. Of course this nutty person could be only one place at any one time, but if the big year were correctly planned (and if the birds behaved) the total number of species could be similar to that for a big year in the whole ABA area (not including Hawaii, which is now included in the ABA area). It's fun to imagine what it might entail. In some ways it would be like a restricted ABA big year, but the restriction would be to two of the most important states an ABA big year birder must visit in order to have a respectable list.

For this outrageous idea to work, it would help if this birder lived in either Texas or Alaska so time could possibly be spent at home—however, on second thought, a birder on such a quest would rarely have time to be home.

The birder would need to decide whether the goal of this year was to get the maximum number in each state, essentially two big years at once, or to get the maximum total number of species, with each state adding its specialties and no effort being made to see a species in the second state once it was found in the other. Or I guess to make it more outrageous, the birder could try to maximize the number of species in each state *and* maximize the total number of species found during the year.

How do I imagine such a year proceeding? Basically, the birder would need to begin birding in both states in January and February. In March and April, as birds begin to arrive in Texas, the big year effort would concentrate there. If the birder were trying to get the maximum number of species in each state, the birder would need to be in Alaska by mid-May at least; however, if the birder were trying to maximize only the total number of species, it would be more important to be in Alaska when vagrants arrive from Asia, especially in late May and again in September and October, which would need to be devoted to Alaskan islands (Adak, Attu, St. Paul, St. Lawrence).

Of course throughout the year, the birder would need to monitor listservs of each state, be in contact with both Texas and Alaska birders, and always be ready to hop on a plane from one state to the other if a rarity turned up.

As the year went on, the birder would regularly fly back and forth between the two states. If the birder were trying to maximize the number of species in each state, he or she would need to be back in Texas toward the end of the year to pick up rarities arriving from the north and would also need to pay attention to what was arriving in Alaska from Asia or the south as birds were moving about.

APPENDIX 1
BIRDS SEEN IN TEXAS AND ALASKA

The following table lists all 637 species seen in my Texas (522) or Alaska (307) big year or in both years, in current taxonomic order. After each name are the date and county of the first Texas sighting of the species (if seen in Texas during my big year) and the date and locale (city, island, or other named location) closest to the Alaska sighting of the species (if seen in Alaska during my big year). The table makes it easy to compare the species seen in the two states, as well as the dates of first sighting in the two states. The table also allows you to easily see which families include birds that are more likely to be seen in Texas than in Alaska (such as doves, nighthawks, hummingbirds, rails, terns, waders, hawks, woodpeckers, flycatchers, vireos, warblers, sparrows, buntings, blackbirds, and orioles), which families include birds that are more likely to be found in Alaska than in Texas (alcids such as murrelets, auklets, and puffins; vagrants from Asia), and which families include numerous birds found in both states during my big years (waterfowl, shorebirds, gulls, owls, and swallows).

Species	Texas	Alaska
Black-bellied Whistling-Duck	1/15 Willacy	
Fulvous Whistling-Duck	1/1 Matagorda	
Greater White-fronted Goose	1/1 Matagorda	4/25 Delta Junction
Emperor Goose		1/1 Kodiak
Snow Goose	1/1 Matagorda	2/28 Juneau
Ross's Goose	1/1 Matagorda	
Brant		5/29 Gambell
Cackling Goose	1/1 Matagorda	5/1 Juneau
Canada Goose	1/1 Matagorda	1/1 Kodiak
Trumpeter Swan	12/29 Hutchinson	1/1 Kodiak
Tundra Swan	1/10 Dickens	4/4 Anchorage
Muscovy Duck	1/4 Starr	

Appendix 1

Species	Texas	Alaska
Wood Duck	1/16 Tarrant	2/25 Sitka
Gadwall	1/16 Matagorda	1/1 Kodiak
Eurasian Wigeon	11/24 Bailey	3/12 Homer
American Wigeon	1/4 Starr	1/1 Kodiak
Mallard	1/8 Castro	1/1 Kodiak
Mottled Duck	1/1 Matagorda	
Blue-winged Teal	1/1 Matagorda	6/6 Anchorage
Cinnamon Teal	1/1 Matagorda	5/1 Juneau
Northern Shoveler	1/1 Matagorda	3/12 Homer
Northern Pintail	1/1 Matagorda	1/2 Kodiak
Green-winged Teal	1/1 Matagorda	1/2 Kodiak
Canvasback	1/16 Hemphill	4/27 Anchorage
Redhead	1/16 Tarrant	1/2 Kodiak
Common Pochard		1/1 Kodiak
Ring-necked Duck	1/1 Matagorda	2/25 Sitka
Tufted Duck		5/15 Adak
Greater Scaup	1/11 Tarrant	1/1 Kodiak
Lesser Scaup	1/1 Matagorda	2/29 Juneau
Steller's Eider		1/1 Kodiak
Spectacled Eider		6/4 Nome
King Eider	4/17 Galveston	5/23 St. Paul
Common Eider		5/16 Adak
Harlequin Duck		1/1 Kodiak
Surf Scoter	11/21 Galveston	1/1 Kodiak
White-winged Scoter	11/15 Travis	1/7 Ketchikan
Black Scoter	11/16 Travis	1/1 Kodiak
Long-tailed Duck	2/16 Rains	1/1 Kodiak
Bufflehead	1/1 Matagorda	1/1 Kodiak
Common Goldeneye	1/1 Matagorda	1/1 Kodiak
Barrow's Goldeneye		1/1 Kodiak
Hooded Merganser	1/8 Hartley	1/7 Ketchikan
Common Merganser	1/10 Hemphill	1/1 Kodiak
Red-breasted Merganser	1/18 Brazoria	1/1 Kodiak
Masked Duck	4/11 Nueces	
Ruddy Duck	1/1 Matagorda	6/23 Kenny Lake

Species	Texas	Alaska
Plain Chachalaca	1/2 Hidalgo	
Northern Bobwhite	1/13 Hardeman	
Scaled Quail	2/6 Reeves	
Gambel's Quail	5/16 Presidio	
Montezuma Quail	5/15 Brewster	
Ring-necked Pheasant	1/8 Castro	
Ruffed Grouse		4/26 Delta Junction
Spruce Grouse		1/11 Anchorage
Willow Ptarmigan		2/16 Anchorage
Rock Ptarmigan		5/15 Adak
White-tailed Ptarmigan		8/27 Summit Lake
Sooty Grouse		4/30 Juneau
Sharp-tailed Grouse		4/25 Delta Junction
Lesser Prairie-Chicken	4/5 Lipscomb	
Wild Turkey	1/10 Hemphill	
American Flamingo	11/11 Aransas	
Least Grebe	1/1 Matagorda	
Pied-billed Grebe	1/1 Matagorda	1/6 Ketchikan
Horned Grebe	1/25 Hudspeth	1/1 Kodiak
Red-necked Grebe		1/1 Kodiak
Eared Grebe	1/15 Kenedy	
Western Grebe	1/7 Reeves	1/6 Ketchikan
Clark's Grebe	1/7 Reeves	
Rock Pigeon	1/2 Hidalgo	*
Red-billed Pigeon	3/2 Starr	
Band-tailed Pigeon	5/11 Brewster	5/2 Ketchikan
Eurasian Collared-Dove	1/1 Matagorda	1/10 Anchorage
Inca Dove	1/1 Matagorda	
Common Ground-Dove	1/2 Hidalgo	
White-Winged Dove	1/2 Hidalgo	
Ruddy Ground-Dove	1/24 Brewster	
White-tipped Dove	1/2 Hidalgo	
Mourning Dove	1/1 Matagorda	
Yellow-billed Cuckoo	4/18 Jefferson	
Black-billed Cuckoo	5/1 Jefferson	

Species	Texas	Alaska
Greater Roadrunner	1/6 Presidio	
Groove-billed Ani	1/3 Cameron	
Lesser Nighthawk	1/15 Hidalgo	
Common Nighthawk	4/19 Galveston	
Common Pauraque	1/14 Hidalgo	
Common Poorwill	5/13 Jeff Davis	
Chuck-will's-widow	3/27 Galveston	
Eastern Whip-poor-will	3/29 Jefferson	
Black Swift		6/10 Hyder
Chimney Swift	3/23 Nueces	
Vaux's Swift		4/30 Juneau
White-throated Swift	1/5 Val Verde	
Mexican Violetear	6/3 Comal	
Green-breasted Mango	1/2 Hidalgo	
Magnificent Hummingbird	6/20 Jeff Davis	
Blue-throated Hummingbird	5/11 Brewster	
Lucifer Hummingbird	5/21 Brewster	
Ruby-throated Hummingbird	3/22 Nueces	
Black-chinned Hummingbird	3/16 Brewster	
Anna's Hummingbird	1/7 Aransas	1/5 Juneau
Broad-tailed Hummingbird	1/11 Jeff Davis	
Rufous Hummingbird	1/11 Tarrant	5/1 Juneau
Allen's Hummingbird	2/23 Aransas	
Calliope Hummingbird	1/18 Harris	
Broad-billed Hummingbird	1/18 Harris	
Buff-bellied Hummingbird	1/2 Hidalgo	
White-eared Hummingbird	6/20 Jeff Davis	
Yellow Rail	4/3 Chambers	
Black Rail	3/28 Galveston	
Clapper Rail	1/3 Cameron	
King Rail	3/29 Jefferson	
Virginia Rail	1/3 Cameron	
Sora	1/1 Matagorda	7/15 Haines
Purple Gallinule	4/17 Chambers	
Common Gallinule	1/1 Matagorda	

Species	Texas	Alaska
American Coot	1/1 Matagorda	2/26 Ketchikan
Sandhill Crane	1/1 Matagorda	4/15 Anchorage
Whooping Crane	1/30 Matagorda	
Black-necked Stilt	1/3 Cameron	
American Avocet	1/19 Galveston	
American Oystercatcher	1/19 Galveston	
Black Oystercatcher		1/2 Kodiak
Black-bellied Plover	1/3 Cameron	5/1 Juneau
American Golden-Plover	3/18 Galveston	6/3 Nome
Pacific Golden-Plover		5/12 Homer
Lesser Sand-Plover		5/22 St. Paul
Snowy Plover	1/3 Cameron	
Wilson's Plover	3/18 Galveston	
Common Ringed Plover		5/28 Gambell
Semipalmated Plover	1/19 Galveston	5/3 Ketchikan
Piping Plover	1/3 Cameron	
Killdeer	1/1 Matagorda	2/27 Ketchikan
Mountain Plover	1/22 Williamson	
Upland Sandpiper	3/30 Liberty	6/22 Delta Junction
Whimbrel	3/18 Galveston	5/6 Gustavus
Bristle-thighed Curlew		6/3 Nome
Long-billed Curlew	1/3 Cameron	
Hudsonian Godwit	4/28 Chambers	4/28 Anchorage
Bar-tailed Godwit		5/16 Adak
Marbled Godwit	1/31 Nueces	5/12 Homer
Ruddy Turnstone	1/1 Matagorda	5/19 Adak
Black Turnstone		1/1 Kodiak
Red Knot	1/31 Nueces	6/5 Nome
Surfbird		1/1 Kodiak
Ruff		5/16 Adak
Sharp-tailed Sandpiper		9/3 Gambell
Stilt Sandpiper	3/6 Cameron	
Curlew Sandpiper		5/24 St. Paul
Long-toed Stint		5/22 St. Paul
Red-necked Stint		5/29 Gambell

Species	Texas	Alaska
Sanderling	1/3 Cameron	5/20 Kenai
Dunlin	1/3 Cameron	4/1 Homer
Rock Sandpiper		1/1 Kodiak
Baird's Sandpiper	3/29 Chambers	6/3 Nome
Least Sandpiper	1/3 Cameron	5/1 Juneau
White-rumped Sandpiper	4/11 Nueces	
Buff-breasted Sandpiper	4/2 Colorado	
Pectoral Sandpiper	3/29 Chambers	5/13 Homer
Semipalmated Sandpiper	3/28 Galveston	5/6 Gustavus
Western Sandpiper	1/3 Cameron	5/1 Juneau
Short-billed Dowitcher	2/23 Nueces	4/28 Anchorage
Long-billed Dowitcher	1/31 Nueces	2/28 Juneau
Jack Snipe		9/14 St. Paul
Wilson's Snipe	1/7 Brewster	4/18 Anchorage
Common Snipe		5/16 Adak
American Woodcock	1/28 Tarrant	
Terek Sandpiper		5/27 Gambell
Common Sandpiper		5/23 St. Paul
Spotted Sandpiper	1/1 Matagorda	5/3 Ketchikan
Solitary Sandpiper	1/3 Cameron	6/23 Fairbanks
Gray-tailed Tattler		8/31 Gambell
Wandering Tattler		5/12 Homer
Greater Yellowlegs	1/3 Cameron	4/13 Anchorage
Common Greenshank		5/22 St. Paul
Willet	1/3 Cameron	
Lesser Yellowlegs	1/3 Cameron	4/27 Anchorage
Wood Sandpiper		5/22 St. Paul
Wilson's Phalarope	4/21 Chambers	7/4 Wasilla
Red-necked Phalarope	8/22 Bexar	5/9 Anchorage
Red Phalarope	10/11 Bexar	5/23 St. Paul
Pomarine Jaeger	11/5 Cameron	6/1 Gambell
Parasitic Jaeger	7/30 Cameron	5/13 Homer
Long-tailed Jaeger	11/5 Cameron	6/3 Nome
Dovekie		5/28 Gambell
Common Murre		1/1 Kodiak

Species	Texas	Alaska
Thick-billed Murre		5/23 St. Paul
Black Guillemot		5/28 Gambell
Pigeon Guillemot		1/2 Kodiak
Marbled Murrelet		1/6 Ketchikan
Kittlitz's Murrelet		5/16 Adak
Ancient Murrelet		5/16 Adak
Cassin's Auklet		6/30 ferry to Dutch Harbor
Parakeet Auklet		5/23 St. Paul
Least Auklet		5/23 St. Paul
Whiskered Auklet		7/2 Dutch Harbor
Crested Auklet		1/1 Kodiak
Rhinoceros Auklet		5/13 Homer (Anchor Pt.)
Horned Puffin		5/23 St. Paul
Tufted Puffin		5/17 Adak
Black-legged Kittiwake	1/3 Cameron	1/2 Kodiak
Red-legged Kittiwake		5/22 St. Paul
Sabine's Gull	9/21 Van Zandt	6/4 Nome
Bonaparte's Gull	1/18 Brazoria	4/24 Anchorage
Little Gull	1/18 Brazoria	
Ross's Gull		10/8 Utqiagvik
Laughing Gull	1/1 Matagorda	
Franklin's Gull	4/5 Hemphill	5/26 Anchorage
Mew Gull	12/31 Tarrant	1/1 Kodiak
Ring-billed Gull	1/3 Cameron	8/20 Ketchikan
California Gull	2/4 Llano	2/27 Ketchikan
Herring Gull	1/3 Cameron	2/20 Seward
Thayer's Gull	2/23 Nueces	1/7 Ketchikan
Lesser Black-backed Gull	1/18 Brazoria	
Slaty-backed Gull		5/22 St. Paul
Glaucous-winged Gull		1/1 Kodiak
Glaucous Gull	3/23 Nueces	5/23 St. Paul
Great Black-backed Gull	3/2 Cameron	
Brown Noddy	6/22 Cameron	
Sooty Tern	6/17 Cameron	
Bridled Tern	6/17 Cameron	

Species	Texas	Alaska
Aleutian Tern		5/13 Homer (Anchor Pt.)
Least Tern	3/18 Galveston	
Gull-billed Tern	1/3 Cameron	
Caspian Tern	1/3 Cameron	5/3 Ketchikan
Black Tern	4/22 Jefferson	
Common Tern	3/6 Cameron	
Arctic Tern		4/24 Anchorage
Forster's Tern	1/3 Cameron	
Royal Tern	1/1 Matagorda	
Sandwich Tern	1/3 Cameron	
Black Skimmer	1/3 Cameron	
Red-billed Tropicbird	6/17 Cameron	
Red-throated Loon	3/19 Grayson	1/19 Homer
Arctic Loon		5/16 Adak
Pacific Loon	2/4 Llano	1/5 Juneau
Common Loon	1/1 Matagorda	1/1 Kodiak
Yellow-billed Loon		1/19 Homer
Laysan Albatross		5/16 Adak
Black-footed Albatross		6/29 ferry to Dutch Harbor
Short-tailed Albatross		7/2 Dutch Harbor
Northern Fulmar		5/16 Adak
Cory's Shearwater	6/17 Cameron	
Short-tailed Shearwater		5/16 Adak
Sooty Shearwater		6/29 ferry to Dutch Harbor
Audubon's Shearwater	6/17 Cameron	
Fork-tailed Storm-Petrel		6/29 ferry to Dutch Harbor
Leach's Storm-Petrel	6/17 Cameron	
Band-rumped Storm-Petrel	6/17 Cameron	
Wood Stork	5/28 Brazoria	
Magnificent Frigatebird	4/27 Nueces	
Masked Booby	6/17 Cameron	
Brown Booby	2/28 Nueces	
Northern Gannet	1/31 Nueces	
Brandt's Cormorant		1/7 Ketchikan
Neotropic Cormorant	1/3 Cameron	

Species	Texas	Alaska
Double-crested Cormorant	1/1 Matagorda	1/1 Kodiak
Red-faced Cormorant		5/18 Adak
Pelagic Cormorant		1/2 Kodiak
Anhinga	1/14 Jim Wells	
American White Pelican	1/1 Matagorda	
Brown Pelican	1/1 Matagorda	
American Bittern	3/7 Nueces	
Least Bittern	1/3 Cameron	
Great Blue Heron	1/1 Matagorda	1/3 Juneau
Great Egret	1/1 Matagorda	
Snowy Egret	1/1 Matagorda	
Little Blue Heron	1/3 Cameron	
Tricolored Heron	1/1 Matagorda	
Reddish Egret	1/3 Cameron	
Cattle Egret	1/15 Kenedy	
Green Heron	3/7 Nueces	
Black-crowned Night-Heron	1/1 Matagorda	
Yellow-crowned Night-Heron	3/22 Nueces	
White Ibis	1/1 Matagorda	
Glossy Ibis	4/17 Galveston	
White-faced Ibis	1/1 Matagorda	
Roseate Spoonbill	1/1 Matagorda	
Black Vulture	1/1 Matagorda	
Turkey Vulture	1/1 Matagorda	
Osprey	1/1 Matagorda	5/9 Anchorage
Hook-billed Kite	1/4 Starr	
Swallow-tailed Kite	5/1 Liberty	
White-tailed Kite	1/3 Cameron	
Mississippi Kite	4/10 Fayette	
Bald Eagle	1/1 Matagorda	1/1 Kodiak
White-tailed Eagle		5/29 Gambell
Northern Harrier	1/1 Matagorda	3/9 Palmer
Sharp-shinned Hawk	1/2 Hidalgo	1/2 Kodiak
Cooper's Hawk	1/1 Matagorda	
Northern Goshawk		1/30 Anchorage

Species	Texas	Alaska
Common Black Hawk	5/10 Jeff Davis	
Roadside Hawk	2/5 Zapata	
Harris's Hawk	1/3 Cameron	
White-tailed Hawk	1/1 Matagorda	
Gray Hawk	1/6 Brewster	
Red-shouldered Hawk	1/4 Starr	
Broad-winged Hawk	3/28 Galveston	
Swainson's Hawk	3/23 Victoria	6/12 Hyder
Zone-tailed Hawk	1/20 Zapata	
Red-tailed Hawk	1/1 Matagorda	4/8 119 mi. north of Anchorage
Rough-legged Hawk	1/8 Lamb	4/8 119 mi. north of Anchorage
Ferruginous Hawk	1/8 Hockley	
Golden Eagle	1/6 Brewster	4/8 119 mi. north of Anchorage
Barn Owl	2/12 Chambers	
Flammulated Owl	5/11 Brewster	
Western Screech-Owl	5/11 Brewster	3/14 Portage
Eastern Screech-Owl	1/4 Starr	
Great Horned Owl	1/8 Hartley	2/13 Anchorage
Snowy Owl		7/5 Utqiagvik
Northern Hawk Owl		1/11 Anchorage
Northern Pygmy-Owl		1/4 Juneau
Ferruginous Pygmy-Owl	9/28 Kenedy	
Elf Owl	5/1 Brewster	
Burrowing Owl	4/4 Briscoe	
Spotted Owl	6/21 Culberson	
Barred Owl	3/30 Liberty	6/8 Ketchikan
Great Gray Owl		10/2 Kenai
Long-eared Owl	1/9 Dallam	
Short-eared Owl	1/12 Tarrant	3/25 Kenai
Boreal Owl		1/23 Anchorage
Northern Saw-whet Owl		2/6 Anchorage
Elegant Trogon	1/15 Hidalgo	
Ringed Kingfisher	1/3 Cameron	

Species	Texas	Alaska
Belted Kingfisher	1/1 Matagorda	1/1 Kodiak
Green Kingfisher	1/4 Starr	
Lewis's Woodpecker	11/26 Culberson	11/18 Petersburg
Red-headed Woodpecker	2/26 Nacogdoches	
Acorn Woodpecker	1/7 Jeff Davis	
Golden-fronted Woodpecker	1/2 Hidalgo	
Red-bellied Woodpecker	1/10 Hemphill	
Williamson's Sapsucker	12/10 Jeff Davis	
Yellow-bellied Sapsucker	1/1 Matagorda	8/4 Delta Junction
Red-naped Sapsucker	1/7 Jeff Davis	
Red-breasted Sapsucker	3/14 Jeff Davis	4/30 Juneau
Ladder-backed Woodpecker	1/3 Cameron	
Downy Woodpecker	1/1 Matagorda	1/10 Anchorage
Hairy Woodpecker	2/26 Nacogdoches	1/5 Juneau
Red-cockaded Woodpecker	2/27 Jasper	
American Three-toed Woodpecker		1/11 Anchorage
Black-backed Woodpecker		1/28 Sockeye Burn, Wasilla
Northern Flicker	1/3 Cameron	1/7 Ketchikan
Pileated Woodpecker	1/1 Matagorda	
Crested Caracara	1/1 Matagorda	
American Kestrel	1/1 Matagorda	4/25 Delta Junction
Merlin	1/5 Zavala	2/2 Anchorage
Gyrfalcon		5/15 Adak
Peregrine Falcon	1/19 Galveston	5/12 Homer
Prairie Falcon	1/9 Dallam	
Monk Parakeet	2/4 Tarrant	
Green Parakeet	2/17 Hidalgo	
Red-crowned Parrot	1/15 Hidalgo	
Northern Beardless-Tyrannulet	1/18 Hidalgo	
Olive-sided Flycatcher	5/3 Cameron	6/8 Ketchikan
Western Wood-Pewee	5/10 Jeff Davis	6/9 Hyder
Eastern Wood-Pewee	4/19 Jefferson	
Yellow-bellied Flycatcher	8/25 Jefferson	6/10 Hyder
Acadian Flycatcher	4/19 Jefferson	
Alder Flycatcher	6/1 Tarrant	6/9 Hyder
Willow Flycatcher	5/3 Cameron	6/9 Hyder

Species	Texas	Alaska
Least Flycatcher	1/18 Brazoria	6/9 Hyder
Hammond's Flycatcher	8/31 Culberson	4/26 Delta Junction
Gray Flycatcher	3/14 Brewster	
Dusky Flycatcher	5/18 Jeff Davis	
Pacific-slope Flycatcher		6/7 Ketchikan
Cordilleran Flycatcher	1/5 Frio	
Buff-breasted Flycatcher	5/14 Jeff Davis	
Black Phoebe	1/7 Brewster	
Eastern Phoebe	1/1 Matagorda	7/12 Nome
Say's Phoebe	1/5 Zavala	6/4 Nome
Vermilion Flycatcher	1/4 Zapata	
Dusky-capped Flycatcher	2/18 Cameron	
Ash-throated Flycatcher	3/2 Starr	
Great Crested Flycatcher	3/28 Galveston	
Brown-crested Flycatcher	5/2 Kenedy	
Great Kiskadee	1/2 Hidalgo	
Social Flycatcher	1/14 Hidalgo	
Tropical Kingbird	5/3 Hidalgo	10/22 Sitka
Couch's Kingbird	1/2 Hidalgo	
Cassin's Kingbird	5/9 Jeff Davis	
Western Kingbird	4/11 Nueces	
Eastern Kingbird	3/18 Galveston	6/9 Hyder
Scissor-tailed Flycatcher	3/5 Brooks	
Fork-tailed Flycatcher	9/25 Travis	
Rose-throated Becard	2/1 Cameron	
Loggerhead Shrike	1/1 Matagorda	
Northern Shrike	2/9 Dallam	1/11 Anchorage
Black-capped Vireo	5/4 Burnet	
White-eyed Vireo	1/2 Hidalgo	
Bell's Vireo	5/7 Tarrant	
Gray Vireo	5/19 Culberson	
Hutton's Vireo	3/15 Brewster	
Yellow-throated Vireo	3/22 Nueces	
Cassin's Vireo	9/7 Brewster	6/11 Hyder
Blue-headed Vireo	1/3 Cameron	
Plumbeous Vireo	5/14 Jeff Davis	

Species	Texas	Alaska
Philadelphia Vireo	4/26 Jefferson	
Warbling Vireo	4/19 Jefferson	6/8 Ketchikan
Red-eyed Vireo	3/18 Galveston	6/15 Juneau
Yellow-green Vireo	4/27 Calhoun	
Black-whiskered Vireo	4/28 Jefferson	
Canada (Gray) Jay		1/14 Anchorage
Brown Jay	1/4 Starr	
Green Jay	1/3 Cameron	
Steller's Jay	2/7 Culberson	1/3 Anchorage
Blue Jay	1/1 Matagorda	
Woodhouse's Scrub-Jay	1/7 Brewster	
Mexican Jay	1/24 Brewster	
Black-billed Magpie		1/1 Kodiak
American Crow	1/1 Wharton	6/10 Hyder
Northwestern Crow		1/1 Kodiak
Tamaulipas Crow	5/2 Cameron	
Fish Crow	3/29 Jefferson	
Chihuahuan Raven	1/3 Cameron	
Common Raven	1/6 Brewster	1/1 Kodiak
Eurasian Skylark		9/23 St. Paul
Horned Lark	1/6 Presidio	6/5 Nome
Purple Martin	1/31 Kenedy	
Tree Swallow	2/6 Reeves	5/2 Ketchikan
Violet-green Swallow	3/15 Brewster	5/2 Ketchikan
Northern Rough-winged Swallow	1/14 Hidalgo	6/10 Hyder
Bank Swallow	2/18 Hidalgo	6/3 Nome
Cliff Swallow	2/18 Hidalgo	6/3 Nome
Cave Swallow	1/31 Kleberg	
Barn Swallow	2/18 Cameron	5/2 Ketchikan
Carolina Chickadee	1/1 Matagorda	
Black-capped Chickadee		1/1 Kodiak
Mountain Chickadee	2/7 Culberson	
Chestnut-backed Chickadee		1/5 Juneau
Boreal Chickadee		1/10 Anchorage
Juniper Titmouse	11/18 Culberson	

Species	Texas	Alaska
Tufted Titmouse	1/18 Harris	
Black-crested Titmouse	1/2 Hidalgo	
Verdin	1/4 Zapata	
Bushtit	3/14 Jeff Davis	
Red-breasted Nuthatch	1/7 Brewster	1/11 Anchorage
White-breasted Nuthatch	1/7 Brewster	
Pygmy Nuthatch	10/20 Culberson	
Brown-headed Nuthatch	2/27 Jasper	
Brown Creeper	1/16 Tarrant	1/2 Kodiak
Rock Wren	1/7 Brewster	
Canyon Wren	2/7 Culberson	
House Wren	1/2 Hidalgo	
Pacific Wren		1/2 Kodiak
Winter Wren	1/13 Grayson	
Sedge Wren	3/28 Galveston	
Marsh Wren	2/12 Jefferson	
Carolina Wren	1/1 Matagorda	
Bewick's Wren	1/4 Starr	
Cactus Wren	1/5 Uvalde	
Blue-gray Gnatcatcher	1/2 Hidalgo	
Black-tailed Gnatcatcher	1/6 Brewster	
American Dipper		1/7 Ketchikan
Golden-crowned Kinglet	1/28 Johnson	1/2 Kodiak
Ruby-crowned Kinglet	1/1 Matagorda	3/12 Homer
Arctic Warbler		6/3 Nome
Siberian Rubythroat		5/24 St. Paul
Bluethroat		6/3 Nome
Red-flanked Bluetail		9/24 St. Paul
Northern Wheatear		5/24 St. Paul
Eastern Bluebird	1/1 Matagorda	
Western Bluebird	1/7 Jeff Davis	
Mountain Bluebird	1/6 Brewster	6/22 Chicken
Townsend's Solitaire	1/8 Lubbock	6/22 Anchorage
Veery	4/18 Jefferson	6/9 Hyder
Gray-cheeked Thrush	4/19 Jefferson	6/3 Nome

Species	Texas	Alaska
Swainson's Thrush	4/17 Galveston	5/21 Kenai
Hermit Thrush	1/5 Frio	5/2 Ketchikan
Wood Thrush	3/29 Jefferson	
Eyebrowed Thrush		5/31 Gambell
Clay-colored Thrush	1/2 Hidalgo	
White-throated Thrush	1/14 Hidalgo	
American Robin	1/1 Matagorda	1/15 Anchorage
Varied Thrush	10/22 Jefferson	1/7 Ketchikan
Blue Mockingbird	1/15 Hidalgo	
Gray Catbird	1/18 Brazoria	
Curve-billed Thrasher	1/5 Uvalde	
Brown Thrasher	1/18 Brazoria	
Long-billed Thrasher	1/2 Hidalgo	
Crissal Thrasher	1/26 Ward	
Sage Thrasher	1/26 Reeves	
Northern Mockingbird	1/1 Matagorda	
European Starling	1/1 Matagorda	1/6 Ketchikan
Bohemian Waxwing		1/10 Anchorage
Cedar Waxwing	1/1 Matagorda	1/16 Anchorage
Phainopepla	1/6 Brewster	
Olive Warbler	5/29 Jeff Davis	
Siberian Accentor		9/7 Gambell
House Sparrow	1/1 Matagorda	
Eastern Yellow Wagtail		6/3 Nome
White Wagtail		5/27 Gambell
Red-throated Pipit		6/1 Gambell
American Pipit	1/1 Matagorda	4/25 Delta Junction
Sprague's Pipit	1/22 Matagorda	
Brambling		1/17 Homer
Gray-crowned Rosy-Finch		1/18 Homer
Pine Grosbeak		1/2 Kodiak
House Finch	1/5 Frio	10/18 Ketchikan
Purple Finch	1/18 Harris	
Cassin's Finch	2/9 Dallam	
Red Crossbill	12/27 El Paso	1/1 Kodiak

Species	Texas	Alaska
White-winged Crossbill		5/3 Ketchikan
Common Redpoll		1/5 Juneau
Hoary Redpoll		1/12 Anchorage
Pine Siskin	1/7 Brewster	1/2 Kodiak
Lesser Goldfinch	1/7 Jeff Davis	
American Goldfinch	1/1 Matagorda	
Lapland Longspur	1/9 Dallam	4/16 119 mi. north of Anchorage
Chestnut-collared Longspur	1/6 Presidio	
Smith's Longspur	2/13 Rains	6/24 Denali Hwy.
McCown's Longspur	1/9 Dallam	
Snow Bunting	12/25 Cameron	1/1 Kodiak
McKay's Bunting		11/28 Nome
Ovenbird	1/14 Hidalgo	
Worm-eating Warbler	4/18 Jefferson	
Louisiana Waterthrush	2/11 Harris	
Northern Waterthrush	4/11 Nueces	5/21 Kenai
Golden-winged Warbler	4/28 Jefferson	
Blue-winged Warbler	4/11 Nueces	
Black-and-white Warbler	1/2 Hidalgo	
Prothonotary Warbler	3/30 Liberty	
Swainson's Warbler	5/1 Freestone	
Tennessee Warbler	4/11 Nueces	6/15 Juneau
Orange-crowned Warbler	1/2 Hidalgo	4/24 Anchorage
Colima Warbler	5/11 Brewster	
Lucy's Warbler	5/10 Brewster	
Nashville Warbler	1/20 Webb	
Virginia's Warbler	3/16 Brewster	
Gray-crowned Yellowthroat	2/17 Cameron	
MacGillivray's Warbler	5/18 Jeff Davis	6/9 Hyder
Mourning Warbler	8/25 Jefferson	
Kentucky Warbler	4/18 Jefferson	
Common Yellowthroat	1/3 Cameron	6/8 Ketchikan
Hooded Warbler	3/22 Nueces	
American Redstart	2/1 Cameron	6/9 Hyder

Species	Texas	Alaska
Cape May Warbler	4/19 Jefferson	11/7 Sitka
Cerulean Warbler	4/26 Jefferson	
Northern Parula	3/18 Galveston	
Tropical Parula	2/18 Hidalgo	
Magnolia Warbler	4/27 Calhoun	6/12 Hyder
Bay-breasted Warbler	4/25 Jefferson	
Blackburnian Warbler	4/22 Jefferson	
Yellow Warbler	4/17 Nueces	5/20 Turnagain Pass
Chestnut-sided Warbler	4/18 Jefferson	
Blackpoll Warbler	4/20 Jefferson	6/3 Nome
Black-throated Blue Warbler	10/5 Denton	
Palm Warbler	3/28 Galveston	10/16 Juneau
Pine Warbler	1/1 Matagorda	
Yellow-rumped Warbler	1/1 Matagorda	1/7 Ketchikan
Yellow-throated Warbler	3/18 Jefferson	
Prairie Warbler	2/12 Jefferson	
Grace's Warbler	5/14 Jeff Davis	
Black-throated Gray Warbler	1/6 Brewster	6/12 Hyder
Townsend's Warbler	3/15 Brewster	5/2 Ketchikan
Golden-cheeked Warbler	4/9 Bosque	
Black-throated Green Warbler	1/3 Cameron	
Rufous-capped Warbler	1/5 Frio	
Golden-crowned Warbler	1/15 Cameron	
Canada Warbler	4/11 Nueces	
Wilson's Warbler	1/2 Hidalgo	5/3 Ketchikan
Red-faced Warbler	8/9 Brewster	
Painted Redstart	5/11 Brewster	
Yellow-breasted Chat	4/11 Nueces	
White-collared Seedeater	1/20 Webb	
Olive Sparrow	1/3 Cameron	
Green-tailed Towhee	1/6 Brewster	
Spotted Towhee	1/6 Brewster	1/5 Juneau
Eastern Towhee	2/12 Jefferson	
Rufous-crowned Sparrow	1/24 Brewster	
Canyon Towhee	1/7 Brewster	

Species	Texas	Alaska
Botteri's Sparrow	5/2 Cameron	
Cassin's Sparrow	1/7 Reeves	
Bachman's Sparrow	2/27 Jasper	
American Tree Sparrow	1/9 Dallam	1/18 Homer
Chipping Sparrow	1/1 Matagorda	6/9 Hyder
Clay-colored Sparrow	1/6 Brewster	
Brewer's Sparrow	1/6 Presidio	
Field Sparrow	1/10 Hemphill	
Black-chinned Sparrow	5/13 Jeff Davis	
Vesper Sparrow	1/6 Presidio	
Lark Sparrow	1/5 Frio	
Black-throated Sparrow	1/24 Brewster	
Sagebrush Sparrow	1/7 Reeves	
Lark Bunting	1/6 Presidio	
Savannah Sparrow	1/1 Matagorda	1/8 Hoonah
Grasshopper Sparrow	4/2 Colorado	
Baird's Sparrow	1/6 Presidio	
Henslow's Sparrow	2/26 Nacogdoches	
Le Conte's Sparrow	2/13 Rains	
Nelson's Sparrow	4/17 Galveston	
Seaside Sparrow	1/19 Chambers	
Fox Sparrow	1/13 Grayson	1/7 Ketchikan
Song Sparrow	1/4 Starr	1/1 Kodiak
Lincoln's Sparrow	1/3 Cameron	1/7 Ketchikan
Swamp Sparrow	1/7 Brewster	12/5 Ketchikan
White-throated Sparrow	1/13 Grayson	1/18 Homer
Harris's Sparrow	1/10 Hemphill	
White-crowned Sparrow	1/4 Zapata	1/7 Ketchikan
Golden-crowned Sparrow		1/8 Hoonah
Dark-eyed Junco	1/7 Brewster	1/2 Kodiak
Pine Bunting		11/28 Gambell
Hepatic Tanager	5/14 Jeff Davis	
Summer Tanager	1/2 Hidalgo	
Scarlet Tanager	4/17 Galveston	
Western Tanager	5/10 Jeff Davis	6/9 Hyder

Birds Seen in Texas and Alaska

Species	Texas	Alaska
Crimson-collared Grosbeak	1/2 Hidalgo	
Northern Cardinal	1/1 Matagorda	
Pyrrhuloxia	1/5 Frio	
Rose-breasted Grosbeak	4/17 Galveston	7/14 Ketchikan
Black-headed Grosbeak	1/15 Hidalgo	6/10 Hyder
Blue Bunting	1/20 Zapata	
Blue Grosbeak	4/18 Jefferson	
Lazuli Bunting	8/20 Jeff Davis	
Indigo Bunting	3/29 Jefferson	
Varied Bunting	5/12 Brewster	
Painted Bunting	4/19 Jefferson	
Dickcissel	4/22 Jefferson	
Bobolink	4/19 Jefferson	
Red-winged Blackbird	1/1 Matagorda	1/29 Anchorage
Eastern Meadowlark	1/6 Presidio	
Western Meadowlark	1/5 Terrell	1/9 Juneau
Yellow-headed Blackbird	1/9 Dallam	
Rusty Blackbird	1/28 Johnson	1/9 Hoonah
Brewer's Blackbird	1/7 Jeff Davis	1/9 Hoonah
Common Grackle	1/1 Matagorda	
Boat-tailed Grackle	2/12 Jefferson	
Great-tailed Grackle	1/1 Matagorda	
Bronzed Cowbird	1/1 Matagorda	
Brown-headed Cowbird	1/5 Frio	6/7 Ketchikan
Orchard Oriole	4/11 Nueces	
Hooded Oriole	1/4 Starr	
Streak-backed Oriole	2/11 Fort Bend	
Bullock's Oriole	5/10 Brewster	6/10 Hyder
Altamira Oriole	1/3 Cameron	
Audubon's Oriole	1/4 Starr	
Baltimore Oriole	4/18 Jefferson	
Scott's Oriole	5/10 Brewster	

*Rock Pigeon was seen in Alaska but is not officially countable there.

APPENDIX 2

Big Year Comparison*

Statistic	Texas (2005)	Alaska (2016)
Bird species	522	307
Previous record	511	287
Miles driven	90,000	30,000 (estimate)
Miles walked	1,264	--
Plane trips	0	86
Most trips taken	Valley: 18 Fort Davis: 12 Sabine Woods: 11	Juneau: 16 Ketchikan: 11 Nome: 7

*Different information was gathered each year, so data are not complete.

APPENDIX 3
MONTH BY MONTH

Month	Texas—2005	NO.*	Alaska—2016	NO.*
JAN	North, Southeast, Valley, West, Panhandle—wintering and resident birds, Mexican and northern vagrants—Crimson-collared Grosbeak, Green-breasted Mango, Black-legged Kittiwake, Rufous-capped Warbler, Social Flycatcher, Blue Bunting	294/294	Kodiak, South-Central, Southeast, Anchorage—wintering birds, leftover Canadian and Asian migrants from 2015—Common Pochard, Northern Pygmy-Owl, Brewer's Blackbird, Spotted Towhee, Brandt's Cormorant, Western Meadowlark, Cedar Waxwing	105/105
FEB	Valley, West, Coastal—Mexican vagrants, more wintering birds—Rose-throated Becard, Roadside Hawk, Streak-backed Oriole, Brown Booby	41/335	Anchorage, Southeast—Northern Saw-whet Owl, Willow Ptarmigan, Wood Duck, American Coot	13/118
MAR	Valley, West, Coastal—Red-breasted Sapsucker, warblers, thrushes	49/384	Anchorage, South-Central—ducks, Western Screech-Owl, Short-eared Owl	6/124
APR	Coastal, Panhandle, Central—warblers, vireos, buntings, shorebirds, Masked Duck, King Eider, Black-whiskered Vireo	54/438	Anchorage, hawk watch, Delta Junction—shorebirds, hawks, Sharp-tailed and Ruffed Grouse	25/149
MAY	Coastal, Valley, West—flycatchers, vireos, hummingbirds, owls, sparrows, western warblers, Buff-breasted Flycatcher, Olive Warbler	41/479	Anchorage, Southeast, South-Central, Adak, St. Paul, Gambell—Cinnamon Teal, Band-tailed Pigeon, swallows, shorebirds, Lesser Sand-Plover, Curlew Sandpiper, White-tailed Eagle, Eyebrowed Thrush, auklets, puffins, warblers	76/225

Appendix 3

Month	Texas—2005	NO.*	Alaska—2016	NO.*
JUN	Gulf, West, Valley—pelagic birds, Red-billed Tropicbird, Spotted Owl	14/493	Gambell, Nome, Southeast, Hyder, Delta Junction, Homer to Dutch Harbor—Bluethroat, Bristle-thighed Curlew, shorebirds, wagtails, flycatchers, vireos, Black-throated Gray Warbler	56/281
JUL	Pelagic—Parasitic Jaeger	1/494	Dutch Harbor, Barrow, Nome, Southeast, Haines—Whiskered Auklet, Short-tailed Albatross, Snowy Owl, Eastern Phoebe, Sora	7/288
AUG	West, Valley, Central—Lazuli Bunting, Red-faced Warbler, Yellow-bellied and Hammond's Flycatchers	6/500	Delta Junction, Southeast, Summit Lake, Gambell—Ring-billed Gull, White-tailed Ptarmigan, Gray-tailed Tattler	4/292
SEP	West, Northeast—Cassin's Vireo, Sabine's Gull, Fork-tailed Flycatcher, Ferruginous Pygmy-Owl	4/504	Gambell, St. Paul—Sharp-tailed Sandpiper, Siberian Accentor, Jack Snipe, Eurasian Skylark, Red-flanked Bluetail	5/297
OCT	North, South-Central, Valley—Red Phalarope, Varied Thrush, Black-throated Blue Warbler	5/509	Utqiagvik, Southeast—Great Gray Owl, Ross's Gull, Palm Warbler, House Finch, Tropical Kingbird	5/302
NOV	West, Valley, Coastal, pelagic—Greater Flamingo, 3 scoters, Eurasian Wigeon, Lewis's Woodpecker	9/517	Southeast, Gambell, Nome—Cape May Warbler, Lewis's Woodpecker, McKay's and Pine Buntings	4/306
DEC	Valley, West, Panhandle, North—Williamson's Sapsucker, Snow Bunting, Trumpeter Swan, Mew Gull	5/522	Southeast—Swamp Sparrow	1/307

*Number new that month/total birds for the year by the end of the month

APPENDIX 4

USEFUL REFERENCES IN PLANNING BIG YEARS

BOOKS

Note: these are the books I used to varying degrees during my two big years (in some cases, newer editions are listed):

Adams, Mark T. 2003. *Chasing Birds across Texas: A Birding Big Year*. Louise Lindsey Merrick Natural Environment Series. College Station: Texas A&M University Press.

Dunn, Jon L., and Jonathan Alderfer. 2011. *National Geographic Field Guide to the Birds of North America*. 6th ed. Washington, DC: National Geographic Society.

Graham, Gary L. 1992. *Texas Wildlife Viewing Guide*. Helena, MT: Falcon Press.

Holt, Harold R. 1993. *A Birder's Guide to the Texas Coast*. Washington, D.C.: American Birding Association.

Kessel, B., and D. D. Gibson. 1978. *Status and Distribution of Alaska Birds*. Studies in Avian Biology No. 1, Cooper Ornithological Society. Lawrence, KS: Allen Press.

Kutac, Edward A. 1998. *Birder's Guide to Texas*. 2nd ed. Houston: Gulf Publishing.

Lockwood, Mark W. 2001. *Birds of the Texas Hill Country*. Austin: University of Texas Press.

Lockwood, Mark W., and Brush Freeman. 2014. *The Texas Ornithological Society Handbook of Texas Birds*. 2nd ed. Louise Lindsey Merrick Natural Environment Series. College Station: Texas A&M University Press.

Lockwood, Mark W., William B. McKinney, James N. Paton, and Barry R. Zimmer. 1999. *A Birder's Guide to the Rio Grande Valley*. Delaware City, DE: American Birding Association.

Peterson, Jim, and Barry R. Zimmer. 1998. *Birds of the Trans Pecos*. Austin: University of Texas Press.

Rappole, John H., and Gene W. Blacklock. 1994. *Birds of Texas: A Field Guide*. College Station: Texas A&M University Press.

The Roads of Texas. 1999. Fredericksburg: Texas A&M University Cartographics Laboratory and Shearer Publishing.

Rylander, Kent. 2002. *The Behavior of Texas Birds*. Austin: University of Texas Press.

Seyffert, Kenneth D. 2001. *Birds of the Texas Panhandle*. W. L. Moody Jr. Natural History Series. College Station: Texas A&M University Press.

Sibley, David A. 2000. *The Sibley Guide to Birds*. New York: Alfred A. Knopf.

Wauer, Roland. 1996. *A Field Guide to Birds of the Big Bend*. 2nd ed. Houston: Gulf Publishing.

Wauer, Roland H., and Mark Elwonger. 1998. *Birding Texas*. Helena, MT: Falcon Publishing.

West, George C. 2008. *A Birder's Guide to Alaska*. Delaware City, DE: American Birding Association.

WEBSITES

Alaska links to checklists and other bird information: Alaska Department of Fish and Game. http://www.adfg.alaska.gov/index.cfm?adfg=birdviewing.checklists.

Alaska listserv: AKBirding (plus there are local listservs and Facebook pages for areas around Alaska).

Texas Bird Records Committee: http://www.texasbirdrecordscommittee.org/ (can find current list of birds of Texas).

Texbirds listserv subscription and archives: http://listserv.uh.edu/archives/texbirds.html (up to 2011).

Texas Parks and Wildlife Department. Great Texas Wildlife Trails, Wildlife Trail Maps. http://www.tpwd.state.tx.us.

INDEX

Page numbers below that are in boldface italics refer to bird illustrations.

ABA: vii; area, 1, 60; big year, vii; checklist, 79; rules, 1, 91, 95
Accentor, Siberian, 31, 45, 59, 107–108, 289, 296
Adak, 17, 31–32, 44–46, 103–104, 106, 130, 132–34, 138, 142–45, 149–50, 153–54, 162, 164, 243–44, 249–55, 257–60, 267, 270, 276–77, 279–83, 285, 295
Adams, Mark, 19
Agler, Bev, 43, 51, 152
AKBirding (listserv), 17, 38
Alaska: Checklist Committee, 145; Range, 32
Alaskan Peninsula, 31–32
Albatross: Black-footed, 32, 54, 55, 56, 106, 259, 282; Laysan, 32, 55, 106, 259, 282; Short-tailed, 32, 45, 55, 106, 259, 282, 296; Yellow-nosed, 45
alcid, 31
Aleutian Islands, 31
Alpine, 123, 153, 207, 212, 214, 231
Amaknak, 42
Amarillo, 128
American Birding Association, vii, 1. See ABA
Anahuac National Wildlife Refuge, 16, 28, 112, 149, 152, 181–82, 191, 209, 234
Anchorage, 23, 33, 44, 46, 60, 105, 113, 129, 132, 135, 137, 140, 145, 148–49, 153–56, 158–64, 167–68, 171, 242, 244–48, 250, 258, 260–61, 263–67, 269–72, 275–77, 279–90, 293, 295
Anchor Point, 44, 152–53, 256, 258, 281
Anhinga, 189, 283
Ani, Groove-billed, 29, 177, 278
Anzalduas County Park, 163, 198, 206–207
Aransas: Bay, 85; County, 189, 277–78; National Wildlife Refuge, 28, 148, 183
Arlington, 26, 160
Attu, 31, 53
Attwater Prairie Chicken National Wildlife Refuge, 28, 153, 173, 181, 185, 233
Auklet: Cassin's, 54, 56, 255, 281; Crested, 31, 56–57, 256, 281; Least, 31, 57, 130, 255, 281; Parakeet, 31, 54, 57, 130, 255, 281; Rhinoceros, 54, 256, 281; Whiskered, 32, 53, *54*, 55, 256, 281
Austin, 27–28, 93, 130–31, 135
Avocet, American, 184, 186, 279

Bailey County, 276
Balcones Canyonlands National Wildlife Refuge, 26, 210
Barrow. See Utqiagvik
Becard, Rose-throated, 45, 94, 286, 295
Bentsen-Rio Grande Valley State Park, 29, 58, 93, 118, 178, 201

Bering Sea, 30, 32
Bexar County, 280
Big Bend NP, 24–25, 40, 45, 59, 65–66, 85, 90–91, 99, 111, 115, 118–19, 122, 147, 155–56, 158, 160, 162–63, 166–68, 177–80, 193, 198, 201, 207, 210, 212, 214, 216, 219, 228–33, 237–38, 241
Bird, Bob, 43, 247
Birder's Guide to Alaska, A, 18, 30
Birding: magazine, 1; *Texas*, 18, 23
Birds in Trouble, 13
Bittern: American 191, 283; Least, 191–92, 283
Blackbird: Brewer's, 33, 58, 125–26, 293, 295; Red-winged, 171, 293; Rusty, 126, 171, 293; Yellow-headed, 70, 239, 293
Bluebird: Eastern, 216–17, 288; Mountain, 2, 32, 66, 119–20, 288; Western, 70, 216–17, 288
Bluetail, Red-flanked, 31, 45, 59, 71, 107, 288, 296
Bluethroat, 31, 78, 268, 288, 296
Bobolink, 238, 293
Bobwhite, Northern, 172–73, 277
Boca Chica, 29, 88, 114, 134, 150–51, 184–87
Bolivar Flats Shorebird Sanctuary, 28, 130, 148, 159, 184, 186, 194, 234
boneyards, 77, 107–108
Booby: Brown, 90, 282, 295; Masked, 52, 89–90, 282
Bosque County, 291
Bowl, 48–49, 69–70, 160, 213
Bowman, Aaron, 16, 54, 171, 245, 261, 264
Boy Scout Woods, 28, 118, 227, 235
Brambling, 33, 270
Brant, 243, 275

Brazoria: County, 276, 281–82, 285, 289; National Wildlife Refuge, 28, 188
Brazos Bend State Park, 28, 102
Brewster County, 207, 233, 277–78, 280, 284, 286–93
Briscoe County, 71, 202, 284
Brooks: County, 209, 286; Range, 30, 32
Brownsville, 29, 52, 58, 95, 166, 172, 193, 199
Brush Country, 27–29, 120, 125
Buddy (Byron) Stewart Park, 171
Bufflehead, 75, 144, 276
Bunting: Blue, 91, 102, 229, 294, 295; Indigo, 57, 67, 178, 237, 293; Lark, 233, 292; Lazuli, 45, 237, 293, 296; McKay's, 31, 78, 271–72, 290, 296; Painted, 57, 67, 237, **238**, 293; Pine, 31, 45, 59, 78, 108, 292, 296; Snow, 44, 57, 78, 142, 272, 290, 296; Varied, 237, 293
Burke, Toby and Laura, 43, 261
Burnet County, 286
Bushtit, 69, 214, 288

Cactus Playa, 143, 171
Calhoun County, 83, 189, 287, 291
Cameron County, 46, 193, 196, 231, 278–87, 290–93
Campbell Creek Estuary Natural Area, 262
Canadian, 113, 164, 206, 239
Canelo, El, 201
Canvasback, 144, 276
Caracara, Crested, 29, 285
Cardinal, Northern, 3, 235, 293
Carpenter: Eric, 5, 8, 16, 19, 36, 130; Larry, 93
Castro County, 276–77

Catbird, Gray, 217, 289
Central: Flyway, 28; Plains, 26–28; Texas, 26, 295–96
Chachalaca, Plain, 29, 68, 172, 277
Chambers County, 185, 278–80, 284, 292
Chasing Birds across Texas, 19
Chat, Yellow-breasted, 68, 227, 240, 291
Chickadee: Black-capped, 32, 213, 266, 271, 287; Boreal, 32, 266, 287; Carolina, 213, 287; Chestnut-backed, 32, 76, 266, 287; Gray-headed, 30; Mountain, 49, 69–70, 213–14, 287
Chicken, 2, 32, 119, 170, 288
Chisos: Basin, 59, 241; Mountains, 24, 228
Christmas Mountains, 179
Chuck-will's-widow, 178, 278
Chukchi Sea, 30
Coastal: Bend, 28; Texas, 295–96
Coffey, Sheridan, 96, 138
Colley, George and Scarlet, 57
Colorado County, 280, 292
Comal County, 278
Coot, American, 35, 76, 112, 278, 295
Cormorant: Brandt's, 35, 75, 106, 282, 295; Double-crested, 90, 154, 282; Neotropic, 189, 282; Pelagic, 260, 283; Red-faced, 57, 260, 283
Corpus Christi, 28, 61, 114, 136
Courtney, Amy, 43, 121
Cowbird: Bronzed, 240, 293; Brown-headed, 35, 58, 77, 127, 293
Crane: Sandhill, 33, 69–70, 74, 130, 148, 214, 279; Whooping, 148, 183, 279
Creeper, Brown, 69, 288
Crossbill: Red, 44, 70, 141–42, 289; White-winged, 76, 271, 289
Crow: American, 35, 77, 119, 287; Fish, 27, 67, 178, 212, 287; Northwestern, 56, 266, 287; Tamaulipas, 95, 287
Cuckoo: Black-billed, 176, 277; Yellow-billed, 67, 120, 176, 277
Culberson County, 284–88
Curlew: Bristle-thighed, 31, 78, 148, 250, 279, 296; Long-billed, 132, 185, 279

Dalhart, 156
Dallam County, 284–86, 289–90, 292–93
Davis: Mountains, 25, 48, 50, 57, 87, 93, 96, 126, 180, 205, 211, 229–31, 235, 237; Mountain Preserve, 93, 111, 160, 162, 166, 170, 205, 207–208, 210, 213–14; State Park, 25, 138, 170, 178, 208
Delta Junction, 23, 32, 44, 116, 140, 143, 148–49, 153, 155, 158–62, 245–46, 261, 265–66, 270, 275, 277, 279, 285–86, 289, 295–96
Denali: 23, 290; Highway, 166–67, 170, 268
Denton: 97; County, 291
Dickcissel, 238, 293
Dickens County, 129, 275
Dipper, American, 76, 267, **268**, 288
Dove: Common Ground-, 68, 176, 277; Eurasian Collared-, 56, 71, 96, 145, 277; Inca, 175, 277; Mourning, 176, 277; Ruddy Ground-, 25, 85, 277; White-tipped, 29, 68, 176, 277; White-winged, 176
Dovekie, 31, 78, 105, 280
Dowitcher: Long-billed, 152, 280; Short-billed, 280

Drumheller, Nat, 43, 133
Duck: Harlequin, 55–56, 244, 276; Long-tailed, 57, 132, 276; Masked, 82, **83**, 240, 276, 295; Mottled, 172, 276; Muscovy, 29, 82, 275; Ring-necked, 129, 276; Ruddy, 32, 110, 276; Tufted, 32, 103, 276; Wood, 34, 109, 118, 276, 295
Dunlin, 151–52, 280
Dutch Harbor, 32, 45, 53, 55–56, 133–34, 153–54, 249, 253–57, 259, 281–82, 296

Eagle: Bald, *vi*, 34, 54, 56, 72, **74**, 75, 103, 106, 154–55, 283; Beach, 110, 114; Fest, 165; Golden, 62, 66, 69, 119, 284; White-tailed, 31, 59, 78, 283, 295
eBird, 17
Edgerton Highway, 32
Edwards: Carol, 146, 166, 174; Plateau, 25–28
Egret: Cattle, 193, 283; Great, 85, 188, 192, 195, 283; Reddish, 193, 283; Snowy, 85, 192, 283
Eider: Common, 243–44, 276; King, 130, 276, 295; Spectacled, 31, 243, 276; Steller's, 243, 276

Fagan, Jesse, 101
Fairbanks, 23, 153, 158–60
Falcon: Peregrine, 159, 285; Prairie, 70–71, 206, 285; State Park, 208
Fayette County, 283
Feldmann, Louann, 16, 113–14, 118, 156, 160, 245–46, 260, 264, 272
Ferry, Alaska, 53, 55, 153, 259, 281–82
Field Guide to the Birds of North America, 18
Finch: Cassin's, 70, 96–97, 120, 289; House, 35, 45, 70, 77, 96, 120, 141–42, 289, 296; Purple, 96–97, 289
Flamingo, American, 44, 83–85, 277, 296
Flicker, Northern, 62, 76, 112, 158, **159**, 285
Flycatcher: Acadian, 207, 285; Alder, 35, 77, 116, 160, 285; Ash-throated, 208, 286; Brown-crested, 208, 286; Buff-breasted, 25, 93, 286, 295; Cordilleran, 98, 207, 286; Dusky, 207, 286; Dusky-capped, 95, 199, 286; Fork-tailed, 44, 93, 286, 296; Gray, 207, 286; Great Crested, 208, 286; Hammond's, 32, 69, 161, 286, 296; Least, 35, 77, 116, 285; Olive-sided, 69, 77, 160, 285; Pacific-Slope, 77, 265, 286; Scissor-tailed, 2–3, 93, 209, 286; Social, 29, 58, 93, 286 295; Sulphur-bellied, 45; Vermilion, 207, 286; Willow, 35, 77, 116, 285; Yellow-bellied, 35, 68, 77, 116, 285, 296
Fort: Bend County, 293; Davis, 24, 203, 216, 220, 232, 294; Worth, 26, 29, 45, 99, 144, 158, 173, 185, 206, 210, 220, 235; Worth Audubon Society, 234
Freestone County, 290
Frigatebird, Magnificent, 53, 188, 282
Frio County, 98, 127, 207, 210, 232, 236, 286, 289, 291–93
Frontera Audubon, 58, 68, 92–93, 95, 101, 124, 168, 203, 206, 217, 220, 227, 235
Fulmar, Northern, 54–57, 259, 282

Gadwall, 129, 144, 276
Gaines County, 113

Gallinule: Common, 183, 278; Purple, 182–83, 278
Gallitano, Lena, 114, 130, 181, 236
Galveston: 178; County, 152, 208, 278–80, 282–88, 291–93; Island, 28, 121, 131, 182, 198, 215; State Park, 181
Gambell, vii, 17, 31, 44–45, 59, 77–78, 104–108, 129–30, 132–34, 136–38, 141, 143–44, 148–50, 152–53, 155, 158–59, 162–64, 242–44, 249, 251–60, 265, 268–72, 275–76, 279–81, 283, 289, 292, 295–96. *See also* St. Lawrence Island
Gannet, Northern, 189, 282
Gee, John, 146, 174
Gene Howe Wildlife Management Area, 26, 71, 113
Glennallen, 32
Gnatcatcher: Black-tailed, 66, 216, 288; Blue-gray, 216, 288
Godwit: Bar-tailed, 32, 250, 279; Hudsonian, 149, 279; Marbled, 149–50, 279
Goff, Matt, 43, 82, 118
Goldeneye: Barrow's, 75, 244–45, 276; Common, 75, **76**, 103, 244–45, 276
Goldfinch: American, 220, 290; Lesser, 220, 237, 290
Goose: Bay, 113; Cackling, 143, 275; Canada, 110, 143, 275; Emperor, 242, 275; Greater White-fronted, 114, 143, 275; Island State Park, 28, 84; Ross's, 171, 275; Snow, 110, 114, 143, 275; Tundra Bean, 45
Goshawk, Northern, 74, 260, 283
Grackle: Boat-tailed, 240, 293; Common, 239, 293; Great-tailed, 240, 293

Granger, 87, 219–20
Grayson County, 215, 282, 288, 292
Grebe: Clark's, 145, 175, 277; Eared, 175, 277; Horned, 110, 145, 277; Least, 175, 277; Pied-billed, 35, 75, 110–11, 277; Red-necked, 248, 277; Western, 35, 75, 145, 175, 277
Greenshank, Common, 31, 105, 280
Grosbeak: Black-headed, 35, 68, 77, 124, 293; Blue, 57, 59, 67, 120, 236, 293; Crimson-collared, 14, 29, 58, 68, 101, 101–102, 227, 292, 295; Pine, 270, 289; Rose-breasted, 20, 35, 45, 57, 66–67, 77, 123–24, 293
Grouse: Ruffed, 32, 245, 277, 295; Sharp-tailed 32, 246, 277, 295; Sooty, 35, 246, 277; Spruce, 245, 277
Guadalupe: highlands, 24; Mountains, 48, 57–58, 122, 160, 166–67, 170, 179, 211, 213–14, 229–30, 232, 235; Mountains National Park, 25, 69–70, 80, 92, 160, 163, 205, 210, 213–15, 230–31
Guillemot: Black, 254, 281; Pigeon, 54–55, 254, 281
Gull: 74; Black-headed, 45; Bonaparte's, 113–14, 281; California, 76, 114, 135–36, 138, 281; Franklin's, 33, 71, 113–14, 281; Glaucous, 114, 130, 136, 281; Glaucous-winged, 114, 136, 258, 270, 281; Great Black-backed, 45–46, 88, 281; Herring, 114, 134, 136, 281; Iceland, 136; Ivory, 30, 45, 72; Laughing, 88, 114, 134, 136, 186, 281; Lesser Black-backed, 186, 281; Little, 88, 281; Mew, 44, 74, 114, 135, 270, 281, 296; Ring-billed, 77, 114, 134–36, 281; Ross's, 30, 45, 72,

257, 281, 296; Sabine's, 31, 44, 78, 134, 281, 296; Slaty-backed, 258, 281; Thayer's, 76, 136, 281
Gustavus, 43, 46, 114, 133, 152, 246, 279–80
Gyrfalcon, 32, 161, 265, 285

Hagerman National Wildlife Refuge, 26, 123, 132
Haines, 46, 112, 158, 166, 265, 278, 296
Hardeman County, 172, 277
Harrier, Northern, 155, 203, 283
Harris County, 87, 180, 213, 278, 287, 289–90
Hartley County, 276, 284
Hawfinch, 46
Hawk: Broad-winged, 61, 198, 284; Common Black-, 24, 90, 160, 283; Cooper's, 70–71, 197, 283; Ferruginous, 26, 70–71, 174, 198, 284; Gray, 66, 198, 284; Harris's, 29, 197–98, 284; Red-shouldered, 198, 284; Red-tailed, 62, 155, 284; Roadside, 91, 284, 295; Rough-legged, 26, 62, 70–71, 155, 284; Sharp-shinned, 155, 283; Short-tailed, 61; Swainson's, 35, 77, 114–15, 284; watch, 61–62, 155–56, 164, 260, 295; White-tailed, 198, 284; Zone-tailed, 50, 59, 66, 91, 99, 284
Hazel Bazemore: County Park, 28; hawk watch, 61, 198
Heinl, Steve, 35, 43, 75, 77, 106, 110, 112, 114, 120–21, 123, 136, 149, 156
Hemphill County, 276–77, 281, 285, 292
Herndon, Mike, 113
Heron: Black-crowned Night-, 193, 283; Great Blue, 85, 154, 188, 283; Green, 193, 283; Little Blue, 193,

283; Tricolored, 85, 188, 193, 283; Yellow-crowned Night-, 194, 283
Hidalgo County, 215, 217, 220, 229, 277–78, 283–93
High Island, 28, 57, 66, 118, 178
Hill Country, 22, 26
Hockey, Petra, 19
Hockley County, 284
Homer, 23, 32, 44, 53, 123, 129–30, 132–34, 136–38, 140–44, 146, 149–51, 153–55, 159–60, 169, 243–44, 248–49, 251–60, 265–66, 270–71, 276, 279–82, 285, 288–89, 292, 296
Hoonah, 34, 43, 46, 58, 126, 171, 244, 272, 292–93
Hornsby Bend, 28, 93, 130
Houston, 27–28, 88, 269
Hudspeth County, 277
Hummingbird: Allen's, 180, 278; Anna's, 35, 76, 146, 278; Black-chinned, 26, 66, 87, 179–80, 278; Blue-throated, 65–66, 179, 278; Broad-billed, 87, 278; Broad-tailed, 66, 87, 179–80, 278; Buff-bellied, 29, 68, 180, 278; Calliope, 180, 278; Costa's, 46; Lucifer, 65, 87, 179–80, 278; Magnificent, 87, 179, 278; Ruby-throated, 26, 57, 67–68, 180, 278; Rufous, 66, 69, 112, 146–48, 180, 278; White-eared, 87, 179, 278
Hunter, Brad, 43, 81
Hutchinson County, 275
Hyder, 28, 35, 44, 46, 58, 75, 77, 114, 116, 118–21, 124, 127, 137, 139, 141–42, 148, 158, 160–64, 166, 170–71, 245–46, 248–49, 265–66, 270, 278, 284–88, 290–93, 296

Ibis: Glossy, 194, 283; White, 85, 188, 194, 283; White-faced, 188, 194, 283

Ingleside, 110, 112
Interior, 22, 32
Irrigoo, Clarence, Jr., 43, 78, 108
Isleip, Pete, 20
Izembek National Wildlife Refuge, 54

Jackson County, 171
Jaeger: Long-tailed, 53, 132, 280; Parasitic, 44, 52, 54, 56, 153, 280, 296; Pomarine, 53–54, 56, 132, 153, 280
Jasper County, 285, 288, 292
Jay: Blue, 68, 212, 287; Brown, 94–95, 287; Canada, 265, 287; Gray, 265, 287; Green, *cover*, 29, 200, 212, 287; Mexican, 59, 99, 115, 287; Steller's, 32, 49, 69, 76, 112, 161–62, 262–63, 287; Western Scrub-, 70, 212; Woodhouse's Scrub-, 70, 212, 287
Jeff Davis County, 278, 283, 285–86, 288–93
Jefferson County, 277–78, 285–91, 293
Jenion, Simone, 20, 37, 39, 42, 69–70, 82, 84–85, 87–88, 93, 97, 102, 113, 137, 166, 168, 174, 180–81, 183, 202, 210, 228
Jesse H. Jones County Park, 28, 96, 163, 227, 269
Jim Wells County, 283
Johnson County, 171, 288, 293
Junco: Dark-eyed, 48, 69–70, 76, 112, 120, 122, 170, 271, 292
Juneau, 17, 34–35, 44, 46–47, 55, 58, 110, 120, 125–26, 132, 138–40, 143–49, 152, 155, 158–59, 161–63, 166, 168, 171, 246, 248, 251, 260, 265–66, 270–71, 275–80, 282–85, 287, 290–91, 293–94

Karges, John, 50
Keene, Laura, 10, 271
Kenai: 32–33, 43, 140, 143, 149–51, 158, 245, 256, 261, 279, 284, 288, 290; Peninsula, 17, 133, 258, 266, 271
Kenedy County, 208, 277, 283–84, 286–87
Kestrel, American, 32, 158–59, 285
Ketchikan, 25, 34–35, 43–46, 58, 75–77, 106, 110–12, 114, 120, 123, 127, 132, 134, 136–39, 142–46, 148–49, 154–56, 158, 160–62, 166, 168, 171, 244, 246, 248–51, 254–55, 260, 265, 267, 271, 276–82, 284–93, 294
Killdeer, 76, 149, 279
Kingbird: Cassin's, 24, 208, 286; Couch's, 29, 68, 118, 208, 286; Eastern, 26, 35, 77, 118, 286; Thick-billed, 45; Tropical, 35, 45, 58, 117–18, 286, 296; Western, 26, 208–209, 240, 286
Kingfisher: Belted, 284; Green, 29, 203, 285; Ringed, 29, 203, 284
Kinglet: Golden-crowned, 288; Ruby-crowned, 2, 288
Kingsville, 172, 193
Kiskadee, Great 29, 68, 208
Kite: Black-shouldered, 196; Hook-billed, 90, 283; Mississippi, 61, 196–97, 283; Swallow-tailed, 195, 283; White-tailed, **195**, 196, 283
Kittiwake: Blacklegged, 29, 56–57, 114, 134, 281, 295; Red-legged, 57, 257, 281
Kleberg County, 287
Knot, Red, 31, 78, 150–51, 279
Kodiak: 32, 34, 44, 103, 129, 131–32, 134–35, 142, 144–45, 154–55, 162, 242–44, 248–51, 253–56, 258, 260, 266–67, 270, 272, 275–77, 279–84, 287–90, 292, 295
Koerner, Jerry, 43, 75, 120, 127, 158, 271

Lagoon: Clam, 250; Westchester, 113, 135, 143–44, 148, 148, 258
La Grange, 196
Laguna Atascosa National Wildlife Refuge, 29, 178, 187
Laidlaw, Howard, 5, 19, 37, 101, 202
Lake: Balmorhea, 134, 145, 173, 175, 231; Bolio, 245; Buchanan, 26, 135, 138; Buskin, 144, 155; Hood, 133, 154; Jim, 111; Kenny, 32, 110, 171; Louise, 103; Marvin, 26, 71, 113, 144, 175, 204; Meredith: 26, 140; Mitchell, 29, 133; Moose, 116; Polovina, 107; Reflections, 167; Rita Blanca, 156; Summit, 33, 43, 247, 296; Swan, 109, 111; Tawakoni, 26, 132, 134; Texoma, 137; Troutman, 252; Twin, 144; Upper White, 71, 129; Ward, 110, 156, 166–67, 265; Worth, 135
Lamb County, 284
Lang, Aaron, 43, 106, 123, 137, 169, 258, 270
Laredo, 29, 91, 102, 207, 214, 222, 229
Lark, Horned, 66, 70, 119, 162, 287
Leonabelle Turnbull Birding Center, 149–50, 152, 189, 191, 194, 208, 221, 227, 240
Liberty: 149, 156, 195, 197, 222; County, 279, 283–84, 290
Lipscomb County, 174, 277
Llano County: 281–82; Park, 135
Lockwood, Mark, 18, 49, 99, 205
Longspur: Chestnut-collared, 220, 290; Lapland, 54, 70, 164, **165**, 290; McCown's, 70, 220, 290; Smith's, 165–66, 290
Loon: Arctic, 106, 282; Common, 137–38, 258, 282; Pacific, 135, 138, 282; Red-throated, 137, 282; Yellow-billed, 33, 258, 282

Los Ebanos Preserve, 58, 99
Lower Rio Grande Valley (LRGV); the Valley, 14, 22, 28–29, 45, 58, 68, 119, 145, 172, 176, 180, 189, 207–208, 212–13, 218, 294–96
Lubbock: 26, 163, 174, 198; County, 288

MacIntosh, Rich, 43, 103
Magpie: 262; Black-billed, 5, 74, 263, 265–66, 287
Mallard, 74–75, 109, 129–30, 276
Mango, Green-breasted, 29, 86–87, 278, 295
Martin, Purple, 212–13, 287
Mason, Jeff, 43
Matagorda: County, 28, 110, 112, 117, 144–45, 149–50, 154–55, 158, 171, 175–76, 183, 192–95, 197–98, 210, 212–13, 215–16, 220, 235, 239–40, 275–93; Island, 46
McAllen, 86, 155, 206, 221
McFaddin National Wildlife Refuge, 28, 66, 167, 181
McNary Reservoir, 145, 175
Meadowlark: Eastern, 26, 100, 238–39, 293; Western, 26, 35, 125, 239, 293, 295
Mendenhall Wetlands, 52, 125, 138, 143, 152, 271
Merganser: Common, 74–75, 276; Hooded, 35, 56, 76, 144, 276; Red-breasted, 75, 276
Meridian State Park, 228
Merlin, 285
Mission, 58
Mockingbird: Blue, 29, 95, 289; Northern, 5, 219, 289
Monahans Sandhills State Park, 26, 219
Morrell, Yve Nagy, 10
Mountain Lion, 59–60

Mount Livermore, 50
Muleshoe National Wildlife Refuge, 26, 71, 110, 113, 129, 144, 149
Murre: 71; Common, 54, 56–57, 253, 280; Thick-billed, 54, 57, 130, 253–54, 280
Murrelet: Ancient, 55–56, 255, 281; Kittlitz's, 32, 55, 255, 281; Marbled, 56, 255, 281

Nacogdoches: 27, 100–101, 203–205, 225, 231; County, 285, 292
Nighthawk: Common, 178, 278; Lesser, 177–78, 278
Noddy, Brown, 88, 281
Nome, 17, 31, 44–46, 58, 77–78, 106, 117, 129–30, 132–34, 136–38, 143–44, 148–50, 152–53, 155–56, 158–59, 161–64, 167–68, 170, 243–44, 247–52, 258, 265, 268–72, 279–81, 286–91, 294, 296
Northeast Texas, 296
Northern: Alaska, 23, 30, 276; Plains, 22, 26–27
North: Padre Island, 84; Slope, 30; Texas, 295–96
Nueces County, 172, 185, 187, 193, 227, 276, 278–83, 286, 290–91, 293
Nuthatch: Brown-headed, 27, 214, 288; Pygmy, 70, 214, 288; Red-breasted, 7, 69–70, 214, 288; White-breasted, 69–70, 214, 288

Oriole: Altamira, 240–41, 293; Audubon's, 241, 293; Baltimore, 57, 67, 120, 241, 293; Bullock's, 35, 77, 127, 293; Hooded, 240, 293; Orchard, 57, 67–68, 240, 293; Scott's, 66, 241, 293; Streak-backed, 102–103, 293, 295

Osprey, 33, 154, 283
Ovenbird, 67, 220, 290
Owl: Barn, 199–200, 230, 284; Barred, 62, 77, 156–58, 284; Boreal, 62, 261–63, 284; Burrowing, 62, 71, 202, 284; Eastern Screech-, 62, 201, 284; Elf, 24, 62, 66, 201–202, 284; Ferruginous Pygmy-, 44, 62, 201, 284, 296; Flammulated, 62, 91, 284; Great Gray, 45, 62, 261, 284, 296; Great Horned, 5, 62, 67, 70–71, 156, *157*, 284; Long-eared, 62, 70, 202–203, 284; Northern Hawk, 62, 260–61, 284; Northern Pygmy-, *xii*, 62, 106, 107, 284, 295; Northern Saw-whet, 62, 263, 284, 295; Short-eared, 62, 74, 158, 284, 295; Snowy, 30, 62, 71, *73*, 260, 284, 296; Spotted, 2, 62, 69, 92–93, 284, 296; Western Screech-, 24–25, 62, 91, 111, 115, 178, 284, 295
Oystercatcher: American, 184, 279; Black, 54, 249, 279

Packery Channel County Park, 28, 176
Padre Island National Seashore, 28, 82, 191
Palmer, 111, 154–56, 160, 266, 270–71, 283
Panhandle, 22, 25–26, 39, 48, 57, 70, 96, 144, 148, 159, 232, 295–96
Paradise Pond, 120, 149–50, 152, 172, 180, 189, 193, 208, 210, 223, 226–27, 240
Parakeet: Green, 206, 285; Monk, 206, 285
Parrot, Red-crowned, 68, 206, 285
Parula: Northern, 67, 222, 227, 237, 291; Tropical, 68, 227, 291
Paso, El: 25, 141, 145, 175: County, 289

Pauraque, Common, 178, 278
Pelagic trip, 44, 52–53, 89–90, 153, 188, 296
Pelican: American White, 85, 189, 283; Brown, 85, 90, 189, **190**, 283
Petersburg, 35, 43, 45–46, 81, 132, 162, 285
Phainopepla, 66, 119, 219, 289
Phalarope: 71; Red, 130, 133, 280, 296; Red-necked, 53–54, 133, 280; Wilson's, 112–13, 133, 280
Pheasant, Ring-necked, 174, 277
Phoebe: Black, 123, 286; Eastern, 31, 45, 58, 78, 117, 286, 296; Say's, 78, 125, 161, 286
Pierce, Barrett, 128
Pigeon: Band-tailed, 24–25, 35, 66, 99, 111–12, 277; 145, 295; Red-billed, 175, 208, 277; Rock, 145,277
Pineywoods, 22, 26–27, 100, 116, 158
Pintail, Northern, 276
Pipit: American, 289; Red-throated, 78, 270, 289; Sprague's, 219–20, 289
Piston, Andy, 114, 123
Plover: American Golden-, 148, 249, 279; Black-bellied, 184, 186, 279; Common Ringed, 31, 104, 279; Lesser Sand-, 31, 59, 104, 279, 295; Mountain, 28, 87, 279; Pacific Golden-, 249, 279; Piping, 184, 186, 279; Semipalmated, 54, 104, 148–49, 184, 186, 279; Snowy, 184, 279; Wilson's, 184, 186, 279
Pochard, Common, 34, 41, 103, 276, 295
Poorwill, Common, 178, 278
Portage, 115, 129, 267, 284
Port: Aransas, 28, 90, 149–50, 152, 180, 188–89, 191, 193–94, 208, 210, 221, 223, 227, 240; O'Connor, 28, 94

Potter Marsh, 72, 74–75, 135, 260
Prairie-Chicken, Lesser, 71, 174–75, 277
Presidio County, 100, 220, 233, 277, 287, 290, 292–93
Ptarmigan: Rock, 247, 277; White-tailed, 33, 45, 247–48, 277, 296; Willow, 246–47, 277, 295
Puffin: 55, 71, 295; family, 60; Horned, *cover*, 31, 54, 57, 130, 256–57, 281; Tufted, 31, 54, 56–57, 257, 281
Puschock, John, 53
Pyrrhuloxia, 236, 293

Quail: Gambel's, 174, 277; Montezuma, **25**, 174, 277; Scaled, 173, 277
Quintana: 88; Jetty, 186; Neotropical Bird Sanctuary, 116, 217

Rail: Black, 181, 278; Clapper, 132, 181, 278; King, 181, 278; Virginia, 182, 278; walk, 17, 181–82; Yellow, 17, 181, 278
Rains County, 165, 276, 290, 292
rare, 79–80
Raven: Chihuahuan, 212, 287; Common, 66, 70, 112, 114, 159, 162, 214, 245, 287
Raymondville, 201
Redhead, 144, 276
Redpoll: Common, 271, 290; Hoary, 271, 290
Redstart: American, 35, 58, 63, 68, 77, 166, 290; Painted, 25, 66, 99, 111, 179, 291
Reeves County, 277, 287, 289, 292
Reid, Martin, 98, 133, 136
Richland Creek WMA, 222

Rio Grande River, 24, 82, 85, 229. *See also* Lower Rio Grande Valley
Rita Blanca National Grassland, 26, 155, 202, 220
Roadrunner, Greater, 29, 66, 119, 177, 277
Robin, American, 96, 159, 289
Rockport-Fulton, 28, 84, 143, 147–48, 180
Rollover Pass, 132, 181, 185
Rose, Patty, 43, 51, 148, 152
Rosy-Finch, Gray-crowned, 270, 289
Rubythroat, Siberian, 31, 59, 71, 104, 107, 288
Ruff, 32, 104, 279
Ruidosa, 174, 202

Sabal Palm Audubon Sanctuary, 58, 94, 97, 166, 168, 177, 189, 197, 203, 205, 211–12, 217, 226, 229, 240
Sabine: Pass, 187, 238–39; Woods, 2, 28, 57, 66–68, 82, 94, 118, 120, 140, 156, 161, 166, 178, 191, 199, 206–207, 211–12, 215, 221–26, 230, 235–37, 240–41, 294
Salineño, 29, 90, 94, 175, 198, 201, 203, 215, 240–41
San Antonio: 28–29, 58, 86, 127, 133, 161, 207, 216–17, 231–32, 238, 249; River, 28
San Benito, 185
Sanderling, 150–51, 279
Sandpiper: Baird's, 152, 280; Buff-breasted, 185, 280; Common, 31, 71, 105, 130, 280; Curlew, 31, 59, 71, 104, 279, 295; Least, 105, 113, 149, 280; Pectoral, 71–72, 152, 280; Rock, 152, 251–52, 280; Semipalmated, 152, 280; Sharp-tailed, 31, 45, 251, 279, 296; Solitary, 153, 280; Spotted, 105, 280; Stilt, 46, 185, 279; Terek, 31, 59, 78, 105, 280; Upland, 32, 149, 279; Western, 280; White-rumped, 185, 280; Wood, 31, 71, 253, 280
San Patricio County, 172, 175
Santa Ana National Wildlife Refuge, 29, 177
San Ygnacio: 29, 91, 102; Bird and Butterfly Sanctuary, 102
Sapsucker: Red-breasted, 35, 57, 62, 138–39, **140**, 285, 295; Red-naped, 63, 70, 205, 285; Williamson's, 45, 63, 205, 285, 296; Yellow-bellied, 32, 62, 115–16, 205, 285
Sarkozi, David, 16, 181
Scaup: Greater, 103, 144, 276; Lesser, 144, 276
Schuette, Scott, 20, 107
Scoter: Black, 56, 130–32, 276; Surf, 56, 75, 130–**31**, 276; White-winged, 75, 130–32, 276
Scully, Peter, 156, 263
Sea Rim State Park, 28, 176, 238
Seedeater, White-collared, 91, 102, 229, 291
Selkirk Island, 163, 170, 175, 225
Seward: 30, 32, 134, 145, 244, 254, 260, 266, 270–71, 281
Shearwater: Audubon's, 52, 188, 282; Cory's, 52–53, 132, 188, 282; Pink-footed, 45; Short-tailed, 55–56, 259, 282; Sooty, 54, 56, 259, 282
Shoveler, Northern, 113, 129–30, 276
Shrike: Brown, 46; Loggerhead, 70, 140, 210, 286; Northern, 57, 140, 286
Simone. *See* Simone Jenion
Siskin, Pine, 69–70, 76, 214, 290
Sitka: 34–35, 43, 45–46, 58, 109, 118,

122–23, 136, 141, 144–45, 155, 158, 162, 164, 244, 249–50, 276, 286, 290
Skimmer, Black, 187, 282
Skylark, Eurasian, 31, 71, 107, 287, 296
Smith Oaks, 28, 192, 195
Snipe: Common, 32, 71, 104, 252, 280; Jack, 31, 280, 296; Wilson's, 153, 280
Sockeye Burn, 63, 160, 245, 264–66, 285
Soldotna, 32, 156
Solitaire, Townsend's, 33, 48, 163, 288
Sonneborn, David, 129
Sora, 112, 278, 296
South-Central: Alaska, 23, 32, 44, 295; Texas, 296
South: Coastal Alaska. *See* South-Central Alaska; Padre Island: 46, 52–53, 57, 88, 90, 142, 154, 158, 166, 181–82, 191; Padre Island Convention Centre, 116, 160, 184, 187, 193; Texas, 22, 57
Southeastern Alaska, 22–23, 25, 28, 33, 35, 44–45, 63, 154, 244, 258, 272, 295–96
Southeast Texas, 295
Southwestern Alaska, 23, 31, 267
Sparrow: American Tree, 26, 70, 168–70, 292; Bachman's, 27, 100, 231, 292; Baird's, 100, 238, 292; Black-chinned, 69, 232, 292; Black-throated, 232, 292; Botteri's, 231, 291; Brewer's, 100, 231–32, 292; Cassin's, 231, 292; Chipping, 35, 48, 77, 170, 292; Clay-colored, 66, 231–32, 292; Field, 232, 292; Fox, 55–56, 76, 123–24, 292; Golden-crowned, 55, 126, 170, 272, 292; Grasshopper, 233, 292; Harris's, 234, 292; Henslow's, 27, 100–101, 292; House, 142, 219, 289; Lark, 232, 292; Le Conte's, 234, 292; Lincoln's, 48, 69, 76, 170, 292; Nelson's, 234, 292; Nelson's Sharp-tailed, 234; Olive, 29, 229, **230**, 291; Rufous-crowned, 48, 59, 69, 230, 291; Sage, 233; Sagebrush, 233, 292; Savannah, 55, 126, 169, 292; Seaside, 234, 292; Song, 76, 270, 292; Swamp, 58, 77, 118, 123, 292, 296; Vesper, 100, 232, 292; White-crowned, 75, 169–70, 292; White-throated, 33, 123, 292
Spenard Crossing, 129, 261, 263
Spoonbill, Roseate, 188, 192, 194–95, 283
Starling, European, 76, 289
Starr County, 276–77, 283–88, 292–93
Stilt, Black-necked, 184, 279
Stint: Long-toed, 31, 59, 105, 279; Red-necked, 31, 78, 251, 279
St. Lawrence Island, vii, 30–31, 58, 77, 104, 142
Stork, Wood, 188, 282
Storm-Petrel: Band-rumped, 90, 282; Fork-tailed, 54, 259–60, 282; Leach's, 52, 90, 282
St. Paul Island, vii, 30–31, 44–47, 57–59, 71, **72**, 104–105, 107, 130, 132–34, 136, 138, 142, 144–45, 150–52, 154, 164, 167, 243–44, 248–60, 265, 267–68, 270–72, 276, 279–81, 287–88, 295–96
Summit County, 277
Surfbird, 251, 279
Swallow: Bank, 54, 163, 287; Barn, 53, 56, 163, 287; Cave, 163, 212–13, 287; Cliff, 120, 213, 287; Northern Rough-winged, 35, 77, 119, 163, 287; Tree, 287, Violet-green, 287
Swan: Trumpeter, 44, 74–75, 128–29, 275, 296; Tundra, 129, 275

Swift: Black, 35, 77, 248, 278; Chimney, 179, 278; Vaux's, 35, 248–49, 278; White-throated, 50, 59, 66, 69, 179, 278

Tanager: Hepatic, 69, 235, 292; Scarlet, 57, 67, 235, 292; Summer, 57, 59, 67, 235, 292; Western, 35, 66, 69, 77, 170, 292
Tarbox, Ken, 43
Tarrant County, 144, 158, 276, 278, 280–81, 284–86, 288
Tattler: Gray-tailed, 31, 45, 252, 280, 296; Wandering, 252–53, 280
Teal: Blue-winged, 33 143, 276; Cinnamon, 35, 58, 110, 276, 295; Green-winged, 74, 110, 129, 276
Tern: Aleutian, 258, 281; Arctic, 32, 54, 74, 258, 282; Black, 53, 88, 187, 282; Bridled, 52–53, 89, 132, 281; Caspian, 35, 76, 114, 282; Common, 187, 282; Forster's, 187, 282; Gull-billed, 187, 282; Least, 186, 282; Royal, 187, 282; Sandwich, 53, 187, 282; Sooty, 52, 89, 281
Texas: Bird Records Committee, 49, 134, 249; Gulf Coast, 52; Ornithological Society, 66, 100, 209; *Ornithological Society Handbook of Texas Birds, The*, 18; Review List, 29
Texline, 26, 71, 96, 120, 145, 163, 168
Thrasher: Brown, 2, 217, 289; Crissal, 217–19, 289; Curve-billed, 29, 125, 217–18, 289; Long-billed, 29, 58, 68, 218, 289; Sage, 70, 219, 289
Thrush: Clay-colored, 29, 217, 289; Eye-browed, 31, 59, 78, 289, 295; Gray-cheeked, 288; Hermit, 69–70, 141, 289; Swainson's, 288; Varied, 75–76, 140–41, 289, 296; White-throated, 29, 68, 95, 289; Wood, 5, 67, 178, 217, 289
Titmouse: Black-crested, 26, 59, 68, 213, 288; Juniper, 44–45, 70, 213, 287; Tufted, 26, 213, 287
TOS: field trip, 203, 205, 214, 231; Handbook, 18, 266. *See also* Texas Ornithological Society
Towhee: Canyon, 48, 69, 231, 291; Eastern, 230, 291; Green-tailed, 66, 122, 230, 291; Spotted, 35, 58–59, 66, 69, 122–23, 291, 295
Trans-Pecos, 22, 24–25
Travis County, 276, 286
Trogon, Elegant, 29, 58, 68, 92–93, 206, 227, 284
Tropicbird, Red-billed, 52–53, 89, 282, 296
Turkey, Wild, 175, 277
Turnstone: Black, 250, 279; Ruddy, 150, 279
Tyrannulet, Northern Beardless-, 206, 285

Unalaska, 56
Upper Coast, 27–28
Utqiagvik, 17, 30, 45–46, 71–72, **73**, 88, 129–30, 132–34, 136, 138, 148–49, 152–53, 159, 164, 243–44, 254, 257–60, 271, 281, 296
Uvalde County, 288–89

Valley. *See* Rio Grande Valley
Val Verde County, 179, 278
Van Horn, 114, 219
Van Vliet, Gus, 43, 110, 116, 119, 121–22
Van Zandt County, 281
Veery, 35, 58, 67, 77, 120, 288
Verdin, 214, 288

Victoria County, 284
Village Creek Drying Beds, 149
Violetear, Mexican (Green), 86, 278
Vireo: Bell's, 210, 286; Black-capped, 26, 65, 210, 286; Black-whiskered, 67, 94, 287, 295; Blue-headed, 211, 286; Cassin's, 35, 44, 66, 77, 118, 286, 296; Gray, 69, 210, 286; Hutton's, 59, 66, 210, 286; Philadelphia, 211, 286; Plumbeous, 69, 211, 286; Red-eyed, 118–19, 287; Warbling, 77, 161, 287; White-eyed, 210, 286; Yellow-green, 94, 287; Yellow-throated, 210–11, 286
Vulture: Black, 195, 283; Turkey, 195, 283

Wagtail: Eastern Yellow, 32, 78, 270, 289; White, 31, 108, 289
Warbler: Arctic, 31, 268, 288; Bay-breasted, 224, 291; Black-and-white, 67–68, 118, 221, 237, 290; Blackburnian, 67, 224, 291; Blackpoll, 5, 63, 167, 291; Black-throated Blue, 67, 97, 291, 296; Black-throated Gray, 35, 58, 64, 66, 69, 77, 122, 291, 296; Black-throated Green, 67–68, 226, 237, 291; Blue-winged, 68, 221, 240, 290; Canada, 68, 227, 240, 291; Cape May, 35, 58, 64, 82, 122, 290, 296; Cerulean, 67, 224, 291; Chestnut-sided, 67, 120, 225, 291; Colima, 24, 59, 65–66, 228, 290; Golden-cheeked, 26, 228, 291; Golden-crowned, 29, 58, 99, 291; Golden-winged, 221, 290; Grace's, 69, 229, 291; Hermit, 45, 66, 69; Hooded, 67–68, 223, 237, 290; Kentucky, 67, 120, 223, 225, 290; Lucy's, 24, 66, 228, 290; MacGillivray's, 35, 63, 69, 77, 166, 290; Magnolia, 35, 58, 64, 68, 77, 121, 291; Mourning, 68, 223, 290; Nashville, 102, 222, 290; Olive, 57, 95, 289, 295; Orange-crowned, 63, 69, 118, 290; Palm, 35, 45, 58, 64, 121–22, 167, 215, 291, 296; Pine, 67, 225, 291; Prairie, 67, 156, 226, 237, 291; Prothonotary, 221, 290; Red-faced, 45, 65, 99, 291, 296; Rufous-capped, 29, 58, 98, 291, 295; Swainson's, 222, 290; Tennessee, 58, 63, 120–21, 240, 290; Townsend's, 50, 63, 69, 167, 291; Virginia's, 229, 290; Wilson's, 55, 63, 69, 168, 291; Worm-eating, 67–68, 120, 221, 225; Yellow, 55, 63, 68, 291; Yellow-rumped, 63, 67, 69, 75, 118, 122, 237, 291; Yellow-throated, 67, 118, 225, 237, 291
Ward County, 289
Wasilla, 280, 285
Waterthrush: Louisiana, 227, 290; Northern, 63, 68, 121, 222, 240, 290
Waxwing: Bohemian, 32, 269, 289; Cedar, 68, 96, 163–64, 269, 289, 295
WBA. *See* Wilderness Birding Adventures
WBC. *See* World Birding Center
Webb County, 290–91
Weslaco, 58
Western: Alaska, 23, 30–31, 53; Plains, 26
West Texas, 22, 25, 44, 127, 295–96
Wharton County, 119, 287
Wheatear: Northern, 54, 71, 104, 268–69, 288; Pied, 46
Whimbrel, 132–33, 279
Whip-poor-will, Eastern, 66, 99, 111, 115, 178, 278; Mexican, 178

Whistling-Duck: Black-bellied, 172, 275; Fulvous, 172, 275
Wigeon: American, 113, 129–30, 276; Eurasian, 33, 44, 71, 129–30, 276, 296
Wilderness Birding Adventures, 17, 31–32, 42, 55, 77–78, 103, 252
Willacy County, 275
Willet, 132, 185, 280
Williams, Allen, 95
Williamson County, 28, 279
Wolfe, Mimi, 101
Woodcock, American, 185, 280
Woodpecker: Acorn, 63, 70, 203, **204**, 285; American Three-toed, 63, 264, 285; Black-backed, 63, 264–65, 285; Downy, 27, 62, 285; Golden-fronted, 29, 63, 203–204, 285; Hairy, 27 62, 285; Ladder-backed, 48, 63, 70, 205, 285; Lewis's, 35, 44–45, 57, 62, 70, 80–81, 285, 296; Pileated, 27, 62, 205, 285; Red-bellied, 62, 204, 285; Red-cockaded, 27, 62, 100, 205, 285; Redheaded, 62, 203, 285

Wood-Pewee: Eastern, 206, 285; Western, 35, 69, 77, 160, 285
World Birding Center, 52, 132
Wren: Bewick's, 48, 59, 70, 215–16, 288; Cactus, 125, 216, 288; Canyon, 50, 59, 69–70, 214–15, 288; Carolina, 215–16, 288; House, 50, 215, 288; Marsh, 67, 215, 288; Pacific, 124, 215, 267, 288; Rock, 48, 50, 70, 123, 214–15, 288; Sedge, 215, 288; Winter, 123, 215, 288

Yellowlegs: Greater, 74, 105, 280; Lesser, 113, 280
Yellowthroat: Common, 5, 67–68, 77, 97, 166, 237, 290; Gray-crowned, 58, 97, 290
Yukon: border, 32

Zapata County, 284, 286, 288, 292–93
Zavala County, 285–86
Zugenruhe Birding Tours, 17, 42